Swing

The Search for my father, Louis Prima

Best wishes –
Alan Gerstel

Alan Gerstel

ISBN: 145652755X
ISBN-13: 9781456527556

Preface

Louis Prima erupted on New York City's music scene in the 1930's.
Born and raised in New Orleans, he took the music of Bourbon Street from
The Big Easy to The Big Apple, where he quickly became known as the
King of the Swingers. He wowed jazz lovers with his virtuosity on the
trumpet, his raspy vocals and his wild onstage antics.

But Louis Prima's reputation as King of the Swingers also extended to
his life off the stage, far from the prying eyes of the public and inquiring
gossip columnists. Over the course of a stellar career that spanned five
decades, he was married five times and had countless affairs with women
eager to share his bed.

Herman Gerstel was a watchmaker and jeweler. He was born and raised
in an Orthodox Jewish family in Romania and was the eldest of six brothers
and sisters. He came to this country as a young adult where he met and
wed his beloved Selma and settled down in a sleepy New Jersey town. They
were simple people who enjoyed a quiet family life rich in conservative
values and a strictly monogamous relationship.

The Gerstels were the antithesis of everything Louis Prima embodied.
The only thing Louis Prima and Herman Gerstel had in common was me.

The law remains very clear: It is illegal to buy or sell a baby. But there was another, more legitimate option to a Black Market adoption… a so-called "Gray Market" adoption. Those private adoptions were sanctioned by the legal system because the babies were not bought. The only money that could lawfully change hands was limited to the birth mother's medical expenses and reasonable attorney's fees. Both sets of parents involved in a Gray Market adoption could also be assured of strict confidentiality because the legal matters were conducted in near-secrecy that left little or no paper trail.

And that's how I became "Alan Gerstel." I was a Gray Market adoptee.

As I began to delve into my past I came to learn how this Gray Market system, wrapped in the facade of legitimacy, was insidiously ripe for corruption. Absent the oversight of an adoption agency to enforce the law, a birth mother with an unwanted child could be enticed to choose one set of adoptive parents over another by the covert payment of a bribe… in cash. In my sordid case, that undisclosed payment led to a treacherous sleight of hand that also obscured the identity of my birth parents.

SWING is a true story of betrayal… of passion… and of payoffs. The characters I write about are real people. Some committed cruel, unthinkable acts at the time of my birth. (Louis Prima was not one of them.) Others accepted bribes from me as I probed into my past. And there are those who may be embarrassed that they were victimized by my deception. So I have altered many names to protect their identities. But make no mistake about it… the story at the heart of this book is all-too-real.

After enduring a childhood saturated with love and affection, I felt a burning need to learn about my genetic identity. Certainly my adoptive parents cherished me, but as an adoptee I couldn't escape the anguish of rejection. The man and woman who created me didn't want me, and in fact, had discarded me. I was haunted by a recurring dream about my birth mother and puzzled by my musical ability and love of performing. I had a strong family bond but couldn't make sense of who I actually was or who I was supposed to be.

As you read on, it's also important to note that I have not been able to confirm every detail of the story that unfolds in the following pages. Gaps exist in the verifiable time line because most of the players have died. Others could not recall specific information that would bridge those gaps. And perhaps two possible sources remain locked up in a prison cell somewhere. So I have created best-guess scenarios to fill in the missing information. In every instance, though, I have tried to remain meticulously faithful to the people involved and the events that transpired.

There are many people to thank for the successful conclusion of my investigation. My Search would have ended hopelessly had it not been for Lou LoScialpo. Lou is the private detective... an adoptee himself... who successfully tracked down his birth parents. Over the years I reached out and employed a handful of private investigators in my Search but not one of them could come close to Lou's uncanny abilities. I was truly fortunate to find this amazing investigative guru who has since become and has remained a close and trusted friend.

It is safe to say I could not have seen my Search through to its conclusion without the undying love and support of my wife, Ronni. My many years of frustration and mood swings put her through an emotional meat grinder, yet she remained by my side through every torturous, perplexing moment. She is so much more than my wife. She completes me. She is my best friend. I am truly blessed to have her as a part of my life.

My friend, Scott Eyman has supported my efforts since I began writing SWING. Scott is a huge Louis Prima fan who not only encouraged me at the onset, but has also given me editorial advice that has improved the book enormously. I am grateful for his input. My thanks also go to my friend and former co-anchor, Claudia Shea, whose assistance in proofreading the text has been invaluable. I must also thank Sunny Quinn for her sage advice.

I would be remiss if I did not thank Fran Yasney for welcoming me back into her life after so many years had passed. She has been a friend and supporter. There is no way to thank her enough. I also cannot say enough about my cousins who stepped in and provided important information during the times my investigation was stalled. Muriel, Alan and his mother, Miriam, were all godsends who helped me make the journey to the truth.

I am also deeply indebted to Gia Prima. Gia has accepted me and embraced me as part of the Prima family. We often joke that even though she is only a few years older than me, she is my "stepmother." But she is so much more. By acknowledging me as the illegitimate son of her late husband she has, in fact, given me legitimacy. She has made it possible for me to make peace with the demons of the unknown that tortured me for so many years.

There are many other people to thank for my success. I trust they know who they are... and also trust they know they have my undying gratitude.

CHAPTER ONE

Far Away In Far Rockaway

The thick salt air embraced Rocco's barrel-chested body like a hot, wet blanket. Skin glistening with a gritty sweat, his torso heaved as his lungs welcomed each moisture-laden breath. Rocco had been in bed since midnight, trying to rein in his nervous excitement. He hungered for a few hours of restful sleep but his mind was racing with anticipation. Sprawled out on his back, Rocco could only listen to the sound of the surf crashing onto the nearby beach as his wife, Rose, remained in a fitful sleep beside him. An oscillating fan rattled noisily on the dresser nearby, swinging from left to right and then back again in a monotonous ineffective ritual, barely moving the humid ocean air across the stillness of the small room.

The sun was beginning to rise on another oppressively hot day in August of 1944, yet Rocco was thankful he wasn't back in their brownstone apartment in the heart of Brooklyn. There, he knew he'd have to endure an even greater torment: the stagnant heat oozing up from the blistering city streets and the smell of rotting garbage filling the alleyways. But here in the bungalows of Rockaway Beach, the breeze off the ocean brought a miniscule measure of relief even on a torrid summer night.

The Rockaways had grown during the 1920's and 30's to become a haven for New York's working class families from the boroughs of Manhattan, the Bronx, and Brooklyn. Each summer, thousands of well-worn bungalows nearest the beach, were transformed into vacation homes for the men and women who worked hard with their hands to support their families. The seven and a half miles of pristine beach were touted as some of the most beautiful on the Eastern Seaboard. The Jews, the Italians, and the Irish returned every summer to the refreshing surf, to the wide, wooden boardwalk that ran parallel to the miles of shoreline, and to the roller coaster and the arcades at "Rockaway's Playland" amusement park.

The accommodations in the one and two-story structures were sparse and cramped and the bungalows may have been in desperate need of repair, but they offered an affordable summer getaway. Each family rented a small room packed with a bed, a dresser, a small table with chairs and a kitchen squeezed into one corner. The Jews had a Yiddish name for the rooms in their bungalows. They were "kochalayns," which literally means "room with cooking." The bathroom was down the hall, shared by the three or four diverse families on each floor who became like "family" as they returned year after year.

The women and children spent their entire summers here from Memorial Day until Labor Day. The husbands didn't have that luxury. They worked all week in the suffocating heat of New York City and went home each night to their lonely, sweltering apartments. But when they finally clocked-out on Friday afternoon, they hopped on the "A Train" and took the subway to the Rockaways where they reunited and relaxed with their families over the weekend.

Rocco and Rose Ferrucci had rented the same second-floor room on Beach 78th Street in Rockaway Beach for several years. They had been married for nine years, and despite the feelings of affection that bound them together, there was something missing in their relationship, a void they could not fill. They could not have children.

It was the early morning of Friday, August 11th. If this had been a normal week, Rocco would have woken to the sound of his alarm clock in his apartment in Brooklyn, getting ready for another day behind the wheel of his delivery truck. But this was a time filled with expectation, and Rocco took time off to remain at his wife's side.

Rocco's body stiffened as the pay phone in the hall began to ring. It was 6:25, and in a flash Rocco leaped out of bed, pulled on his pants, and stumbled toward the door. Rose began stirring and opened her eyes. "Maybe this is it," he said as he threw the door open and rushed down the hall to the phone.

"Hello, this is Rocco" he said as he fumbled with the receiver and it's tangled, unforgiving cord. "I think it's starting," said a woman with a thick Hungarian accent on the other end of the line. Rocco paused, struggling for a moment with the reality of the four words he had just heard. He could feel his heart pounding. "Should we get a cab?" he asked. "I think it's still too early," the woman replied. "I'll call you back." The line went dead before Rocco could formulate another question.

The 29-year-old truck driver stood there at the pay phone, receiver still in his hand, as his mind started racing. He found himself distracted for a moment by a torrent of perspiration running down his back, but then refocused sharply as if he'd been jolted by the nagging reality that any slip-up would unravel his plan. He hung up the receiver as he played out the day's critical details in his mind one more time while walking quietly back to his room.

Rose was already dressing. She had also sensed the phone call was the one they had been waiting for. Who else would call before 6:30 on a Friday morning, she thought, as she raced around, trying to find her blouse and her shoes. "No need to panic," Rocco reassured her as he came back into the cluttered room and quietly closed the door behind him. "She said it's starting. She doesn't want us to do anything yet. We have some time. But we should be ready when the time comes."

They both froze for a moment and then looked at each other tenderly. Rocco took a few steps toward Rose and they held each other tightly, lingering in a warm embrace. "Maybe we should wash up while we have a chance," she suggested in response to their mutual body odors that had festered overnight. "Good idea," Rocco responded, "but let's use the bathroom one at a time so that one of us can listen for the phone."

As it turned out, they had no need to rush. The phone didn't ring again until well after 9 o'clock. And when it finally did, it only rang once. Rocco bolted and opened the door only to see Mrs. Schwartz from the room down the hall in her drab pink robe and brown slippers with her hair wrapped in large rollers. "Heh-loh-oh," she sang into the phone, "What's that? … oh… oh wait a minute." She turned to see Rocco anxiously making a beeline toward her. "It's for you," she announced suspiciously as she handed him the receiver.

Rocco fumbled with the phone nervously as he grabbed it from Mrs. Schwartz with a forced smile and nod of appreciation. "Hello," he said cautiously as he watched Mrs. Schwartz shuffle back to her room. The voice with the Hungarian accent responded, "It's time. I think you should call a cab and come over here right away if you want to be any help." Rocco managed to blurt out, "We'll be right there." He pushed the cradle of the pay phone down and released it, put a nickel in the coin slot, and dialed the number for the Yellow Cab Company which had been pasted on the side of the phone. "I need a cab right away at 170 Beach 78ᵗʰ Street," he said as he fidgeted nervously. "Where to?" came the response. "St. Joseph's

Hospital," he replied, "and right away." The cab dispatcher fired back, "Five minutes," and with a click the line went dead.

Rocco turned almost frantically to see Rose standing outside the doorway of their room anxiously. "Do we have everything?" he asked as Rose rushed back inside to grab her purse. Without waiting for an answer, Rocco said breathlessly, "Let's go!" Rose dashed out of the room and quickly closed the door behind her before they both rushed down the stairs.

They had less than a block to walk. But the path took them past several other bungalows and dozens of inquisitive people with prying eyes sitting on their porches directly alongside the sand-swept sidewalk. The numbered streets like Beach 78th Street ran perpendicular to the boardwalk. And the block closest to the seashore where the Ferruccis lived was the most popular and most populated. Everybody there knew everybody and everybody's business. But the Ferruccis didn't want to attract attention. So they gripped each other's hand tightly and paced themselves to walk quickly but without a sense of panic, nodding and smiling nervously to the neighbors they passed.

As they approached number 170, they spotted a young, pregnant woman, Dorothy, sitting uncomfortably on a wooden chair tucked away on the front porch. An older woman stood by her side holding a small brown leather suitcase. Dorothy's belly was rotund and taut and looked like it might burst as she perched there sweating and breathing heavily. The older woman, Margaret Weltsch, handed the suitcase to Rocco and said in her Hungarian accent, "Here, she will need this." She went on warmly, "You are such good friends to be able to help her today. You must be nice people to be here when she needs you the most." Rocco fidgeted and checked his watch just as Rose spotted the Yellow Cab turning the corner onto 78th Street. She rushed to the sidewalk and flagged it down.

It took the combined efforts of both Rocco and Margaret to lift Dorothy out of her chair. The trio then took a few halting steps before Dorothy stopped and winced in pain. She took a breath and then addressed Margaret sincerely, "I can't thank you enough for everything. But I'll see you again after I leave the hospital." Margaret nodded as Dorothy continued, "And please tell Frances for me that I am going to the hospital now. She'll want to know." "That's all right, sweetheart. I'll tell her. Not to worry," Mrs. Weltsch replied as she and Rocco shuffled her to the cab, "and don't you worry either. Everything will turn out all right."

Rose took Dorothy's arm from Margaret and helped maneuver Dorothy into the back seat of the cab. She and Rocco then went around to the other side and climbed into the back seat alongside her. "St. Joseph's Hospital," Rocco commanded.

Margaret Weltsch stood there and watched the cab chug along to the end of the block, turn right at the corner, and disappear out of sight. She didn't know much about Dorothy's friends except that they had a room down the block and they seemed like such sweet people to help her. She was puzzled, though, why she had never seen them in each other's company before and why they suddenly became involved in Dorothy' life.

Each bumpy metallic groan was an irritating counterpoint to the sweet music coming from the cabbie's radio. Lily Ann Carol was singing "I'll Walk Alone," accompanied by Louis Prima's orchestra. The song was an anthem for the soldiers serving overseas in World War Two. "Til you're standing beside me," Lily Ann warbled tenderly, "I'll Walk Alone." Dorothy couldn't tolerate another minute. "Awghhhh... Off... turn it off," she blurted out in misery. The cabbie complied without question as the cab continued bouncing along toward its destination with its windows wide open to let the ocean air blow across its sweaty occupants.

The cab came to a halt in front of the Emergency Room of St. Joseph's Hospital. Rocco rushed inside while Rose paid the cabbie and then opened the passenger door on Dorothy's side. They waited only a few moments before Rocco came bursting back through the Emergency Room doors with a nun dressed in white, followed by an aide with a wheelchair. The nun and the aide then helped Dorothy shift from the cushioned back seat of the cab to the wheelchair with its hard, wooden seat. Dorothy let out another groan. The nun took her hand and reassured her that, "God will be looking over you today."

The cab pulled away as the aide began pushing the wheelchair toward the Emergency Room doors with a parade of people in its wake: the aide, the nun, Rocco, and Rose. The nun leaned over and asked Dorothy: "Are you comfortable?" "What do you think?" Dorothy snapped back sarcastically. "That's how God would want it," said the nun, oblivious to the sarcasm. "Behind every joyous event in our lives like the birth of a baby there is always pain." Dorothy groaned.

Once inside, they stopped at a desk with a sign that read "Admitting." Another nun in a starched white habit sat behind the sturdy desk with a large ledger book open in front of her. Rocco stepped up. "My name is Rocco Ferrucci and my wife here is going to have a baby," he said in a wooden fashion, trying to mask his deceit. The nun responded, "Then let us get the information we need so we can make your wife more comfortable." Rocco gave his "wife's" name as "Rose Ferrucci." His name was Rocco Ferrucci. Their address was 343 Vernon Avenue in Brooklyn. The lady who was accompanying them was Rocco's "sister" he stated in a more relaxed voice.

The ruse played out very easily because this was New York City during World War Two and very few people had a driver's license or any other proof of their identity. Rocco, being a commercial truck driver, was the exception. He could prove his identity using his trucker's license. The nun used a fountain pen to record the information in her ledger book. Her handwriting was crisp and neat with occasional flourishes. "Rose Ferrucci's" admitting time, she noted in her book, was 10 AM.

Nearly three hours passed. Rocco and Rose sat in the Waiting Area but they barely spoke, afraid that they might be overheard. Every few minutes one or the other would pace across the room and back. Rocco went over the details of their plan again and again in his mind. But each time, he concluded that he had thought of every possibility. He reassured Rose with a smile and a wink.

At last, the sound of footsteps echoed faintly from down the hall. They grew louder as Sister Margaret approached the waiting area. "Congratulations, Mr. Ferrucci," she said. "You are the father of an adorable baby boy." Rocco's eyes met Rose's. They smiled a little smile and let out a sight of relief. "When can we see our baby?" he asked excitedly but then added clumsily, "And of course, when can I see my wife too?" "You and your sister can see them both in a little while," Sister Margaret said reassuringly. "Remain here for now. I'll come back and get you when your wife is ready."

The sound of Sister Margaret's sensible shoes chattered down the hall as she left them. Rocco squeezed Rose's hand. "It's working," he said as he gazed at her lovingly. "It's all going to work out just fine."

CHAPTER TWO

The Adoption Conversation

The adoption conversation began in a most unremarkable way. My mother was sitting at one end of her French Provincial crushed-velvet couch covered with clear plastic slipcovers and I was sitting on the other. She was knitting a sweater. I was looking at pictures in a book. My father was relaxing comfortably in the ornate chair across from us reading his favorite newspaper, The New York Daily News. I became aware that my mother and father glanced uneasily at each other. Then it happened again. They said nothing so I said nothing. I kept turning the pages and pretended I wasn't aware of the awkward environment. Several minutes passed before my mother put her knitting in her lap and shifted closer to me on the couch. I didn't really understand what was happening but I began to feel the apprehension a five-year-old could only sense yet not truly understand.

My mother reached over and took hold of my hand and squeezed it in hers. "You know, Alan dear," she said tenderly, "we love you more than anything else in the world, Daddy and me." There was another awkward silence as I nodded my head in automatic agreement. I was looking directly at my mother's face but my mind was racing uncontrollably as it tried to get a handle on this odd moment in time. My father startled me when he added to my growing concern from across the room. "Listen to what your Mother is saying," he said very directly. "This is very important... an important thing for you to know." My mother looked at my father and neither said anything. For me, time seemed to stand still.

My mother finally squeezed my hand harder and said, "You are a very special boy, Alan. You are so special... Daddy and I wanted you so much... and we love you so much. We wanted you so much that we picked you out from all the other babies in the hospital." "Yes, that's right," my father chimed in somewhat abruptly. "We picked you out because we wanted only you."

I couldn't begin to grasp what I was being told yet I had an avalanche of questions I felt too awkward to articulate. Is that how babies are made, I asked myself? But my inner dialog was interrupted again when my mother repeated, "You are special. We knew you were special the minute we saw you," she cooed. Then with a seemingly greater urgency she continued, "We went all the way to St. Joseph's hospital in Far Rockaway. You were born in St. Joseph's hospital... on August 11, 1944... and that's where we picked you out. We saw all the other babies there and we picked you... We chose you... and we adopted you. We adopted you and we took you home with us when you were ten days old."

My mother then gave me a big hug as she said, "Daddy and I want you to know that... and we want you to know how much we wanted you and how much we love you. We don't want any other children... only you. You will always be our only child... because we love only you."

I stared at her momentarily because I really didn't know how to react to this exaggerated and bewildering outpouring of affection. "I love you too mommy," I said innocently. My mother's tender words had genuinely bathed me in the warm feeling of affection. But at that moment I was a very confused little boy.

That conversation about being adopted was the only conversation my parents and I ever had about adoption and what it meant. There were no follow-up talks when I was a few years older and might have understood more about how I became Herman and Selma Gerstel's child... the only child they could love... their "only child." It was as though the conversation about being "picked out from all the other babies in the hospital" never took place. I intuitively sensed that I should never question it. The subject of my adoption was never mentioned in our household again. Never.

I grew from a little boy into a teenager smothered by my mother's love and affection. My father was a watchmaker and owned a jewelry store in our hometown of Westwood, New Jersey. He was as much married to his store as he was to his wife. He was the Provider and he did his job well. He just wasn't around very much to play the role of the traditional father in raising his son. We never went fishing or to a ball game or talked about "guy" stuff. I have no doubt, though, that he loved me. He was just never very expressive about it.

My mother was the classic homemaker, always busy around the house, always tending to my needs, always keeping me clean and well fed. As I progressed through elementary school I felt consumed by her love. But even with her constant adoration, an amorphous, imperceptible feeling of loneliness began to seep into the recesses of my subconscious. To counter that dark feeling, I developed the veneer of a happy, extroverted, very talkative young man. And I duped everyone with my ongoing, outgoing performance.

Though my parents remained mute on the subject of adoption, my inquisitive mind eventually ferreted out the difference between a biological child and an adopted child. Once I understood that difference I gradually began to interpret my parents' uncomfortable silence about my adoption as a mark of shame. There is something so terrible about being adopted I thought, that the mother and father who profess so much love for me never want me to talk about it. So I didn't. I kept those "unspeakable" thoughts bottled up deep inside.

But the dark feelings that lurked in the crevices of my soul came to light as I slept. During my teenage years, a recurring dream played out again and again. I would be walking down a street of cozy-looking homes nestled in a quiet suburban neighborhood. There was nothing specific about the way the houses looked. The neighborhood could have been out of "Leave It To Beaver" or "The Partridge Family," unremarkable except for the cheery, carefree feeling it exuded. The houses were cookie-cutter perfect in a bright and colorful cartoonish way. They also appeared to be warm and friendly. But I wasn't basking in the glow of that warmth in my dream. I was on a mission. I was looking for a specific house number and I was determined to find it.

The adrenaline was flowing along with the anticipation as I spotted the number, walked up to the front door and knocked. I was so fixated on my mission that I gritted my teeth in my sleep as I waited for someone to open that door. After several knocks, an attractive but matronly woman finally answered. "Yes?" she questioned. I looked at her steely-eyed. "I'm your son," I lashed out. "I want you to see what you threw away. I want you to eat your heart out because I am successful, and popular, and happy. And you... you gave me away when you should have kept me and loved me."

Then my verbal assault ended and I stared at the woman and waited. My anger would elicit some vague response from her. But even though the dream played out countless times, I could never recall her specific words. When she finished whatever it was that she said, I would wake up feeling furious, frustrated, and filled with self-loathing.

During those same teenage years, I began to develop an uncontrollable inner dialog that questioned why I had certain talents, certain desires to perform in front of an audience that just didn't seem to mesh with my mother and father as well as all my other relatives, for that matter. I needed to know what fueled the fire of my creative energy. Over time, that specific question became all-the-more puzzling as I considered the non-artistic background of the family that adopted me.

While I was still in elementary school my mother informed me that I was going to take piano lessons. We had an upright piano that had remained dormant in our living room for as long as I could remember and my mother suddenly became determined that I would learn how to make music with it. I studied with Mrs. Hollander, a spinster who lived in the neighborhood. She was very sweet and, over time, I became somewhat accomplished playing the uninspired etudes and minuets she selected for me.

When I reached junior high school my parents decided that I should also learn another instrument, one I could play in the school band. I was excited by the prospect and had no hesitation. My instrument of choice was the trumpet. There was something hip and jazzy about it and the thought of "blowing my horn" fed the fantasies of my musical soul. But when I announced my decision to my parents, they were emphatic in their disapproval. In fact, they would not hear of it. "It's too loud and it will make your lip look like Louis Armstrong's lip, all out of shape," they claimed, "Take up the clarinet instead." They were my parents. They won. I took clarinet lessons and later added the saxophone. I never played the trumpet nor even dared mention it again.

I thrived musically, playing saxophone in the Westwood High School Marching Band, the Dance Band and the Orchestra. But even those musical experiences were too regimented for me and left me unsatisfied. Then, quite unexpectedly, some friends approached me about starting a

Dixieland Band and asked me to join them on clarinet. We called ourselves "The Dixie Cups."

We relished our new identity and felt we were free to let loose. Finally, we had a chance to make music without the constraints of a Music Teacher instructing and conducting us. And was it ever a spiritual experience!! We played "Basin Street Blues," "When the Saints Go Marchin' In," and other classic New Orleans Dixieland tunes. Our unofficial leader played a mean trombone and was, by far, the best musician in our group. After an especially inspiring rehearsal he took me aside and said, "You know, Gerstel, you have the best sense of rhythm of any Jewish guy I have ever heard, even in a professional band. You just never miss a beat, no matter what."

That compliment hung with me. It haunted me. I couldn't quite shake it, nor did I really want to, because it really seemed to strike a nerve. After eight or nine years of playing music I had been told I had something special. Did that compliment really mean something? Did it define who I was or who I wasn't? And what impact could it possibly have on me and my feelings about myself? Those questions rumbled around in my brain and then would vanish, only to reappear later in the far reaches of my psyche where they played little tricks on my mind before they drifted into hibernation again.

I continued playing in the "Dixie Cups" but I also took on the role of the emcee in school talent shows. I was the Deejay at school dances and performed in school plays. I relished each opportunity to appear before an audience and found ways to emulate some host, some comedian, or some actor I had seen in films or television. I was "Mr. Entertainment" at Westwood High School. I also became the "go to guy" for advice in how to polish a performance.

On one occasion, I came to the aid of some friends who had formed a folk-singing group similar to the Kingston Trio. They asked me to sit in on a rehearsal and critique their music. They were terrific but were not "selling it." So I shared with them the lesson I had learned from personal experience: Have a good time while you're performing and it will be infectious. The audience will respond to the good vibes you generate and have a good time along with you. It worked. My recommendations injected new life into the group and their performances wowed their audiences.

I clearly embraced my public role as a musician and performer but I was also trying my best to gain control over my feelings of despair. As time passed, though, I found that I couldn't really get a real grip on the emotions I didn't fully understand so I had to learn an alternative method of coping: I would divert my mind from the dark thoughts that were smoldering inside me by staying manically active in my daily life. I found that managing the pain became like stuffing a genie back into the bottle. The genie would threaten to erupt and manifest itself physically, but that created an even stronger desire to force it back into the bottle and lock the cap on tight.

Though I was gregarious and outwardly happy, never revealing the anguish that raged inside, I was also super sensitive to criticism and even comments made in jest. During my teenage years, a number of friends and acquaintances would kid me about my nose. It wasn't THAT big but it was larger than I would have liked. One person said it "looks like an Italian nose." Another said it was crooked. Those comments, and so many others, made me self-conscious about my prominent facial feature and prompted me to examine it closely many times in the bathroom mirror. Does it really look Italian, I would ask myself, and why does it look so crooked? I thought about it again and again and finally got up the nerve to tell my parents that I wanted to get a "nose job." Surprisingly, my parents didn't object.

Once my "crooked, Italian nose" became history in the operating room, I had a surge of self-confidence and more positive feelings of self-esteem.

But, as it turns out, the cosmetic surgery was only a quick fix. As the weeks and months passed with my new nose, I discovered that the change in my outward appearance did nothing to cut through to the innermost reaches of my soul and numb the pain.

When it came time to decide on my future, the cliché rang true. My parents felt that a nice Jewish boy would grow up to be a Doctor, a Lawyer or a CPA. But I had other ideas. I wanted to be an Actor. And I was accepted at Boston University's School of Fine Arts where I immediately felt at home. I enrolled in acting classes, speech classes and dance classes, but my greatest joy came from singing lessons... many, MANY singing lessons. To this day, if I could do anything I want (and I actually had the raw vocal ability), I'd want to be a singer.

Summers during my college years were spent working in Summer Stock. I had found my "calling" by attending theatre classes at Boston University and I couldn't wait to satisfy my cravings by actually working in a real theatre. Those cravings were satiated during the summer after my freshman year when I was hired by Storrowton Music Fair in West Springfield, Massachusetts as the Technical Director. I worked with stars like Martha Raye, Milton Berle, Keely Smith and Andy Devine. The next summer I toured with the legendary Diahann Carroll and I worked with Martha Raye again.

"Maggie," as her friends called her, was a warm, vivacious performer and a larger-than-life person. Martha Raye had been a huge film star back in the 1930's, 40's and 50's, but you would never know it from her demeanor. She was sweet, she was funny... and to my surprise, this woman could really sing! One night at a cast party that lasted into the wee hours of the morning, Maggie sang the soulful "Little Girl Blue" accompanied by a lone piano player. When she finished, there wasn't a dry, sober eye in the place. I was among the smitten, and with cheeks still moist from tears, I walked over to her with my arms outstretched and said fervently, "Maggie, I'd love to wrap you up and take you home with me." Martha Raye looked at me warmly with an impish smile and with impeccable comic timing, cupped her hands under her well-endowed bosom, nudged her breasts upward, and defused my ardor by confessing, "Alan, I'd love to go home with you... but I don't know how you'll wrap up the boobs."

Each summer brought bigger career challenges and each theatrical experience intensified my love of my chosen career path. But the more successful I became, the more vocal my father became in his disapproval of my choice of profession and of me personally. He expressed his frustration and his disappointment with me on any number of occasions.

During one summer, I toured with several shows as a Technical Director. One of my duties was to drive the scenery truck between theatres and supervise the installation and the breakdown of the scenery. As you might expect, I didn't dress in a suit and tie. I usually wore faded jeans and a wrinkled polo shirt. And when I stopped home for a visit, my father went into a blustery rage over my appearance. He pointed a finger at me as he blurted out almost comically, "Bum.... Beatnik.... Truck Driver!!" It would have been funny had it been uttered by a ranting nightclub comedian, but to me it spoke volumes about how my father felt about me. He was comparing me to the people who he held in the very lowest esteem.

There was the one outburst, though, that was clearly an outrage no parent should ever utter to an adopted child... ever! His words cut deeply into my fragile feelings of self-worth and made a mockery of his pious facade as a loving father. He was angry and frustrated about something I had done or the way I was dressed, and he looked at me steely-eyed. With a venom that regurgitated from his raging bowels, he lashed out at me with words that shattered whatever was left of my self-esteem, "I told your mother we should have picked a girl!" At that moment I realized he clearly regarded me as nothing more than the merchandise he'd purchased for his jewelry store.

CHAPTER THREE

Rocco and Rose and Herman and Selma

"Baby Boy Ferrucci" was born at 12:37 PM on Friday, August 11, 1944, only two and a half hours after Dorothy McDonald arrived at St. Joseph's hospital in labor. Another hour and a half passed before a nun approached Rocco and Rose in the Waiting Room. "If you'll follow me Mister Ferrucci, I can take you and your sister to the nursery to see your baby," she said as they started walking down the hall. "Your wife is a little out-of-sorts right now and wants to be alone." Rocco looked at the nun quizzically. "Oh, I wouldn't worry, though," she added reassuringly, "sometimes it is God's will that a new mother needs to heal by herself."

Rocco and Rose looked at each other as they each silently questioned Dorothy's refusal to see them, but their concerns were assuaged at the nursery where they were introduced to their son being held by a nun behind a large glass window. They squeezed each other's hands tightly, almost too tightly, as they cooed and pointed at the newborn being held up in front of them. They had to keep up the charade. They couldn't let on that they would soon be taking this little baby back to their apartment in Brooklyn to become their own. They made faces and pantomimed trying to touch the infant through the window as their joy overwhelmed them. The nun indicated that she needed to put the newborn back in his bassinet so Rocco and Rose blew kisses, squeezed each other tightly, and then walked away anxiously awaiting the day they would be holding that baby in their arms.

Their enthusiasm, though, was not shared by the baby's mother who was recovering in a room just down the hall. The antiseptic white walls of Dorothy's room stood as a nagging reminder: she was far from the pulsating glitz and glamour of the clubs on 52nd Street. "Swing Street", as it was called in early years of the 1940's, was home to the dynamic jazz that defined the war years in New York City. Dorothy was tall and beautiful so it was no surprise that the 21-year-old became a favorite of the musicians who performed there. She was a "hostess" and worked at the smoke-filled clubs that were owned by the Mob.

Dolly, as she liked to be called on "The Street," was hired to keep the high-flying patrons happy and she did whatever it took to please. If it meant going home with a wealthy customer, she would figure how to make it pay off in cash or in favors. The club managers would target the big spenders they wanted Dolly to please and the bosses paid her handsomely... in cash... for her tireless efforts. Lying in her hospital bed, Dorothy ached to return to 52nd Street. But for now she could only dream of the excitement raging in the heart of midtown Manhattan as she tried to appear maternal while awaiting another feeding of her newborn baby boy.

"He is really a very adorable, very healthy baby," cooed the young nun who entered the room with the blanket-wrapped child. "I just know how happy he must make you." Dorothy responded with a forced smile and a grunt as she tried to readjust her position in the bed. "Are you still in pain, dear?" the nun asked as she gently passed the baby to his mother.

"Yes, but I am getting used to it," Dorothy said without much emotion. There was so much more that Dorothy wanted to tell the nun about this baby boy and what his birth really meant to her. She remained silent, though, and forced another smile even as she was doing the math and calculating the cash she would be making off her unwanted pregnancy. Maybe her career was on "hold," but Dolly was a hardened survivor. She was going to come out of this with a bundle of bills to put in her hidden stash jar.

Before her pregnancy, Dolly's life had revolved around the pulsating nightclub scene that brought 52nd Street to life night after night. But here along the seaside in Far Rockaway, life didn't pulsate. It ambled along with an easy-going gait. Dorothy spent her final days and weeks before giving birth reading magazines, helping Margaret Weltsch with the light housework, and lying on the beach. Margaret was the perfect hostess and Dorothy was taken with her hospitality and her cooking. This 21-year-old Catholic girl had never had the likes of stuffed cabbage, goulash, or blintzes. Margaret was a wonderful cook but an even better baker. She could make strudel and rugalach and linzer tortes better than anyone in the neighborhood. The food was foreign to Dorothy but she quickly developed a taste for it. As Margaret would put it, "What's not to like?"

The weekdays at the seashore passed with a near-certain regularity that bordered on monotony. And no one needed a calendar to tell when the weekend arrived. Beach 78th Street was a very quiet street in a quiet neighborhood during the week. But the population along the street exploded on Friday night as husbands and lovers arrived from their jobs in the heart of the City.

Still, the sight of a stunning, tall, very pregnant, single woman in the tightly-knit neighborhood on Beach 78th Street did not go unnoticed by others. Hardly. Dorothy McDonald had tongues wagging in the bungalows up and down both sides of the cracked, buckled pavement. These people had seen photos in glamour magazines but they had never seen anyone like Dorothy in the flesh. In fact, they had never seen anybody in "show business" except for Margaret Weltsch's daughters, Frances and Edie. They too had that eye-popping, glamorous appeal that dazzled curious onlookers and stood in stark contrast to the bland housewives who spent their days cooking, cleaning, and caring for their families.

Ruth and Louis Paul, along with their teenage daughter, Miriam, were among the Hungarian crowd that found summer solace on Beach 78th Street. One of Ruth's sisters, Fritzi, her husband Jack, and their teenage daughter, Muriel, rounded out the numbers. They all knew Margaret Weltsch from the neighborhood in the Bronx. They all spoke English well but they chatted in Hungarian every chance they had. It created a special bond and a way to keep secrets from those who didn't understand their native tongue. It was a way to talk about Dorothy without Dorothy understanding a word they said.

Ruth and Fritzi had another sister, Selma, who lived in not-too-distant New Jersey. Selma and her husband, Herman, could not have children of their own, and after nearly ten years of marriage, they were looking for a baby to adopt. After Dorothy moved in with Margaret Weltsch, Ruth found an excuse to invite Margaret over to her kochalayn... alone. She interrogated Margaret sweetly and learned that Dorothy was not keeping the baby. Ruth wasted no time calling her sister Selma. "Zelma," Ruth said, using the familiar, ethnic pronunciation of her name, "Zelma, a wonderful thing has happened and maybe, just maybe, you could adopt a little baby of your own.

Even as that conversation was taking place, Rose Ferrucci was striking up a conversation with Dorothy on the beach. It began with benign comments about the weather but turned quickly to Dorothy's pregnancy.

Rose wanted to know all about the baby and what plans Dorothy had for the baby after she gave birth. "So why are you so interested in hearing about my baby?" Dorothy asked Rose pointedly. "What's so special about my baby?" Rose looked at Dorothy with tears welling up in her eyes. "You are so lucky. You can have children. You don't know what it's like to want a baby so badly and not be able to have one."

Then Rose stopped abruptly. "I'm sorry," she said. "I'm being too forward. I shouldn't be telling you all this. It's really much too personal." Rose averted her eyes and took a step to leave but then turned back. "I hope we can talk again," she said awkwardly. Dorothy nodded her head in agreement.

The two women passed on the street and on the boardwalk several times that week and each time they stopped to chat. Rose asked how Dorothy was doing and how her baby was doing. And each time the talk became more personal with Dorothy feigning a growing vulnerability, a growing desperation over what was to become of her child. She remembered Rose's comment about not being able to have a baby and she sensed that Rose might be the pigeon that could make her pregnancy pay off.

Rose could hardly wait for Rocco to arrive in Far Rockaway on Friday night. She had been immersed in thought every day since she met Dorothy and she formulated her own plan to help fill the void in their lives.

The minute Rocco opened the door Rose threw her arms around him with gusto. She hugged him and kissed him over and over again before Rocco even had a chance to put down the bag he was carrying. "Oh, Rocco, Rocco," Rose said excitedly, "How was your week? How was the ride on the subway tonight? Did you get bread?" But before Rocco could muster even a tentative response, Rose continued, "Oh, Rocco, I have such wonderful news. I am so... I can't wait to tell... I think... Oh Rocco... maybe we can adopt a baby."

Rocco paused a moment to take in Rose's last words as Rose stared at him intently. It was Rose, though, who broke the moment of silence when she blurted out, "Here, let me take the bag," "No, no, honey… wait… wait for a moment," Rocco insisted. "Wait. Calm down. What are you saying? But wait… wait… first let's sit down… let me hear what you have to say. But easy… take it easy, honey."

Rocco put the bag of groceries on the table and sat down in a chair across from Rose who was already sitting and fidgeting excitedly. She told Rocco about Dorothy and about the baby. And she told Rocco about the plan she devised. "What if we offered to pay this woman's doctor bills and hospital bills? Maybe she would let us adopt her baby."

Rocco Ferrucci was a sensible man, a man grounded in life's realities. He and Rose had a modest savings account but he knew there would always be someone with more money and more connections that could outbid them for the baby. Rocco was the bread-winner and the protector and he didn't want Rose to get hurt. "Think about it honey," he said warmly, "think about…. What are the odds… What are the odds that we could be that lucky? We can't afford to pay what some rich people could pay… to get this child. I don't want you to get your hopes up."

"Rocco Ferrucci," Rose said in a firm, stern voice, "now you listen to me. I know what I'm talking about. I've been talking to this woman and this can happen… this good thing can happen to us." Before Rocco could gather his thoughts and respond, Rose went on. "This woman needs money. She has no friends who can help her. She doesn't know a lot about these things. We can pay her what we can and I'm sure we can make it worth it for her and nobody else has to be involved." But Rocco disagreed, "Yes, Rose, somebody else does have to be involved. There will be lawyers and judges and people asking questions. It's not that easy. It won't be that easy for us."

A depressing silence settled on the small room as Rocco and Rose each pondered the harsh reality of the words Rocco had just uttered. It was so quiet they could both hear the rumbling sound of the waves rolling onto the nearby shore. Rose felt the crackle of excitement give way to an emotional surrender. She let herself sink into the realization that with lawyers and judges come rich people. And a truck driver and his wife are no match for those rich people. The rich, she knew, could always outbid them.

Rocco could see his wife's suffering. He could feel her pain of disappointment. But as he reached out to touch her hand to comfort her, his thoughts reverberated with a newfound clarity. "Wait.... No... wait...," he stammered. "Rose, wait. I... maybe... there's a way... a way that we can do this without getting the lawyers involved.... a way... a way without questions." He went on... even as he was formulating the plan in his mind. They would check this pregnant woman into the hospital as if she was Rocco's wife. She would be Rose Ferrucci. How could the hospital verify it? The hospital would have to take their word and so the baby would be named "Ferrucci." They could tell people back in the neighborhood that they adopted the child and who would know? Who would bother to check up on it? Far Rockaway wasn't exactly right around the corner. "But this woman," Rocco cautioned, "this woman... what did you say her name was? ... Dorothy... This woman, Dorothy... she will have to agree to this." Rose reassured Rocco that she was certain Dorothy would agree.

Late Saturday morning, Rocco and Rose sat in the rocking chairs on the porch of their bungalow near the beach. They were on a mission: They were hoping they could spot Dorothy and strike up a conversation with her. After about an hour had passed, they spotted Dorothy waddling toward the boardwalk with a blanket and small beach umbrella. But there were prying eyes sitting on the porch of the bungalows nearby. "Wait... let's not talk to her here," Rocco cautioned. "The beach is a better place to talk." Rose agreed, so they sat for another minute and then casually sauntered down the street and walked up the steps to the boardwalk and over to the ocean side.

They had no trouble spotting Dorothy. She stood out like a neon sign, sitting under her umbrella with her blonde hair and her expansive belly.

Rocco and Rose walked across the sand toward her. Rose made the first contact and then introduced her husband to Dorothy.

"My wife tells me that you are short of cash?" Rocco said to Dorothy compassionately. Dorothy reluctantly admitted that she was. "Maybe we can help," he went on. "What are you planning to do once you have the baby?" Dorothy played her role well as the penniless, single pregnant woman. "I guess I'll have to give my baby up for adoption," she said almost tearfully. "I don't have, as you know, any money… and I can't afford to keep my baby or even go see the doctor as much as I should." Rocco seized on the moment to present his offer. He and Rose would pay for Dorothy's care and even take her to the doctor for checkups. They would pay her expenses. They would take her to the hospital and pay the hospital bill. And in return, if Dorothy would agree to claim she was Rose Ferrucci when she checked into the hospital and give them her baby when she checked out, they would pay Dorothy one-thousand dollars in cash… (a very substantial amount of money at the time.)

It appeared to be the perfect scheme. No lawyers, no legal adoption, no rich people who would have an edge over Rocco and Rose. And this way, Dorothy would get a thousand bucks in cash, unrecorded and untaxed, the kind of money she was used to. Dorothy readily agreed to the deal. So before Rocco left Rose to go back to work early Monday morning he left her with some extra money to take Dorothy to the doctor and pay for an exam. Rocco also promised to bring more cash back with him the following weekend.

The next weekend Rocco made good on his promise. "How did it go this week, sweetheart?" he asked Rose anxiously when he arrived on Friday night. "Did you take Dorothy to the doctor?" Rose was feeling the sweet contentment of a surrogate mother and told Rocco, "Yes, dear, everything is fine. The doctor said the baby is doing well and should be due in about three weeks. And that Dorothy… she is such a sweet person. I feel so sorry for her, having to give up her baby..." "But you know...." Rocco interrupted sternly. "It's the right thing to do.... and it's the only thing to do. You know that, Rose."

Though Rose naively cared about Dorothy she had no way of knowing that Dorothy only cared about Dorothy. And she had no way of knowing that another couple was about to appear in the picture who would also want Dorothy' child.

"Sweetie, sit down, I have something I want to talk to you about," Margaret Weltsch cooed. Dorothy took a seat at the table in Margaret's kochalayn. "Here, sweetie," she said as she passed a plate of rugulach over to Dorothy, "Have a little nosh. It'll be good for your baby." Dorothy obeyed. She had learned there was no way to say "no" to a Hungarian mother who prided herself on her culinary skills. "Have you decided what you want to do when your baby is born?" Margaret asked. But Dorothy was savoring a mouthful of the tasty rolled-up pastry and before she could respond Margaret continued, "Because I know a family who would love your baby and care for your baby and would love to adopt your baby." The remaining chewy pastry in Dorothy' mouth gave her a moment to consider how she would reply. She hadn't told Margaret about her deal with the Ferruccis. She hadn't told anyone. So it was easy to innocently ask, "But how will I know these people will be able to afford to care for my baby? How will I know they will have the money for clothing and food?" Margaret put Dorothy's mind at ease. "Darling... sweetheart... I wouldn't think of talking to you about these people unless I knew about them. They own a jewelry store in New Jersey. I'm sure they can afford everything your baby would need."

Margaret added more of an inducement somewhat conspiratorially, "And I'm sure they would take care of your money needs too." "Oh really," Dorothy replied with fake innocence. "Well, I would hate to talk about money when it comes to my baby... but I haven't been able to work for months… and I do have a lot of bills to pay." They talked a bit more before Dorothy McDonald and Margaret Weltsch reached an "understanding" that Margaret could now convey to this family that wanted Dorothy's child.

Selma Gerstel was at home when she got the collect call from her sister Ruth in Far Rockaway. "Zelma… oh, Zelma, "Ruth said excitedly into the phone, "this woman… the pregnant woman who is staying with Margaret Weltsch… Zelma, she wants you to adopt her baby… that's what she told Margaret." Selma was overcome with joy. "I can't tell you how happy this… this wonderful news makes me," Selma practically shouted back at her sister. "Let me call Herman and see what we should do now. How long… how much time before this woman will have the baby?" "I'm not sure, Zelma… I think maybe just a few weeks from now. I will find out…. And I will find out what we should do next," Ruth responded before the two sisters hung up.

Selma called her husband's jewelry store immediately and told him the news. "That's really wonderful news," Herman told her, "I am so happy dear as long as you are happy. Maybe we should even go out to dinner tonight to celebrate?" They both agreed that a celebration was in order that evening. But Herman Gerstel was also a pragmatic, shrewd businessman. He expected that he would have to pay a lot of money to get this baby that his wife wanted and he wanted assurances that he would be getting what he paid for. So he walked around the corner to the office of his friend Robert Minsky.

Robert was an attorney and the two men knew each other well. "You don't have to go through an adoption agency, Herman. But you do need a lawyer and you have to make this adoption legal through the courts in New York State," Robert told Herman in his no-nonsense style. "And what do you know about this woman? How do you know the baby will be healthy? You need to make sure you protect yourself and your money. But you and Selma have to stay out of it. Trust me. I have done this before.

Don't get involved with that woman yourself. It could mean trouble. Find someone who can be a middle-man so you and Selma don't get too personally involved. I'll help you all I can but you must listen to what I am telling you."

Herman Gerstel was many things but he was not a stupid man. He knew who to trust and he trusted Robert Minsky. Herman was also a religious man who was on the Board of Directors of Temple Emanuel in Westwood, New Jersey, and a trusted friend of Rabbi Samuel Schwartz. Because he knew the Rabbi so well, he knew that the Rabbi and his wife had rented an apartment for a month-long vacation getaway... in... Far Rockaway! That meant Rabbi Schwartz was in the perfect location to be an intermediary. Herman called Rabbi Schwartz, who readily agreed to do anything in his power to help.

Herman and Selma drove to Far Rockaway that Sunday to meet the Rabbi at the office of a lawyer who was a close friend of Robert Minsky... so close a friend that he agreed to a weekend meeting. Together they crafted a deal: The Rabbi would go to Margaret Weltsch's bungalow, sit down with Dorothy and offer a proposition. The Gerstels would pay $2,000 for her baby but not all at one time. She would get $500 right away if she would go to the lawyer's office and sign a document agreeing to relinquish her rights to the baby. The Rabbi would go to the hospital and give her another $500 after the baby was born and a doctor examined the baby and found it was healthy. And the lawyer would give her the additional $1,000 in cash when she signed over her rights to the Gerstels and left her baby with them.

Rabbi Schwartz fulfilled his mission. Dorothy could not have been happier with the proposition. She was due to have her baby in less than two weeks and she would walk away with $3,000 in cash. She... and only she... knew that this new deal with the Gerstels meant she was going to "burn" the Ferruccis, but she concluded that a total of $3,000 trumped

$1,000 any day. She rationalized her treachery by convincing herself that if she had to suffer through this pregnancy for nine months, everyone was fair game.

The Rabbi reported back to Herman and Selma who were anxiously awaiting word in Ruth's bungalow just down the street from Margaret's. They were ecstatic when the rabbi told them Dorothy agreed to the arrangement. But as they sat around the table chatting excitedly in Hungarian and English, Selma suddenly fell silent. "What is it Zelma? I can tell that something is bothering you," Ruth said. At first Selma said nothing, but the burden of silence was too much to bear. "I have to see her," Selma said stoically. "I have to see what she looks like." The room fell silent. No one could find the right words to say. Selma went on, "But I don't want to meet her. I just need to see her, to know what my baby's mother looks like... that's what I need to do" Ruth reacted quickly, telling her sister, "Don't be silly, Zelma," what's the difference?" Selma responded stoically, "I just have to."

Rabbi Schwartz had seen Dorothy head off to the beach after he struck the deal with her, and despite his reservations, he reluctantly offered to point Dorothy out to Selma if she would go along with him to the beach. Selma nodded in agreement. So while everyone else remained in the room, Selma and the Rabbi walked to the beach. It was a beautiful summer day that brought thousands of people out to the surf and sand. But it wasn't difficult to pick Dorothy out from the crowd. "There she is," exclaimed the Rabbi as he pointed to a rotund woman sitting by herself on beach blanket near the lifeguard stand. "Please wait here, Rabbi," Selma said reassuringly, "I'll be right back."

Selma took off her shoes and left them on the boardwalk next to the Rabbi and sauntered across the sand and down to the water's edge. She dipped her feet into the surf and let the waves splash on her legs as she turned around several times seemingly to get refreshed from each surge of salt water. But with each turn she took another look at the mother of her child, and with each turn, she seemed to be more and more in tune with what this woman was going through. She finally acted as if she had enough of the water and slowly walked back toward the boardwalk gazing at Dorothy as often as she could. Dorothy had her head tipped back with her eyes closed as she was "taking in the sun." She was never aware of Selma's intense gaze.

The non-encounter only took a few minutes but it was all that Selma needed. She had felt the urge to somehow bond with this woman and in some way experience a pre-natal relationship with the baby the woman was carrying. She needed to see the biological mother of her soon-to-be child in the flesh to feel some sort of emotional attachment. What she experienced was satisfying enough. Dorothy remained unaware of Selma's gaze but Selma had made the connection. It was the only time the two "mothers" would ever cross paths.

CHAPTER FOUR

Where Did I Begin?

The nagging despair I felt during my childhood blossomed into a firestorm of doubt during my college years, and that doubt consumed many long hours as I tried to remember a time in my life, ANY time in my life, when I felt truly happy or even a small sense of contentment. Could it have been at a birthday party? When I played the Handsome Prince in my second-grade school play? When I got my first bicycle? What about my first girlfriend... my first kiss? Nothing clicked. Though I relived the events of my life again and again, I could not remember, nor did I fully understand, what it meant to let my emotions soar and to be truly happy.

My military tour of duty in Vietnam ultimately forced me to face my demons. The year was 1966 and I was drafted right out of college during the height of the build-up for the war. I probably could have avoided the draft if that's what I really wanted. I could have stayed in college, gotten married, or had a psychologist intervene on my behalf and claim I was mentally unstable and therefore unfit for military service. And that would have been very close to the truth for I was tormented by ongoing, vague feelings of self-loathing. Somewhere deep down inside I convinced myself that going off to war would change me. It would toughen me and help me deal with my troubling emotional baggage.

During the previous four years while I studied Theatre at Boston University and worked in Summer Stock, I continued evading the ugly reality that I was a troubled young man who desperately needed help dealing with the issues that were crippling him emotionally. During those years I maintained the same intense schedule that I had created for myself in high school. And whenever I couldn't immerse myself in enough projects to divert my mind I could always numb myself with alcohol. I was never a slave to the spirits but there were those rare idle times when I needed a healthy glassful of Canadian Club to force the adoption genie back into its bottle.

It took the U-S Army, and specifically my year of service in Vietnam, to dismantle the emotional defense mechanism that had served me so well for so long. There were no theatres in Vietnam. No television. No accessible telephones. No real diversion… except for fear, the fear that I might not make it through the next mortar attack.

The one true moment of diversion came in a phone call I received from Saigon. This was 1968 and I was in the middle of a war zone. Communications were rudimentary at best and getting a "phone call" was unheard of. Yet here I was, rushing over to HQ, where I was handed a phone. Martha Raye was on the other end. "Alan, I finally tracked you down," she said in that almost breathless voice of hers. "I've been looking for you because I need someone to help me out on my USO tour." Martha Raye supported the troops in Vietnam even more than Bob Hope did. She was there for months at a time, with little or no fanfare, just trying to raise the spirits of the men and women who were so far from home. "But I got some bad news, kiddo," she went on. "I'm here in Saigon and the Big Brass won't let me snag you from your unit. Hell, I'm an honorary Major and I got no pull. I'm sorry we can't work together again. But I wanted you to know I tried my best."

I too was terribly disappointed because touring with Maggie would have provided that much-needed diversion I was lacking. She was such a joy to be with and I was truly disheartened that I wouldn't be spending the upcoming weeks and months alongside this special lady. But I was honored that Martha Raye was such a dear friend that she tracked me down in that miserable South East Asian country in the middle of a horrible war because she wanted me to be with her as a part of her tour.

Then there was marijuana… some of the most potent marijuana in the world. I tried drinking the alcohol that had served me so well in the past but in the intense heat and humidity of Vietnam it only served to make me sick. And what's worse, it made me sick before it numbed my senses. So, along with legions of fellow soldiers marijuana became my drug of choice. My friends and I would take a regulation U-S Army pillowcase down to our local village and visit "Connie," a Vietnamese lady who ran a barbershop there. She filled the pillowcase with marijuana and sewed it up for 60-dollars. "The Pillow," as we called it, serviced my friends and me for many months. I smoked a joint or two every night after work hours and on my days off.

The marijuana numbed my senses and took the edge off my anxiety but it could only bring temporary relief to the searing emotional pain. It did, though, give me the insight to finally recognize that I needed professional help and I made a commitment that when I returned to the States… IF I returned to the States… I would seek therapy. And I did.

I spent many hundreds of hours "on the couch" talking with Dr. Charles Streicher. He was an amazing psychiatrist who taught me how to handle my father's emotional bullying and my rejection issues. Oh, certainly my mother loved me, and on some level, my father too. My mother, in fact, overwhelmed me with love and affection as far back as I can remember.

She truly accepted me into her life wholeheartedly and even lived her life to meet my needs.

But there was still a catch: Someone... SOMEONE... didn't want me. Someone gave birth to me and then gave me away. And all the love my parents showered on me could not compensate for that feeling of abandonment. I felt unworthy. I felt worthless. I was, in fact... a bastard. It took many years, but Dr. Streicher gave me my life back, a life without that searing inner pain.

That absence of hurt also unleashed a torrent of feelings that needed to be satisfied by a woman who would show me that I was truly worthy of love and affection. I was nearly 30 years old when I met and fell passionately in love with Ronni Richman, whose parents were in a Community Theatre production I was directing. Ronni had been dating another guy for six years, but fortunately for me, Ronni fell as hopelessly in love with me as I had fallen for her. So when she had to make a decision between the two of us, she chose me. I certainly didn't feel unwanted and unworthy anymore!

Finally, in May of 1976, five months before I was to marry this woman who had captured my heart, I began the process of learning who I really was. I began the Search for my birth parents. Dr. Streicher told me there's a connection that comes with marriage and that adopted men in particular develop a need to learn who they really are before sharing a life of uncertainty with another person. Ronni was extremely supportive. She encouraged me to delve into the past and unravel the mystery surrounding the origins of my birth.

I started the search for my genetic identity by looking back at what I knew about my birth. Several facts had remained etched in my mind since I was five years old: I was born in St. Joseph's Hospital in Far Rockaway on August 11, 1944 and I was adopted when I was ten days old.

The first step would be a simple phone call to St. Joseph's Hospital to ask about my birth records. But the more I thought about it, the more the simple act of making a phone call paralyzed me with doubt. The questions erupted. What if my parents found out? I knew my mother would be devastated. What would I say to whoever answered my call at the hospital about not having a birth certificate? Would the hospital staff question me suspiciously and would I be able to handle the probing and possible rejection? The questions went on. What would happen if I were successful in locating my birth parents? Would they reject me yet a second time? And then, the overriding questions: Why was I... a "nice Jewish boy"... born in St. Joseph's, a Catholic hospital? And why had my parents, who were religious Jews, gone to a Catholic hospital to pick me out "from all the other babies in the hospital?" I had no idea how my questions would be answered but I think more than anything else I feared being turned down, being rejected again in every step of the journey I knew had to begin with a simple phone call.

After weeks of procrastinating, I finally overcame my fears and doubts and picked up the phone and dialed. I asked the "Information" Operator in New York City for the listing of St. Joseph's Hospital in Far Rockaway in the Borough of Queens. There was no immediate response but during the moment of silence I could hear the sound of the operator flipping pages to try to find the number. She was exhaling heavily into her headset and then began to vent her frustration as only a New Yorker can do, with an accent that is unmistakably "New Yawk." "I'm sorry, honey, I can't find no listing for St. Joseph's Hospital in – where'd you say again?" she asked. "Far Rockaway," I repeated in a hesitating voice. "Far Rockaway," she echoed. The saliva was drying up in my mouth.

Then a flash of discovery must have resonated in the operator's mind because her demeanor softened. "I've been around here for a long time, sweetie, and I think that – that Long Island Jewish Hospital - is where St. Joseph's used to be. In fact, yes, that's it. Yes, uh-huh, that's it," she said with a startling clarity even as I could hear the sound of the pages in front of her flipping again. "Here it is," she said as she gave me the number for Long Island Jewish Hospital. Then she finished off the call by giving herself a pat on the back, "You know, you were lucky to get me on duty tonight. Not many people would remember that St. Joseph's Hospital closed down years ago." With a sense of relief and the saliva flowing again, I thanked her profusely for her good work and hung up.

"Hey, this isn't going to be so bad," I thought to myself. "I can do this." The next day, I confidently called the number for Long Island Jewish Hospital only to get a confirmation that St. Joseph's had indeed closed down years before and that all records from St. Joseph's were transferred to St. Anthony's, which was also the Catholic Medical Center for Brooklyn and Queens.

My mind buzzed with a Rubik's Cube of possibilities: What strange cosmic force was at work here? And how did I play into this grand scheme? I was a nice Jewish boy who was born at a Catholic hospital that, in turn, became a Jewish hospital. What are the odds? And what does it all mean... if it truly means anything at all?

I called "Information" again and got the number and the address for St. Anthony's. Then, empowered by my success with St. Joseph's, I called St. Anthony's and asked how to go about requesting medical information. The hospital operator transferred me to the Medical Records department where I was told to mail in a request along with ten dollars for processing. I put the request in the mail the same day. In my letter I spelled it all out. "I was born August 11, 1944 in St. Joseph's Hospital according to my Birth Certificate #9740, which was filed in the Queens office of the New York City Department of Health. I was adopted when I was ten days old and I'd like to see the medical records of my birth mother if they exist."

The only Birth Certificate I ever had was an "Amended Certificate by Adoption." It confirmed that I was born on August 11, 1944 in St. Joseph's Hospital in the New York City Borough of Queens, according to Certificate Number 9740. But it listed my parents as Herman and Selma Gerstel... my adoptive parents. It made no mention of my birth parents. Yet here I was, holding it and staring at this Amended Birth Certificate. It was an official document issued by the Department of Health and it seemed logical to me there had to be a paper trail that would lead back to my birth parents. So I wrote to the New York City Health Department, the agency that had issued my Birth Certificate. It seemed easy enough. I spelled out my entire story once again, and asked for any medical records for my birth mother.

The journey was underway and I was confidently taking charge of my Search and looking back into the past to uncover the truth. I would find out who my birth parents where, discover how I came into this world, and ferret out the reason why the man and woman who created my genetic identity chose to give me away. I felt the answers to my questions were within my grasp.

As it turned out, I was being spectacularly naïve. I truly believed that anyone with even a semblance of compassion would want to help adoptees in their search for their origins. It seemed to me that everyone would see it as an honorable mission, a life-saving mission to make adoptees whole again. But I quickly learned that The System was riddled with perverse laws enacted specifically to thwart adoptees from learning the truth.

In rapid succession I heard back from St. Anthony's and from the Department of Health. St. Anthony's responded to my inquiry with a form letter saying "no records can be found regarding the birth of Alan Gerstel or his mother." No records? What about my Amended Birth Certificate? Did my parents lie to me so many years before? Or was I being lied to now by some nameless, faceless hospital clerk who took some perverse pleasure in rejecting my request before even looking into it? But I only had one day to ponder those questions before I received a response from the Department of Health. It was equally unhelpful. But its form letter contained a hand-written note at the bottom: "all we have are Birth Certificates. Adoption Records are sealed permanently. If you wish a B.C. please fill in the app (application) and remit fee."

"Adoption records are sealed permanently." Those five hand-written words opened my eyes to a sobering and very demoralizing fact of adopted life: All adoption records in the State of New York are under lock and key and requests from adoptees are routinely denied to protect the identity of the birth mothers. So here I was... butting heads with an unsympathetic, unyielding bureaucracy. I was trying to uncover information from a system that was established solely to deny me and everyone like me.

I had run headlong into my first reality check. And because I was so naïve about the system it was like a sucker punch that brought me to my knees. What would I do now? I had just begun my Search and I had already reached a dead end. The connection to St. Joseph's Hospital was all that I had except for my Birth Certificate... my "Amended" Birth Certificate. I had conquered the fears that kept me from taking the first tiny, tentative steps only to find that the task ahead of me would take a Herculean effort. Yet my need for answers was becoming more desperate because the questions that filled me with insecurities and self-doubt were finally surfacing in my psychotherapy and I realized for the first time that the questions about my identity were the source of the emotional difficulties I suffered for so many years.

Dr. Charles Streicher was not only my therapist, he was also incredibly helpful as a practical resource. He offered to call the New York City Department of Health, affirming that he was my doctor and that it was "medically necessary" for me to get my birth records. And Dr. Streicher was remarkably persistent. As the weeks passed he showed me his notes indicating he had been transferred to at least a half-dozen different people in the Health Department. The final answer, though, even to a medical professional was "no." He was told "Birth Records are sealed. Your patient

needs to hire an attorney to petition the court to have the records unsealed."
Dr. Streicher, as I said, was persistent and he went on to call a number of
other doctors and even a lawyer who told him that the legal route would
be a waste of time. In New York State, sealed birth records are just not
unsealed.

Yet Dr. Streicher plugged on. He reached a clerk in the Medical Records
Department at St. Anthony's where my records were now stored. Mr. Luis
Andre told Dr. Streicher that "records are filed according to the mother's
maiden name" and if we could provide a maiden name he could probably
find the records. Talk about a Catch-22!!! How could I provide my birth
mother's maiden name if I didn't know if she was married or single? And
how would I have a hint of her name at all if my birth records are sealed?
It all seemed to be a cruel practical joke and I was being made the butt
of scorn. Weeks before, I had been wildly optimistic, but then the cold,
negative responses to my queries plunged me into the depths of despair.

CHAPTER FIVE

The Street That Never Sleeps

Dolly's legal name was Dorothy Jeannette McDonald. Her mother named her after the singer Jeannette MacDonald, who became famous for her sweet, warbling operetta duets with Nelson Eddy in the 1930's and 40's. Growing up, Dolly felt that it was her destiny to become famous as an entertainer. And to that end she moved to New York at the age of 18 to try to make it as a Big Band singer. She knew her looks could open doors and she figured the best doors to open were on 52nd Street where she could hob-nob with the jazz musicians who gave that street its fame and its flair. She hung around the clubs, adding a touch of sexy glamour, doing the managers' bidding, and keeping the customers happy. In return, she could become very close with a multitude of musicians as she tried to weave her way into their bands. She even went "on the road" with some of them and would do anything to get into the good graces of the bandleader who might let her step up to the microphone and take a shot at stardom. In the era of rock and roll, Dolly would have been known as a "groupie."

Once Dolly learned she was pregnant, though, life as she knew it began to change dramatically. As her belly grew so did her liability to her bosses who eventually dropped a wad of cash in her hand and told her to take some time off and come back after the baby was born. "There will always be a place here for Dolly," they promised. "Don't sweat it, kid. We'll see ya around." Dolly expected to be back in the club scene after she gave birth and slimmed down again but she was especially downhearted because she had made serious inroads into Louis Prima's band, one of the most popular Big Bands of the day. And now she could feel the connection to Prima's band slip away.

Dolly spent the last months of her pregnancy and gave birth in Far Rockaway because of her friendship with her next-door neighbor at 301 West 46th Street in Manhattan. The apartment building was just blocks from "Swing Street" and catered to the young women who worked the club scene. It had a Concierge at the front desk much like a hotel but the Concierge was more of a bouncer who kept the riff-raff out and shielded the girls from unwanted advances. Her neighbor, 16-year-old Frances Duze', lived next door with her husband, Thomas. Frances Weltsch Duze' had married with the blessings of her mother, a Hungarian woman whose life was steeped in Old World tradition. Back in Budapest it was not unheard of for a girl to marry in her teens. In fact, it was a fairly common occurrence. But it was not an accepted practice where Francis grew up on Morris Avenue in the Bronx. There, other Hungarian families looked upon Frances and her older sister Edie as Show Girls who worked in the questionable "club scene" that was so far removed from the daily life in the working class neighborhood.

Frances was a stunning, sophisticated-looking blonde, who could easily have been mistaken for Betty Grable. She had the upturned hair style, the knockout body, and a winning smile of a younger Grable and she attracted men like a magnet. She and Thomas Duze' had been an "item" for a year before they were married. But Thomas Duze' was devout in his faith and his faith was womanizing. Even Frances, with her good looks and shapely torso couldn't keep him from straying. Very late one summer night in August of 1943, Frances returned home to 301 West 46ᵗʰ Street unexpectedly to find her husband practicing his faith with another woman.

Frances was young but she was no dummy. She slipped out of her apartment quietly without waking her husband and his "friend" and went next door where she knocked softly on Dorothy' door. Dorothy had just gotten home herself and readily let Frances in. "That louse," Frances blurted out. "That creep is sleeping in my bed next door with some floozie. And he's going to pay for that. He's going to pay!" She asked her friend Dorothy to be her witness and they both returned to Frances' apartment to confront her husband. "Hey, louse," Frances screamed. "I'm not in Far Rockaway anymore!" Thomas bolted upright. His female partner also awoke in a panic and tried to cover her naked body with the sheet. "I have a witness. I have a witness, you creep." Thomas Duze' was speechless. He knew he wasn't in a position to argue. Thomas Duze and his female companion got dressed hastily and rushed out the door without saying a word.

That incident helped cement the relationship between Dorothy and Frances. Dorothy agreed to be a witness in Frances' divorce case and she appeared in court and signed papers testifying to the events of that night. During the court proceedings, Dorothy met France's mother, Margaret, who expressed her deep gratitude and praised Dorothy as a good friend who didn't let her daughter down. So it came as no surprise that when Dorothy got pregnant Margaret Weltsch would extend a helping hand.

The summer heat in New York City was no place for a woman to endure the final months of her pregnancy. So when Dorothy became "with child" in the Fall of 1943 and then left the glamour of 52ⁿᵈ Street in the late Spring,

Margaret invited her to join her in the relative comfort of Far Rockaway. There Dorothy could give birth, far from the sweltering summer stench of the City and the wagging tongues who wanted to know who the father was but could only guess. Dorothy packed her suitcase and stuffed several large shopping bags with her personal items, then closed up her apartment in Manhattan in early June when she was 7 months pregnant. She took the subway to Far Rockaway with Frances at her side and moved in with Margaret Weltsch. She gave birth on August 11th.

On Saturday, August 12th, the day after the baby was born, Rabbi Schwartz paid a visit to St. Joseph's Hospital along with Herman and Selma Gerstel. They told the nun at the Main Desk that they were friends of the family and they asked to see the baby in the nursery. But the Rabbi also asked some questions, very innocently, about the baby's well-being. He was told the child was the picture of health and would have no problem going home with his mother on schedule, ten days after his birth date. Herman and Selma lingered at the nursery window enraptured by the sight of the child being held up in front of them. Even when the nun put the baby back in his little hospital bed, they stayed and looked on lovingly. Rabbi Schwartz, meanwhile, left them at the nursery to visit Dorothy in her hospital room where he presented her with an envelope containing $500 in cash.

Nearly every day that week the Ferruccis checked up on Dorothy and her baby. But it was no surprise to Dorothy that no one from the Club Scene came to visit her. After all, that's one of the reasons she came to Far Rockaway... to get away from the prying eyes that would see her at her most unattractive self... big-bellied and bloated. So it was a real shock when Jimmy Vincent walked through the door of her hospital room. Jimmy was the drummer in Louis Prima's band and Louis Prima's best friend. He came for a visit on Wednesday, five days after Dorothy had given birth. "Hey toots," Jimmy announced as he strutted into Dorothy's room.

"Good to see ya." Dorothy brightened up and ran her fingers through her hair to make herself a little more presentable. "Hi Jimmy," she responded in the seductive voice that had won the hearts of countless men. "How ya been holding up?" "Still jiving," he said with a big smile. "But you know the boys in the band is all missing you. They wanna see you back in the groove." Dorothy lifted her chin a bit and smiled a great big smile. "It won't be long now," she said. "I'm outta here on Sunday. And hey... by the way Jimmy... how's Louis doing?" Jimmy took a moment to weigh his answer and then responded cheerily, "Louis is doing good too.... In fact, he told me to give you his best."

Jimmy shuffled his feet and then sat on the bed next to her. "I got something for you and I want you to wear it," he told her. He handed her a small box which she opened to reveal a gold cross on a gold chain. "And this is the real thing, nothing gold-plated about this gift," Jimmy bragged. "Gee Jimmy, thanks," she said as she took it and clasped it around her neck. "But you didn't have to do that." Jimmy took a breather as he struggled for just the right words to say... words that would conceal the real reason he made this hospital room visit. He looked down at the floor and then looked up at her and took her hand. "You know, kiddo, all of us hit it off pretty good on the West Coast last year, you and me and Louis and the rest of the guys," he said awkwardly, "and I wanted to give you that cross to... uh... to show you how special you meant to me... uh... personally." Then he paused again before he took a deep breath and blurted out, "I'd like it if you would marry me."

The air in the room seemed to stand still. Neither Jimmy nor Dorothy appeared to be breathing. Dorothy was stunned but desperate to turn Jimmy down while not alienating him. Finally she managed to speak. "Oh Jimmy, you're a sweetheart, but I can't marry you. I just can't get tied down because of this baby. I gotta keep plugging away. Hell, I can sing circles around that Lily Ann Carol... and you know it! And Louis knows it too! I just wish he'd give me a shot." She then took a breath and continued softly, "Oh Jimmy, you're so sweet to ask me. But ya gotta know... that I just can't get tied down. You know I still care for you as a friend, don't you? It has nothing to do with that. I just gotta try."

A gust of ocean breeze blew into the room and seemed to defuse the tension in the air. "I gotcha, babe. Hey, no harm in trying, right?" Jimmy said with an underlying expression of relief. "No harm, Jimmy," Dorothy replied sweetly. They talked small talk for a while. Dorothy played with the cross around her neck. She thanked Jimmy again. Then the room fell silent. Jimmy used that silence as his cue to leave.

Dorothy spent the rest of the week especially antsy to get out of St. Joseph's and onto "Easy Street." When the Ferruccis came by on Saturday, August 19th, they brought along an envelope. It contained $1,000 in cash. Dorothy thanked them and then told them the doctor wouldn't let her leave the hospital with the baby until Monday morning, a day later than planned. The Ferruccis said that wouldn't be a problem and, in fact, it would give them extra time to get things ready in their apartment back in Brooklyn.

Dorothy, though, left St. Joseph's with her baby on the morning of Sunday, August 21st, exactly ten days after she had given birth... as originally planned. She took a cab back to Margaret Weltsch's bungalow on Beach 78th Street knowing full well that the Ferruccis would be in Brooklyn preparing for their baby's homecoming. Margaret, though, knew nothing of Dorothy's deal with the Ferruccis. She only knew that Dorothy was going to leave her baby with her, so she and Frances created a makeshift crib out of an open dresser drawer. Nothing fancy... just towels lining the empty drawer. Dorothy arrived with her baby and placed him in the homemade crib. She was leaving the baby there for the Gerstels to pick up a short time later. The two mothers would never have to meet.

As she was getting her remaining belongings together Dorothy began to sniffle and then to sob. It was the first time anyone had seen a hint of emotion from this woman, the first time she seemed to react to the fact that she was leaving her flesh and blood behind. Frances went over, put her arm around Dorothy's shoulder and told her reassuringly, "I know it must be tough, leaving your child like this. But it's the best thing for him and the best thing for you too." Her soothing words snapped Dorothy back into reality. She looked at Frances and said coldly, "I'm not crying because I'm leaving the kid. I'm crying because of the nine months he took out of my career." The iciness of the response took Frances and her mother by surprise. They didn't know quite how to respond.

Dorothy thanked Mrs. Weltsch again for her kindness. She thanked Frances too for helping her escape the wretched summer heat of the City while she awaited the birth of her baby. Then she picked up her bags, side-stepped around the table and made her way over to the door. She opened it and walked out without ever looking back at the people who had been so kind to her, or to the baby she carried in her womb for nine months. Dorothy took a cab to the lawyer's office where, without a hint of emotion, she signed the necessary papers that gave the child a name while relinquishing her rights to it. She collected another envelope stuffed with cash and took the subway back to her old haunt in Midtown Manhattan leaving "Baby Boy McDonald" nestled inside a dresser drawer in a bungalow on Beach 78th Street.

CHAPTER SIX

The Great Bar Mitzvah Connection

My Search was only several months old and I had already hit the brick wall of bureaucracy. I was disheartened but eventually took some comfort that it was still early in the game. I vowed to forge ahead. As I pondered the path I should explore next I realized that someone must have known something about my adoption because I was raised in a small town where everyone it seemed, knew each other's business. My father was also well-known as a jeweler and a founding member of Temple Emanuel in the little town of Westwood, New Jersey, so I tried charting every local connection, every link between my father and the past. I used a legal pad and scribbled every name, every event I could remember, anything that might lead me to someone who had precious information about my birth.

One event that eventually came to mind was my Bar Mitzvah. I recalled that my coming-of-age ceremony and celebration was held Labor Day weekend, a full three weeks after my 13th birthday on August 11th because I was told, many people were out of town for the summer... (including my relatives who vacationed in Far Rockaway.) I vaguely recalled a Rabbi who I had heard mentioned in connection with my bar mitzvah but I couldn't get a handle on his name or his connection to me.

Coincidentally, a close friend happened to be the current Cantor at Temple Emanuel and had access to its records. I shared the story of my Search with him and made him aware that any inquiries had to be very discreet to keep word from getting back to my father. The Cantor checked the temple records but could not find anything going back into the 1940's. So he questioned an old temple member, a friend of my father, about the succession of rabbis at the Temple and "who would have been the rabbi in 1944?" The first name to surface was Rabbi David Lieber.

I checked the library and located a Rabbi Lieber in Los Angeles and then wrote him, leaving out any mention of my adoption just to be cautious. I only introduced myself and asked if he had served at Temple Emanuel in 1944. Rabbi Lieber responded graciously and said he was the rabbi at Temple Emanuel from 1947 to 1948 but he also told me that he couldn't, unfortunately, name any of his predecessors.

Further subtle inquiries at Temple Emanuel turned up the name of Rabbi Schwartz. "Rabbi Samuel Schwartz. I remember that name!" I told my friend, the Cantor, when he called me with the news. I remember a Rabbi Schwartz who attended my Bar Mitzvah yet I was never told who he was or what his connection was to the family. I thought it was very strange. But what was even stranger was that he actually lit one of the candles on my Bar Mitzvah cake, an honor reserved for close family members and friends. So, I reasoned, he must have been an important person in the minds of my parents.

I knew my parents had an album of Bar Mitzvah pictures in their apartment and wondered if they might not also have hidden away some paperwork about my adoption. When they took off for a weekend getaway, Ronni and I sprang into action. We slipped into their apartment using the spare key I had and checked every conceivable spot. The apartment wasn't large and there weren't any hiding places. Yet, we came up empty-handed. I felt certain that my father would always cherish my adoption papers. They were the bill of sale for his most precious piece of merchandise. So how could they have vanished? Then it hit me! Years before, in 1968, while I was serving in Vietnam, crooks had broken into the safe in my father's jewelry store and literally cleaned it out. My father kept the store's most expensive jewelry in there as well as all his important papers. My adoption papers were likely taken along with everything else.

Ronni and I, though, did find a treasure during our search: my Bar Mitzvah album. The thick book of photographs was just as I remembered it. One section contained thirteen photos of thirteen people lighting the thirteen candles on my Bar Mitzvah cake. Since they were all my close relatives I knew every one of the people intimately... until I got to the picture of a man I didn't recognize. He had a big smile and was beaming with pride. It was Rabbi Schwartz!

My friend, the Cantor, located a Rabbi Schwartz in Indianapolis, Indiana. "Schwartz" is, of course, a common Jewish name. There was no certainty this was THE Rabbi Schwartz we were looking for but I took a shot. I composed a letter saying that I hope I was writing to the Rabbi Schwartz who served Temple Emanuel in 1944. And I decided to play it straight. I told him that I was searching for my birth parents, that I felt a real need to do so, and that I was hoping to keep my Search a secret from my parents to keep from hurting them.

Within a week, I received a heartwarming reply: "Dear Alan," Rabbi Schwartz wrote, "I am the Rabbi Schwartz for whom you are looking! And I'll be happy to provide any information I recall." I took a deep breath and read on. "I was vacationing in Rockaway Beach when I received word from your father about a baby boy who had just been born and who was available for adoption. Unfortunately, I do not remember the names, only the circumstances.

1. The arrangements were handled legally through a state welfare officer, an attorney, and a judge (who formalized the adoption one year later at the conclusion of the probationary period.)

2. Your biological mother was a tall, beautiful woman, a vocalist in a band. Your biological father was the leader of the band, and since they believed that they were not in a position to be married at that time, they felt that you should have a stable, cultured atmosphere in which to grow.

3. Your biological mother was in excellent health. At the time, as an infant, you were examined by a pediatrician and found to be in excellent health, responding normally to the world around you.

4. In the presence of the social worker representing the state, your biological mother formally declared that she wanted you to be raised in the Jewish faith.

5. Your father and mother were kind, gentle, and honorable people, "pillars" of the Jewish community in Westwood. Therefore, I had no hesitation in recommending that they be granted you as their son. I always considered them as good friends, happy to be liked and well regarded by them. If there are any other questions you may have, please do not hesitate to call.

Very sincerely, Samuel Schwartz."

I read the letter again… and then again! It unleashed a torrent of emotions. It answered so much yet said so little. My mother was a singer in a band. My father was the leader of the band. No wonder I had musical talent! No wonder I enjoyed being on a stage, entertaining people. It was in my genes. It was who I am!

But the words in the letter were just a taste. They were only a beginning, a beginning that invoked a torrent of questions. Who were these people? Where did they perform? What kind of music did they play? Would people know who they were? Were they famous? Why were they "not in a position to be married at the time?" Thoughts swirled around inside my head wrapped in a torrent of questions about the possibilities. Who did I look like? Did I somehow resemble some famous entertainer? After all, I was an actor, a musician, an emcee who liked to make an audience laugh. Who did I resemble? How did I come to be?

Then, as if to answer my wildly speculative questions, I came across the March 31, 1980 edition of "People" magazine at a newsstand. It had a photo of Alan King on the cover. I was a fan of the comedian but knew little about his life. Immersed in the emotional frenzy that had me grasping at the straws of my origins, I bought a copy and began to read. The article said that Alan King was raised in Brooklyn. He "was doing everything — playing the drums when I could get a job, singing with another kid." He organized a combo to play weddings and bar mitzvahs. Could it be? Was this some kind of sign? I read the article over again and again. Alan King's real name was Irwin Kniberg. He played in a combo, "a band." The possibility was intriguing. But then I checked his age and found that he would have had to be 17 or 18 when I was born. That made paternity unlikely, though still a possibility. I tried to justify this implausible theory in my mind. Perhaps his age was why they were "not in a position to be married at that time."

I decided to call Rabbi Schwartz and ask him if the name "Irwin Kniberg" rang a bell. The rabbi had been kind enough to include his phone number on his letter to me when he urged me: "do not hesitate to call." Rabbi Schwartz seemed pleasantly surprised to hear from me and genuinely concerned about trying to help. "Irwin Kniberg?" he asked, "no, that doesn't ring a bell. It was so long ago that I can't say that I really remember much." He said that he could say with certainty that my birth mother was under 25 at the time. He never met my birth father but he assured me that he was told my father was not married at the time. I'm not certain why he put such an emphasis on that fact. Maybe he wanted me to feel that the only sin my parents committed was that they loved each other very much and that they consummated that love without the benefit of marriage. My birth father, though, had not committed the sin of adultery. The rabbi wanted to assure me of that. We ended the conversation on a pleasant note and he told me to call back at any time.

Months passed as I mulled over the information Rabbi Schwartz had provided again and again. I eventually dismissed my desperate fascination with Alan King because of the comedian's age at the time of my birth and also because I eventually concluded it was unlikely, no matter how much I massaged the facts, that my birth mother, who the rabbi said was "under 25", was dating a 16-year-old. Their ages just didn't make a relationship seem plausible.

With every passing day I had more questions, more probabilities that I wanted to explore. But the Search was emotionally draining. I was trying to cope with rejection issues caused by my birth and adoption and my Search was adding even more opportunities for rejection. Every time I reached out and talked to someone I was risking rejection again. Rabbi Schwartz was the exception. But even he added to my emotional baggage. He remembered some specific details, enough to send me on wild fantasies like the one I had about Alan King. But he couldn't remember anything that would give me solid information I could use with the Department of Health or St. Joseph's Hospital. He had met my birth mother... but he couldn't remember her name... only that she was "a tall, beautiful woman.... under 25." The information was tantalizing but far less than satisfying.

At this time in my life, through the late 1970's and early 1980's, I was trying to make it as an actor and was lucky enough to get enough roles in regional theatres and on television to pay the bills. I appeared in small parts in several Soap Operas and performed many evenings in various theatrical productions. That gave me the time I so desperately needed for my Search. During one session with my acting coach, as she was urging me to delve into my inner emotions for a scene I was working on, I shared the story of my Search. She was fascinated by the possibility that my birth parents had a background in entertainment and suggested I speak with a lawyer. She knew one specifically who had talked with her in the past about "adoptions" and "adoptees." Greg Turner turned out to be a nice guy and was very sympathetic though he really didn't know how to help. But he mentioned a private investigator that he knew and also told me he had done some work for an adoptee, Jenny Sandusky. He would call her and get back to me.

Several days later, Greg did as he had promised and told me that Jenny Sandusky had agreed to speak with me and that, in fact, she was a member of a group called ALMA… The Adoptees Liberty Movement Association.

My call to Jenny was truly a wake-up call. She had searched for her birth parents and had been successful and she was more than willing to share her knowledge. Some of what she had to say, though, twisted my stomach into a knot. "You will never get the information sealed in the Department of Health records, Alan," she told me bluntly. "It just isn't going to happen… because of the laws designed to protect birth parents." She also cautioned, "Never, ever tell anyone that you were adopted. Bells will ring and anyone who might otherwise agree to help you, will back off, knowing that they may be breaking the law. They may even feel that your biological mother has the right to her privacy." Barbara recommended without hesitation that I use stealth in all my inquiries.

Then she imparted a piece of basic, yet terribly vital information about my Birth Certificate Number that really blew me away. "Despite all efforts to keep birth records secret," she almost whispered, "New York State really screwed up. Your Amended Birth Certificate has the same number as your original Birth Certificate." That was interesting information, I thought, but I was puzzled by its relevance... until she continued, "The archive section at the New York Public Library has all the New York City birth records listed by year... in individual volumes. You just need to match up the number on your birth certificate with the same number in the 1944 Book of Birth Records and you will come up with a name." She also told me that the head librarian there was sympathetic to adoptees and would assist with my research.

At last, something tangible... a seemingly sure-fire method that might yield a hint of valuable identifying information to kick my Search into gear!

Ronni, my wife and best friend, was so excited that she eagerly volunteered to help. We drove into Manhattan, parked in a lot on the West Side, and walked across town to the library. I felt a cool breeze rush against my face as we walked east on 42nd Street and I could feel my heart pounding harder with each step. I squeezed Ronni's hand in anticipation. We both felt confident that we were really on to something this time.

The New York Public Library is a cavernous structure that inspires a reverential silence once you pass between the massive sculptures of lions flanking the expansive front steps and through a set of massive metal doors. Ronni and I found a room marked: "Geneology Department" and walked up to a pleasant-looking man at the desk. "Is this where I can find birth records for the City of New York?" I asked in a hushed voice. He looked up at us with a reassuring smile and said, "Just fill out one of these forms over here giving the years that you'd like to check and your seat number and we'll be happy to get them for you. And if you have any questions you come right back up here and I'll try to answer them for you." This must be the guy, I thought, that Barbara Sandusky had told me about.

Ronni and I chose a seat at one of about a dozen long tables lined up across the room, took note of the seat number, and filled out a simple form. We requested the birth records for the year 1944. A few minutes later, the books arrived at our seat. Yes, book(s)!!! "Birth Records for 1944" was split into two volumes, each containing about 600 pages of information. Ronni took the book marked "A through K." I picked up "L through Z." We opened the books to find about 75 names on every page with every page broken into six columns: Sex, Date of Birth, Borough of Birth, Birth Certificate Number, and Name. The anticipation grew as Ronni and I reviewed the task ahead. "With so many entries, the easiest thing to do is to focus on the column for birth certificate numbers," I said, "and we want number 9740." I theorized that if we found a match for the birth certificate number we should also be able to match the sex, borough of birth, and date of birth.

The initial rush of anticipation was quickly dimmed by the tedious routine that followed. Page by page, I would run my finger down the dozens of numbers looking for 9740. Ronni performed the identical task alongside me. An hour passed and I hadn't made it out of the "L's, and was barely closing in on the letter "M." Who could fathom that so many people were born in 1944 in New York City with a last name beginning in "L?" I began to do some simple math in my head and realized that Ronni and I might not even reach the page with my birth certificate number on it today. The library might close before we finished and we would have to make the trip from New Jersey back into the City on another day. I started moving my finger faster down each page. I also urged Ronni to forge ahead.

The boredom was mind-numbing. I forced myself to remain focused on each four-digit number as I scanned down each page. But I'd find my eyesight blurring as my vision would go out of focus from the repetition of number after number after number. I'd have to stop and hold my finger on the last number that remained clear and then shake my head to clear my vision. Then I'd blink several times, take a breath, and force myself back to the column of numbers that played tricks on my mind as well as my eyes. Was the number I was reading 4947 or was it number 4974? I'd have to stop and reassure myself before I continued to plod on. I didn't want to pass by number 9740 without realizing it.

Another half-hour passed.... and then... the magic number appeared: 9740!!! I stopped and looked again. I challenged myself mentally that 9740 was indeed the correct number. My heart was racing as I let my finger scan horizontally across the page to the first column to the right of number 9740... A Male... born August 11, 1944... in the Borough of Queens... with Birth Certificate Number 9740... was named "Frank McDonald!!!!"

Without taking my eyes off the page I reached over and clutched Ronni's arm but I could only grunt. "Uh... Uh," I babbled at Ronni incoherently. She looked at me strangely. "I found it," I managed to say as my throat muscles relaxed enough for me to speak. Ronni leaned over. Our eyes met and locked. "My name is Frank McDonald!!!" I blurted out. Ronni took a breath and then looked down at my finger pointing to the name on the page. After a brief moment of recognition she looked up at me with a glimmer in her eye. "Does that make me Ronald McDonald?" she asked gleefully. Her joke broke the tension of the previous hour and a half and we both felt the relief as we chuckled under our breaths. Then we both looked over the page again... very carefully. We wanted to be sure that we weren't hallucinating. We needed to be certain that the information was correct. It was. Everything added up.

"Frank McDonald," I said incredulously to Ronni, "Somehow I never thought of myself as a Frank McDonald." I guessed that McDonald was my birth mother's name since Rabbi Schwartz had told me that she was not married. But why "Frank"? Who was the Frank in her life that had motivated her to name me Frank? Could that have been my father's name? Or was it just someone she had admired? Those questions lingered, but without question, Ronni and I had made real progress. I now had my mother's maiden name to give to the medical records department at St. Anthony's.

Despite what Barbara Sandusky had told me I thought I might try another shot with the New York City Health Department. So I wrote to the Health Department as "Frank McDonald," born in the Borough of Queens on August 11, 1944, and said I had lost my birth certificate and wanted a copy. I reasoned if I could get my hands on that original birth certificate it would list both my mother's name AND my father's name plus addresses and other valuable information. I knew it was a long shot but I had to take it anyway. Just five days later, though, I received a form letter from the Department of Health with a check in the box for "insufficient information." Clearly, they had discovered my ruse and I ran into a dead end there… again.

St. Anthony's Hospital also proved elusive. My psychiatrist wrote to Mr. Andre in the Medical Records Department again using the name "McDonald" as the requested "mother's maiden name." Mr. Andre sent back a form letter stating: "No record found after careful search." Dr. Streicher, though, would not be put off. He wrote another letter to Mr. Andre detailing my "psychological problems brought on by not being able to find my biological mother." Another similar form letter followed.

It seemed that every "up" in my Search was followed by a crushing "down." But I felt I was making headway, and despite the setbacks, I would soon learn the identities of my birth parents. The progress I was making kept me motivated to press on, but with each new bit of information came a nagging fear that my birth parents would reject me all over again. Roger Grimsby, a television News Anchor in New York City, once told the story of being adopted and finding his birth mother. His on-air comment summed up my own fear: "She didn't want me THEN. She doesn't want me NOW." I realized my birth parents might feel that same way about me.

Rabbi Schwartz had remembered so much yet so little. But I thought that I might be able to jog his memory with my name at birth so I called him again. "Does the name Frank McDonald mean anything to you?" I asked him urgently. "That's my birth name and also my mother's maiden name." Unfortunately, neither name rang a bell with the rabbi. But he told me he remembered that my birth mother had long hair and was very pretty and that he met with the lawyer handling the adoption twice. That lawyer could certainly be helpful to me and it occurred to me that he might still be practicing so I encouraged Rabbi Schwartz to remember his name. Again, he drew a blank, and could only say that his office was on the second floor of a building in Far Rockaway. I thanked the rabbi again for his kindness.

I spent the next days endlessly reviewing what I had discovered. In the end, I concluded that if my birth was indeed recorded in Health Department documents there must be a record of my birth at St. Anthony's despite the written denials. So I decided to approach Mr. Andre myself and confront him in person. I had to be certain that he was telling me the truth, and at the same time, I wanted to motivate him to exhaust every possibility in his search for my birth records. The most effective way to be certain of the truth, I thought, would be a bribe. Mr. Andre didn't make much money working in the Records Department, I thought, and an offer of money would be a welcomed gesture. After weighing the options, I settled on one-thousand dollars in crisp, one-hundred dollar bills. Yes, it was a lot of money at the time but the future of my Search was now resting on the information in my birth records. If Mr. Andre maintained that he could not find my records I had to know that he was telling the truth. He might pass up a hundred-dollar bribe and maybe even five-hundred dollars. But I felt if he had to forfeit one-thousand dollars because he truly couldn't find my birth records, I knew I could believe him.

"Mr. Andre," I said into the phone, "this is Alan Gerstel. I've been writing to you for some time and so has my psychiatrist... trying to get my Birth Records." There was a pause on the line so I went on: "I was adopted... and I wrote you asking if you could find my birth records. I was born on August, 11. 1944..." He cut me off in mid-sentence to say, "Yes, I remember and I also remember that there were not records to be found. I'm sorry I cannot help you." I responded in the most convincing voice I could muster, "Mr. Andre, I know that you have tried but I am hoping that you will try a little harder. May I come and visit you at your office? There is something I would like to discuss with you."

I obviously piqued his curiosity because Mr. Andre quickly agreed to meet with me in his office at St. Anthony's Medical Center... about an hour from my home in New Jersey... at 11 O'clock the following morning.

This was a make-it-or-break-it step to find out, once and for all, whether my birth records did indeed exist and if they contained information that would identify my birth parents. If Mr. Andre couldn't locate them I would have to head in a different direction. But I wasn't even certain I could find another direction. So I walked myself through every step, considering how I would approach Mr. Andre and what I would say. It seemed fairly straightforward until it occurred to me that I was probably breaking the law. What if Mr. Andre ratted on me? What if he took my money and lied to me at the same time? I broke into a cold sweat as I realized I was clearly entering an arena of intrigue that could be filled with unexpected and unwanted consequences. But I couldn't back off now. And I wouldn't take Ronni with me. Not this time. I didn't want Mr. Andre to feel threatened by TWO strangers arriving at his office. No. This had to be a one-on-one conversation.

I left my home at 9:30, an hour and a half before I was due to meet with Mr. Andre. But oddly, there was little traffic, so I got to St. Anthony's with forty minutes to spare. I ran my routine over and over again in my head to make sure my bribe would appear to be more of a payment for services rendered than an illegal payoff for information I was not supposed to have. About ten minutes before the appointed time, I got out of my car and walked the half-block to the hospital entrance. I asked for the Records Department and then followed the directions I was given.

The Records Department of St. Anthony's was in the dungeon-like basement of the decades-old hospital. I took a creaky elevator down to the basement, turned right, and walked down a corridor lined with large, well-worn, baskets full of crumpled bed sheets. Then I passed several offices, turned left down a corridor, and then right into an area labeled "Records." It was a large area packed with files containing hospital boxes. The wire shelves that cradled those records ran almost up to the ceiling, nearly scraping the steam pipes that ran haphazardly across it. Those shelves were massive and probably three car-lengths long and at the end of the corridor framed by these paper-stuffed shelves was a solitary door. I could make out the small letters on it: "Luis Andre- Medical Records." I felt very much alone and was only aware of the sound of my footsteps scuffling quietly on the concrete floor as I approached. I knocked and opened the door. "Mr. Andre?" I asked the solitary man seated behind a large desk. "I'm Alan Gerstel," I said without waiting for an answer

Mr. Andre welcomed me into his office and gestured to me to close the door behind me. He was of Caribbean descent, possibly from Haiti. But he spoke perfect English and had probably been born here in the United States if not at least raised here. "I am pleased to meet you," he said, "why don't you sit down?" He offered me the plain, functional wooden chair next to his desk while he took his seat again behind his desk. "Mr. Andre," I said carefully, "I am adopted and I am becoming obsessed with trying to find out things about my birth parents… things that would just make me feel better about myself. It's so bad that I even see a psychiatrist… you know, the doctor who's also been in touch with you. I know you have looked hard but I am asking you to look harder. It is worth so much to me that…uh.. uh…."

This was the moment of truth! Could I pull it off? I was on the verge of backing down from the bribe until I realized I didn't know what else to say to him. So I just laid out my story and prayed he wouldn't throw me out or even call the police. "Mr. Andre," I said to him in my most sincere voice, "I am desperate otherwise I wouldn't be here talking to you. I know I am asking you to do more work on my behalf and I don't expect you to work without getting paid. So I am offering to pay you one... thousand... dollars if you can find my Birth Records."

Mr. Andre reacted as if my offer was nothing special but his rapid response told me he was taking the bait with a vengeance. "I have some very good other ideas where I might look. And I will do what I can to help you," he said, looking across the room at the piles of clutter on the opposite wall. Boxes of papers were stacked on top of each other, surrounding a row of filing cabinets and overstuffed filing drawers. "Give me some time and I will be thorough in my searching," he promised me. I gave Mr. Andre my phone number again and began to get up to leave. He also rose and showed me to the door as he reassured me, "I will do the best that I can. I can promise you that." "I'll wait to hear from you," I responded, "and I hope you have good news." I walked through the door and it closed behind me.

I headed back through those dingy corridors with my heart racing. I did it!!! I pulled it off!! There were no problems and no hitches. And as I reviewed the conversation I just had with Mr. Andre in my mind I realized that he had gotten mightily interested in my case once he heard that thousand-dollars bandied about. He was very cool, though. He never showed excitement about the money, just a newfound determination. He also never questioned me about how the transaction would take place IF and WHEN he found my records. I walked out of the hospital, got back in my car and drove home to New Jersey.

That same night, Ronni and I went to the musical "42nd Street" on Broadway. We needed to put all of the details of my Search into a tiny, imaginary box for a while and a huge hit musical proved to be the perfect diversion.

The drive home after the show took almost an hour. We arrived at about 11:45, still feeling vibrant in the aftermath of our "42nd Street" experience as we played back the messages on the answering machine. The first message started with the mechanical voice saying, "Eight Forty Five... PM." It was followed by a voice: "Hello. Hello. This is Mr. Andre... and I think I found something. So maybe you will call me in the office tomorrow. I think so.... Good night." I froze! Ronni froze! She looked at me and grabbed my arm. We both erupted with joyous excitement over what we heard. My mind began racing. "This is it!" I told her. "This is where we hit the mother lode. I just know I'm on the right track now. I can feel it!" The music from "42nd Street" rushed back into my mind like an avalanche and I began to belt-out the lyrics of the upbeat toe-tapping song "We're in the Money."

I woke early the next morning after a restless night of anticipation tempered by the uneasiness of past experience. Would I get the information I need? And would it lead to my birth mother... or turn out to be another dead end? I waited until shortly after 9 o'clock to call Mr. Andre. His now-familiar voice answered the phone: "Medical Records," he intoned. "This is Alan Gerstel, Mr. Andre," I said anxiously, "I got your message when I got home last night." "Oh yes," he said, "I think I have what you are looking for. I have the Birth Records for a baby boy who was born on August 11, 1944, and they must be for you since no other babies were born in St. Joseph's on that day." I pounced. "When can I see you?" I asked. "Any time," he replied. "I'll be there in less than two hours," I said hurriedly before hanging up.

The first stop was the bank where I withdrew one-thousand dollars in crisp one-hundred dollar bills. I put the cash in a bank envelope and put the envelope in my pocket. Then I stood there and began to tremble just thinking about what I was about to do. I was about to give away one thousand dollars! I stopped and swallowed hard and then reached into my pocket and squeezed the cash-filled envelope. Did I really want to do this? "Can I afford to toss away that much money?" I asked myself. An inner voice echoed back, "Can you afford not to?" Whatever I felt about the money and what I was doing with it quickly became a moot issue. I would pay off the bribe to Mr. Andre because I had to. I really had no choice.

I arrived at St. Anthony's shortly before 11:30... meeting my self-imposed deadline to get there before Mr. Andre went to lunch. He welcomed me into his office and shut the door behind me before sitting down. He then gestured for me to take a seat in the chair next to the desk. As I sat, I reached into my pocket, took out the envelope, and handed it to Mr. Andre. He nodded, then took the envelope and slipped it into his inside jacket pocket without looking inside it or saying a word about it. He must have felt he could trust me. I have no other explanation for his apparent indifference to counting the money or even checking to see if the envelope contained any cash at all.

Mr. Andre opened a large, well-worn record book on his desk and produced two 3 by 5 index cards that he had stuck in between the pages. The muscles in my body tensed in anticipation as he put one of the cards down on the desk in front of me. The card had "St. Joseph Hospital" printed on top and then spaces for "Name," "Address," "Religion," etc. It had been filled out neatly in longhand with occasional flourishes. I imagined a nun with perfect penmanship had been assigned to record the vital information. But I quickly became puzzled by what I saw. On the line alongside the "name" was "Ferrucci, Rose." She lived at 343 Vernon Avenue in Brooklyn. She was a 22-year-old... white... Catholic... married housewife. Rabbi Schwartz, though, had said that my birth mother was a singer in a band and that she was single. There's no way she could fit the profile of a "married housewife." But she WAS admitted at 10 AM on

August 11, 1944, and was discharged at 10:30 AM on August 21… ten days later. That fit with what my parents had told me: I was adopted when I was ten days old.

Then, at the very bottom of the card, written in parentheses, were the words: (Correct Name Dorothy McDonald.) I was utterly confused… and looked over the information on the card again. How did Rose Ferrucci have her name changed to Dorothy McDonald? But before I could ask Mr. Andre, he stood up and ushered me to a nearby filing cabinet. "This is why I couldn't find any records for you," he explained as he riffled across the tops of the cards in the file: "There is no listing for a Dorothy McDonald along the top of the pages, I only saw the name "Ferrucci, Rose" at the top of the one card as I was going through them."

Mr. Andre then handed me the second index card he had taken from the large book on his desk. It was the record of my birth and was eerily similar to the first card. My name was listed as: "Ferrucci, Baby Boy." I was also listed at 343 Vernon Avenue in Brooklyn. I was a white, Catholic, newborn, whose occupation was listed as "Infant." I was born at 12:37 PM on August 11, 1944, and was also discharged at 10:30 AM on August 21, 1944. At the very top of the page, someone had written: "(Summer) 170 Beach 78th St. R'way Beach." At the very bottom of the page was the notation: "Correct name McDonald, Baby Boy." The word "pay" was written in the lower right hand corner of both cards. "That means someone paid the bill in cash before they took you home," Mr. Andre explained.

As I was trying to digest what I was reading on these cards, Mr. Andre went back to his desk and pointed to the entries in the large record book there. "Here's more," he said. "It is the master record book of every patient in the hospital." It too, was filled out in a flowing cursive longhand. The original information there was also crossed out. "Rose Ferrucci" became "Dorothy Jeanette McDonald." It gave her corrected age as 21 with a birth date of "12-31-22"… and indicated she was "single" instead of "married" and a "singer" instead of a "housewife"! She was also Catholic. My father was listed as "Rocco Ferrucci" at the same address. Under a listing for grandparents were "Joseph McDonald" and "Jean McDonald."

I asked Mr. Andre why he wasn't able to find my mother's name originally in this large record book. He told me that it has been used in some court case and was in the hands of lawyers for several years. True or not, I wanted to believe him because he had ceased being the heartless bureaucrat who had sent me those sterile form letters that said there was no record of my birth. Instead, he was the recipient of a cash-filled envelope and was cooperating with me, sharing information, and at least acting like he really understood the importance of my birth records. "I can't thank you enough for this information," I told him. "It gives me some solid information, though I am still puzzled about the change of names." "That is quite unusual," he said, "I have rarely ever seen these records changed like that... and there is really nothing in the records to indicate what happened."

Mr. Andre then gave me photocopies of the index cards and the record book, and he even handed me a paper with his home phone number on it. "I want you to call me if you have any questions about that information," he said as we walked toward his office door. "In the meantime, I will look more and see if I can find out anything else. It is difficult, though. These books and papers are so old." I shook his hand as I told him, "I want to tell you again how much I appreciate your help." I then walked through that door that said "Medical Records" and it closed behind me.

I had gambled a thousand dollars... and oh... my... God... had it ever paid off!!!

Once through his office door and into the hospital's basement hallways, I began to feel an overwhelming madness overtake me!! My life is now validated, I told myself, as I took the elevator to the lobby and walked out the front door of the hospital. I am now a real person!! I know that I have a history... confusing as it might be at the moment!!

Then I began trying to feverishly process the information I had in my hands. I was walking along the sidewalk that ran parallel to the hospital as I began imagining why Rose Ferrucci changed her name to Dorothy Jeanette McDonald. I began to speculate that she must have been in trouble with her family and maybe used a phony name until her identity was somehow uncovered. Maybe her boyfriend left her on her own. Maybe her parents threw her out. I guessed that she must have had a rough time because she was single. So, at that moment, rather than being angry at her for abandoning me, I felt truly sorry for her.

My father's name, though, was never changed. He was Rocco Ferrucci and he wasn't married to Rose Ferrucci... or if he was, he cheated on her with Dorothy McDonald. Somehow, I never imagined my father's name being Rocco Ferrucci. I had never even met a "Rocco" before in my life and I pictured him as some character out of "The Godfather." The further I walked away from the entrance to the hospital, the more emotional I became and the more the facts and fantasies fermented inside me. I quickened my step as my car came into view. I quickly unlocked the door, sat down in the driver's seat, and locked the door again.

Then I erupted! My body shook and I began to sob uncontrollably. I had uncorked the bottle, releasing the genie that would tell me who I am. And now, at this moment, I knew who I was. At least, I thought I knew. I sat and shuddered for several minutes before I could pull myself together and drive home.

The next day, I called attorney Greg Turner to tell him what I had uncovered. Greg was impressed with what I was able to accomplish. "But now," he said, "You need some professional help." He gave me the phone number of a private investigator he knew. I called Bob Fitzpatrick the next day and shared my story. He told me that he would run a DMV check on a Dorothy McDonald with New York State. "If she's alive and living in New York State she probably has a car and we'll find her through the state driving records," he said reassuringly. We then talked about his fees which weren't cheap. A complicated Search like mine would rack up many thousands of dollars in hourly fees, he said. So to save money, Bob suggested I take on some investigative responsibilities myself. (I think he was impressed at my motivation and my moxie in bribing Mr. Andre.) His idea seemed to make a lot of sense since I was so driven by my Search anyway.

Bob recommended that I go to the two addresses I had gotten from the hospital records: 343 Vernon Avenue in Brooklyn, and 170 Beach 78th Street in Rockaway Beach. "Take note of the kinds of neighborhoods they are," he advised me, "the age of the buildings and any indication that some older people still live there and get back to me. You'd be surprised by how many people live in the same apartment or same neighborhood for decades. And it's just possible that someone living there may still remember the Ferruccis or Dorothy McDonald and know what happened to them. You do the initial investigation and if you come up with anything, I'll follow-up with a personal visit." The excitement began raging inside me! I was taking an active role in my Search again AND I was going to go back to the places that were the roots of my being.

CHAPTER SEVEN

The Hand-off

Watchful eyes peered out from behind the drawn curtains of an apartment on Beach 78th Street just across from Margaret Weltsch's bungalow. Those vigilant eyes spotted Dorothy arrive with her baby in the early afternoon hours and leave just a few minutes later without the child in her arms. Then, several minutes after Dorothy's cab chugged away from the oceanfront neighborhood, a woman scurried through a back alley to the concrete staircase of a bungalow on Beach 77th Street. She clomped up the stairs and into a room where a group of people had gathered. "She's gone," the woman said breathlessly. "I watched... and I waited... just to make sure she wasn't coming back." Every movement in the room came to a standstill. The three men sitting around a table playing cards, froze. One of the players, Louis, had just taken a puff on his cigarette and seemed incapable of exhaling. To his right at the table, his brother-in-law, Jack looked straight ahead as if he hadn't heard a thing. And another player, Hy, lowered his cards to look toward the three women gathered on a couch and a chair and the man sitting with them. The paralysis of the moment shattered when Herman and Selma Gerstel reached out to clutch each other's hands, stood abruptly and hugged. At the same moment, Selma's sisters, Ruth and Fritzi wrapped their arms around each other in a big embrace. It was hard to tell who among them had the bigger grin. The card players applauded, and Louis finally exhaled an extended stream of cigarette smoke.

As the room buzzed with excitement, Selma was actually the first to speak coherently. "Can we go see him now?" she asked almost breathlessly. "I have to see him and hold him." But her husband expressed more caution than emotion. "How do we know that she has really gone?" he asked. "How do we know this woman won't come back?" Everyone in the room seemed to chime in at once. "Oh Herman…don't worry… that's not going to happen… She just wanted the money… You'll never see her again," their many voices overlapped in a cacophony of Hungarian-dialects as they sought to reassure him. "Let's go, Herman," Ruth said with a nod of her head as she took Selma's hand, "let's go see your new baby boy."

The men at the card table wished Herman and Selma well as they picked up their cards and continued to play while the procession of three giddy sisters, including Selma and her husband, made their way out of the cramped room, down the stairs, and through the alley and across the street to Margaret Weltsch's bungalow.

"Come in, come in," Margaret Weltsch greeted them warmly. "Oy, he's such a little cutie pie. And he's so good." The foursome pushed forward but Selma got to the dresser first to see her son lying on a soft pink towel in the dresser drawer. Frances was hovering over the child, holding out a little plastic ring for the baby to try to grip with his little fingers. Selma reached down to pick up the baby and began to cry when she put her arms around the little boy. "Zelma, oh Zelma," Ruth said lovingly as she put her arms on her sister's shoulders to steady her. "It's all right. It's wonderful… it's a wonderful thing. Go ahead. Pick him up."

Herman moved in to comfort his wife. He had a broad grin on his face. "It's a mitzvah... that's what it is, Selma. This is what we have been praying for," he said to her softly. "I know, I know," Selma replied. "I just can't believe this miracle has come true. I can't believe he is really ours." She stroked the baby's forehead and then picked him up tenderly and held the baby against her. The baby let out a burp and the room erupted in laughter. With the remnants of tears still streaming down her cheeks, Selma laughed along with everyone else.

The women all took turns holding the baby and making the appropriate cooing sounds. Herman tried holding the baby too but couldn't find quite the right position to support the baby's head properly. He quickly gave up and handed the boy back to his wife. Selma took the baby and cuddled him lovingly, almost suffocating him with rapturous affection. This is what was missing in her life. This is what she had wanted for so long.

There was a soft knock on the door. Margaret opened it eagerly to find Rabbi Schwartz standing there. "I'm Rabbi...," he began to say as Herman spotted him and cut him off. "Rabbi Schwartz, come in. Come in," Herman said eagerly, "This is the man who made it all happen. And I'm so glad you could join us here because you were such a part of making this mitzvah possible." Rabbi Schwartz smiled and puffed out his chest like the proud papa himself as he spotted the baby and walked over to Selma, who was holding the child up for him to see. "Oh, Selma, this is such a rich, wonderful moment in the eyes of God. I wish only nachas (good things) for all of you," he said with the spiritual voice one would expect from a man of God. He used his index finger to tickle the baby's chin and then turned his attention to Herman and to business. "She signed all the papers, Herman. I just came from Liebovitz's law office where she signed everything and I'm hoping to tell you, you will never see her again." "Well, I'll see her again." Frances chimed in innocently. "I'll probably see her tonight when I get back to my apartment. She lives right next door." Margaret scowled at her daughter prompting Frances to go on the defensive. "But I don't think you will have to worry about Dorothy," she assured everyone. "She doesn't even want to remember that she got pregnant and had a baby. For her, it is all over." Margaret echoed her daughter's sentiment and everyone in the room breathed a collective sigh of relief.

"Well, let's not stay around her to find out. I think it's time to go," said Herman in his very no-nonsense voice. "Let's take our baby home. We don't need any unpleasant surprises." Everyone knew Herman so by the tone of his voice they knew he meant business. They gathered their belongings and began to move toward the door. Selma stopped for a moment and turned to Margaret. "This is a beautiful thing that you have done for us. We can never repay your kindness," she oozed with joy. "Ah, it was mine pleasure, a real pleasure," Margaret responded. "And it all started with my darling Frances here. She is the one where it all began." Selma gave Frances a kiss on the cheek as she passed her and the procession of three women, one man, and a baby headed down the stairs to the street. Rabbi Schwartz shook Herman's hand. "Mazel Tov," he said again. "I have no words to thank you, Rabbi," Herman responded. "But I want to honor you for what you have done for us. Enjoy the rest of your vacation. We'll talk more when you come back to Westwood."

Ruth, Fritzi and Herman, along with Selma and her baby all walked cautiously to Herman and Selma's borrowed car parked nearby. They remained on the lookout, fearing that Dorothy might still return, but nothing happened to spoil the joy of the moment. Selma got into the car still holding the baby tightly to her bosom. Herman got into the driver's seat and started the engine. Ruth and Fritzi rolled down the passenger-side window before closing the door. They reached in and touched the baby once again as they reassured Selma that everything would be all right.

"We'll call you in a few days," Ruth said to Selma, "... in a few days to see how you are doing and how the baby is doing." "And you have our phone numbers here too," Fritzi added. "Please let us know what your friend, Doctor Goldberg, says when you take the baby in for an examination. Not that I think there is anything to worry about, mind you." Selma continued to gush, "I'll call... we'll call...but meantime he is a beautiful baby and such an adorable baby and I love him so much I could just squeeze him," Ruth and Fritzi blew kisses and waved as Herman slipped the car into gear and drove off with a ten-day-old baby in Selma's arms. It would be the last time they would venture to Far Rockaway for 12 years.

The next day... Monday, August 22nd... Rocco and Rose returned to Far Rockaway from their apartment in Brooklyn and headed straight to St. Joseph's Hospital. They were flush with excitement at the expectation of finding Dorothy waiting with their baby. Instead, they learned they were victims of an unthinkable act that they never even considered as a possibility. The nun at the main desk told them that Dorothy had checked out with her baby the day before.

Rocco and Rose were in a state of shock as they took a cab to 170 Beach 78th Street and Margaret Weltsch's bungalow. No one answered their repeated knocks on the door. No one was home. Rocco was enraged. Rose was inconsolable. They knew they had been duped. It wasn't the money. It was the loss of a baby, a baby they had wanted so badly.

But even as the Ferruccis were mourning the loss of their baby that Monday morning, their names were being altered on the documents that could tie them to the child. The lawyer, Marv Liebowitz, made a trip to St. Joseph's Hospital himself to speak with the Administrator, Sister Marie. The two had known and trusted each other for many years. In fact, Marv had helped Sister Marie place the children of other single young women with loving families in the past. He told her about Dorothy and called her "a frightened, unhappy girl," who had given a phony name when she checked in to delivery her baby because of the shame and the disgrace it would bring on her family. Sister Marie understood entirely but she still wanted to know, "What happened to Dorothy's baby?" Marv showed her the legal paperwork that the baby had been adopted "by a loving family" in New Jersey and that Dorothy had named the baby and had signed over all her legal rights. Sister Marie assured her friend that she would personally make the changes on the appropriate hospital documents so that the adoption could proceed without complications. There would be no legal question about the baby's name at birth.

CHAPTER EIGHT

That Old Black Magic

Though I had committed myself to taking on the legwork in the investigation into my past, I was wracked with indecision. I was obsessed with learning the identity of my birth parents but the reality of what I might find was weighing heavily on my mind and paralyzing my actions. Psychologists would call it an approach-avoidance experience. "Rocco Ferrucci" didn't sound like someone who was warm and fuzzy. I asked myself over and over again, who are these people? And what happened between the time I was born as "Baby Boy Ferrucci" and the time I became "Baby Boy McDonald?" Also, how and when did I become Frank McDonald? I was curious but also fearful of what I might find or how the Ferruccis would react to whatever happened at St. Joseph's Hospital so many years before.

Several weeks passed as I wrestled with my feelings but my curiosity eventually won out. I convinced myself that I had gotten too far into this

Search to back off now so I summoned the determination to press on. I started by buying several maps of New York State and New York City and went over them carefully. I was not at all familiar with Brooklyn and it had been many years since I had last gone to Far Rockaway as a child. I used the street reference guide on one map and I found Vernon Avenue in Brooklyn and plotted a route to it. I then mapped a route that went from Brooklyn directly to Far Rockaway and Beach 78th Street.

Maps in hand, Ronni and I headed out on a chilly December day to face my past. I needed Ronni and every bit of support she would give me and I also needed her eyes and ears to help me digest and remember what I was about to experience. We drove from New Jersey, through Manhattan, and crossed the Brooklyn Bridge. As we followed the plotted path on our maps we watched the neighborhoods deteriorate block by block. We turned one corner and then another before we spotted the street sign that read "Vernon Avenue." As I turned onto the street we were stunned to encounter a neighborhood that looked like a bombed-out German city at the end of World War Two. "Make sure your door is locked," I cautioned Ronni as I checked my own door lock. At one time, it must have been an attractive working-class neighborhood judging by the four-story brownstone buildings that remained. But the Vernon Avenue of 1980 had plunged into disrepair. Only about one out of every four buildings was still standing. And those remaining buildings looked as if they had been abandoned and were now used as "shooting galleries" where the junkies crashed when they were strung out on heroin. In between the buildings still remaining were piles of bricks and stone and even larger piles of rubble.

It was about noon and no one was on the street, yet Ronni and I felt uneasy. I had to remind us both that this was Brooklyn. This was one of the five Boroughs of the City of New York. "How could the City allow this?" I asked Ronni incredulously. "I've never seen anything even remotely like this except in history books," she replied as she gasped at the remnants of the once-proud community. I slowed as we passed a building about halfway down the block. We spotted a number next to the front door. It read "339." "Keep going a little further," Ronni urged, "It should be up ahead on the right here." We drove past a vacant lot filled with piles of cement and bricks before coming to the next building on the same side of the street only to see the number "347." I stopped the car but kept it in gear with my foot on the brake pedal as we looked back at the vacant lot and realized that the piles of bricks and cement were all that was left of the building that once was 343. "I guess that's it. It's over. 343 Vernon Avenue is a thing of the past," I said as I resigned myself to the reality. "There's nothing here to give us anything to go on."

Ronni continued to gaze out the window and raised a tantalizing question. "I wonder what it was like in 1944 when Rocco and Rose lived here?" she mused. "I wonder if you and I would have ever met if you grew up here on Vernon Avenue?" If my parents hadn't adopted me from Rose Ferrucci or Dorothy McDonald or whatever her name was, Fate might never have drawn Ronni and me together. Each of us would likely have gone through life never even knowing the other person existed.

"Time to move on," I said to Ronni who was already refolding the map to uncover the routes that would take us from Brooklyn to Far Rockaway. "Let's just get out of here," she said. "This neighborhood gives me the creeps." I already had my foot on the gas pedal.

If Vernon Avenue was a stunning disappointment, Far Rockaway was an unimaginable nightmare. It only took about a half-hour to get there from Brooklyn but as we drove along Rockaway Beach Boulevard near the elevated subway that ran parallel to, and about four blocks from the beach, I became increasingly dismayed. There was nothing... acres and acres of nothing. No bungalows, no cottages and no two-and-three story apartment buildings that I remembered so vividly from my childhood. Not even any vegetation... nothing but sand... and strips of cracked and crumbled asphalt where streets used to form black pavement paths down to the beach. Ronni and I could see the boardwalk several blocks away. It still stood proudly and ran along the beach as far as the eye could see in stark contrast to the barren stretch of real estate that was once home to a vibrant, caring community of summer residents. The remnants of the remaining paved streets formed a huge surrealistic checkerboard that ran the three to four blocks between us and the beach and several miles into the distance. I was so utterly devastated I had to pull to the side of the road and stop to collect my thoughts. "Honey, I don't... I can't... uh... this is nuts," I said incredulously. "The bungalows... the... everything was right here... It was here... I can't... I... this is not happening."

(I later learned that the City of New York demolished every building along this beautiful stretch of beach back in 1960's with plans to redevelop it with low-income housing and nursing homes. Once the buildings were gone, though, there was no affordable summer housing for the thousands of families to spend their summers and without the influx of those summer visitors, businesses shuttered. A City budget crunch put all development plans on "hold," which left the area barren and blighted for decades.)

Ronni and I sat silently in our car for several minutes trying to grasp the enormity of our disappointment. We had hoped for some clue, and just as we did with Vernon Avenue, some connection to the past. I hoped that maybe some "old-timers" might still be around who might perhaps have rental records... notations... anything that might help in my Search. Instead, we found a wasteland... a barren expanse of sand that not only dashed my hopes of finding a connection to my birth but also a destitute vision that shattered my dreams of long ago when my parents eventually took me to spend a Sunday "at the beach."

"This is 117th Street," I said dejectedly as I pointed to the street sign still standing on the corner ahead of us. "Let's continue along Rockaway Beach Boulevard to Beach 78th Street. After all, that's where it all played out." Ronni nodded in agreement so we started driving the remaining 39 blocks. As we counted down the numbers on the street signs, we spotted two large apartment buildings near the boardwalk that seemed out of place in the midst of this lifeless wilderness. Then, as I turned down a street leading to the boardwalk and closer to the beach where I vividly remembered playing as a youngster, the route turned into an obstacle course, forcing me to zig-zag down the patches of pavement that were still negotiable. As I navigated around the drifting sand that encroached on, and nearly covered the remaining roadway, I also had to maneuver around the years of accumulated litter.

But as Ronni and I approached the block that should have been 78th Street, we found that the street signs seemed to skip from 79th Street to 77th Street with those two large apartment buildings in between. We were unsure and drove several more blocks thinking we had somehow missed 78th so we turned around and checked the street signs again. "It should be right here, honey," Ronni said with determination. "This is where it's supposed to be" "I know, I know," I shot back. "But it's not!" Beach 78th Street had vanished like some eerie scene out of "The Twilight Zone." It no longer existed. Gone was the entire neighborhood along with the street address listed on my hospital records. It was if some great conspiracy was underway to shut the door on my past, bolt it, and make sure that it could never be opened again.

But we had come this far and the boardwalk was still inviting so we drove toward the beach and stopped to park where the remaining pavement was entirely covered over by the drifting sand. A short walk took us to the sand-dusted wooden stairs that led up to the boardwalk. Even though it had been neglected for many years, that long stretch of wooden boards looked as if it had been frozen in time. Ronni and I walked across to the other side and gazed at the deserted beach and the wind-whipped ocean water beyond. It was exactly as I remembered it from my childhood. And oddly, the street signs along the boardwalk remained intact… including the sign for Beach 78th Street. As we paused, I took a moment to remember. To the east the beach curved back out of sight, and to the west I could still make out the ferris wheel and the faded wooden sign that proclaimed "Rockaway's Playland." The sights and smells and sounds from my early years came flooding back. But as I took a deep breath of ocean air I could only experience the fond memories in my mind. There was no tangible evidence of what once was.

As Ronni and I stood there breathing in the salty ocean air, the pieces of the puzzle seemed to fall into place. My mother's two sisters, I remembered, had vacationed every summer in Far Rockaway when I was young. They must have stayed in this general vicinity because I seemed to have such a connection to that spot. I remember my parents bringing me there for Sunday visits during the summers when I was about twelve or thirteen years old and I vividly recalled playing on the beach and swimming in the rough waters. Then it dawned on me that my parents had probably learned of my birth from one of their relatives who summered there and that information likely put the events into motion that led to my adoption. At any rate, it could explain why a "nice Jewish boy" like me was born at St. Joseph's Hospital in Far Rockaway. And it could also explain how I ended up with my adoptive parents.

Within an hour of returning home, I called Bob Fitzpatrick to share my bleak news. But he was even more disappointed than we were as he had just heard back from the New York Department of Motor Vehicles, which had no driving record for a Dorothy McDonald. So what do we do next? "Okay, so we both struck out," Bob told me with an air of confidence, "but we still have lots of avenues to pursue. How about her career? She was a singer, wasn't she?" "I don't know for certain," I responded, "but that's what she put down on my birth records." "Then maybe she's listed with one of the entertainment unions," he said with assurance. Give them a call and see what you get."

So I called the New York Local 802 of the Musician's Union, the American Guild of Variety Artists (AGVA), and the American Federation of Television and Radio Artists (AFTRA). None had any listing for a Dorothy McDonald. Bob, meanwhile, planned to call all the dozen or so "Ferruccis" listed in the Brooklyn phone book to see if any of them were related to a Rocco and Rose Ferrucci and could lead us to them. Ronni wrote to the New York City Department of Health claiming to be "Dorothy McDonald," born December 31, 1922, to request a replacement copy of her birth certificate. But again, the response was "no records found."

Several weeks passed before I heard from Bob Fitzpatrick again only to learn that he called all the Ferruccis in the Brooklyn phone book and was met with indifference or downright anger. "If any of the Ferruccis living in Brooklyn know Rocco and Rose," he said confidently, "they aren't talking." Bob and I bounced some ideas back and forth trying to decide what avenue to explore next, but there was no clear path ahead. Since Bob didn't make any headway with the Ferruccis, he proposed a course of action that would prove to be a huge undertaking. He suggested that I systematically write to all the "McDonalds" listed in the Brooklyn and Queens phone books. "We have to find your biological mother," Bob insisted, "but if I have to make phone calls to all the McDonalds it will cost you a heck of a lot of money." Bob theorized that, even though a lot of time had passed, my birth mother might not have left the area. If she had left, he said, she likely left relatives behind who could identify her.

Bob then laid out the plan of attack: I was to compose a form letter asking if the recipient knew the whereabouts of a Dorothy McDonald. But I was not to say why I was looking for this woman because that might scare someone off. I would then make copies of the form letter and mail each of them with a self-addressed stamped envelope. The most important thing, he said, was to place a number on the return envelope under the stamp and cross-reference those numbers to the list of names.

That way, if I got an anonymous reply that was worth following up, I could determine who sent it by cross-checking the number under the stamp with the list of names.

Clever... but as it turned out... daunting. I went to the local public library where I found every phone book I needed. A check of the Brooklyn phone book revealed 251 listings for "McDonald"!! When I agreed with Bob Fitzpatrick to undertake this task I clearly did not realize what was ahead. I paused for a moment as I scanned down the list of names. The chore ahead would be overwhelming. But I felt there was no other recourse and I knew that Bob was right. We HAD to find my birth mother. At least we knew her name, her birth date and age, and a claim that she was a singer in a band. We had no knowledge about my birth father, though, except that Rabbi Schwartz remembered he was the leader of the band she sang in. He would be far more difficult to locate, and without any unaltered hospital records naming him as my birth father, probably the only person who could identify him would be my birth mother. If I wanted to make more headway I had to send out those letters.

I photocopied the pages in the phone book with the "McDonald" listings and took them home where I then began the laborious task of typing a list of every name and address and assigning each name a number from 1 to 251. I also typed those names on envelopes and typed my return address in the upper left hand corner. The return envelopes were trickier. I typed my home address... Alan Gerstel, 23 Buena Vista Avenue, Hillsdale, New Jersey 07642... then estimated where the stamp would go in the upper right hand corner, and typed a corresponding number in that space, which I later covered with a stamp. I checked a few envelopes by looking inside and found I could indeed make out the impression of the typewritten number printed beneath the stamp. Without looking as carefully, though, no one else would notice that number.

I then composed my letter, which was dated April 23, 1981.

Dear Mr. or Mrs. McDonald,

I am trying to locate Dorothy Jeanette McDonald, 58 years old, who was born to Joseph McDonald and Jean McDonald on December 31, 1922. She lived in Brooklyn or Queens, and during the early 1940's, she was a singer in a band.

If you have any idea who she is or where she is, please fill out the form below and mail it back to me. It is very important to me that I find her. Thank you in advance for your trouble.

Sincerely, Alan Gerstel.

On the lower third of the page I typed in a form for the respondent's name, address, home and business phone numbers, and comments. But I also knew that, even if they did not wish to identify themselves, I could determine who they were by using my coded number system.

I took the letter back to the library and began feeding nickels into the Xerox machine to make 251 copies. That chore in itself took more than an hour. Then I stuffed the envelopes with the letters and included the secretly-numbered return envelopes. I mailed them all at one time... and then waited.

A week passed before I got the first reply. It merely stated: "No knowledge." Several other responses trickled in, and though some were pleasant enough, no one claimed to know anything about a Dorothy McDonald. As I mulled over the responses, I decided to move ahead and send more letters, this time to all the McDonalds in Queens. After all, Far Rockaway was in the Borough of Queens and it shared a common boundary with the Borough of Brooklyn. My new task was equally time-consuming.

While I was waiting for responses from the latest batch of letters I drove to the Brooklyn Board of Elections to check on any McDonalds living at 343 Vernon Avenue in Brooklyn in 1944. The helpful clerk couldn't find any listing for a McDonald there. But he started reading down the list of the names of registered voters at that address when he read the name "Ferrucci." I stopped him abruptly and asked him for the first name. "There are two Ferruccis registered to vote at that address," he said. "Rocco and Rose." I asked him if he could provide me with their complete voter information. He said he could and then disappeared out of sight.

While I waited for him to return with copies of the voting records for Rocco and Rose my mind began swirling again as I tried to digest this newest information. The clerk told me that Rocco and Rose lived at the same address, so I theorized that Rose must be Rocco's mother because Rabbi Schwartz told me that my birth father was not married at the time. But given the confusion created by the hospital records of my birth I was having real doubts about the Rabbi's memory and what information was truly accurate.

The clerk returned with the completed records that indicated Rocco was 29 years old when he registered to vote on October 14, 1944... and he was married! He worked for a trucking company in New York City. Rose was 25-years-old and she was also married. So much for the theory that Rose was Rocco's mother, I thought. So, I agonized... what DID happen? Could it be that Rocco and Rose were married to each other and yet Rocco "knocked up" someone else, someone named Dorothy McDonald? And was it possible that he was going to raise me as "Baby Boy Ferrucci" along with his wife who was NOT the mother of his child? Rocco, I thought, must have been rotten and even cruel to do something like that. But then my suspicions turned to another anomaly. The voting records showed that Rocco worked for a trucking company yet Rabbi Schwartz told me my birth father was a musician. So what was he? Was he a musician? Or maybe he was a truck driver who supplemented his income by working as a musician on weekends? I was overcome by questions and could not stop my mind from the frenzied stabs at solutions that bounced from one possibility to another like a ping-pong ball.

Sparked by the voting information I got on the Ferruccis and the confusing questions it raised, I wrote to the Queens Board of Election to see if Dorothy McDonald had registered to vote in Far Rockaway. As far as I knew, it was only a summer bungalow colony but Dorothy could have lived there year-round. It certainly appeared that she didn't live on Vernon Avenue in Brooklyn so I figured it was worth a shot. But just several days later I got a reply indicating that no records could be found. And the responses from the letters I sent to the McDonalds in the Borough of Queens were as disappointing as the ones I received from Brooklyn... only a handful of responses... each claiming they had no knowledge.

I found myself truly puzzled by the conflicting information I uncovered and without conscious thought found myself running an endless number of "what if?" scenarios through my mind. None of them, though, produced any more clarity. I had so much "information" yet so little "knowledge." Dorothy wasn't born in New York City... Didn't have a driver's license... She didn't vote... She wasn't a member of an entertainment union... The Department of Health claimed it didn't have a birth certificate in her name...And no other McDonalds in the vicinity of Brooklyn and Queens seems to know who she was.

I struggled to overcome my frustrations in the face of conflicting facts and first-hand accounts. But I remained compelled by the taste of the truth I gleaned from my hospital birth records and even by the confusing voting information about the Ferruccis. I didn't trust the Health Department's negative response to Ronni when she requested Dorothy McDonald's birth certificate. But I knew from experience that there was another way to be certain Dorothy was not born in New York so I made another trip to the New York Public Library and its Genealogy Department.

It took me many long hours to search the Birth Records for the year 1922 but I couldn't find any listing for the birth of Dorothy McDonald and that seemed to confirm the response from the Health Department. So

I asked the friendly, supportive clerk if the library had records for births outside of the 5 boroughs, figuring that I might be able to track her down in upstate New York or on eastern Long Island. The clerk told me that birth records at the library were limited to the Five Boroughs of New York. But then he asked me somewhat secretly if I was "Searching." I confessed that I was and poured out my frustration over locating accurate information on Rocco, Rose, and Dorothy. He knew his stuff. He suggested checking out the Brooklyn City Directory even though it was last printed in 1934.

City Directories, I learned, were much like our current phone books but they contained personal information on the people listed. The library had transferred the 1934 Brooklyn City Directory to microfilm to preserve it and the Directory clearly listed Rocco and Rose Ferrucci... indicated that Rocco was a peddler... and listed him as "head of household." Rocco and Rose had married young. In fact, Rose was only 16 when they did and Rocco had been some kind of salesman before he turned to the trucking business. The City Directory also indicated that, at the time, they lived at 1725 99th Street, apartment 1. There were also listings for Vitorio, Jessica, and Benedetti Ferrucci living in the same apartment.

I called Bob Fitzpatrick to give him an update on the Ferruccis. Since the information was lacking any real clues to their whereabouts, he proposed that I send out more letters with return envelopes and hidden code numbers to all the Ferruccis in Brooklyn and Queens. Fortunately, unlike the hundreds of "McDonalds," I only had 21 "Ferruccis" to include in my mailing. But none of them was a "Rocco". I wrote:

Dear Mr. or Mrs. Ferrucci,

I am trying to locate Rocco Ferrucci, who was born in 1915 (I did the math from the Voting Records) and was married to Rose Ferrucci. In 1943, Rocco and Rose Ferrucci lived at 343 Vernon Avenue in Brooklyn. He worked for a trucking company in New York City and was also a musician.

I dropped those letters in the mail on April 24, 1981.

It was time again to wait for a response, and that in turn, cranked up my frustration level a few more notches as it churned up those puzzling questions: If Rocco and Rose were married, how then did Dorothy McDonald, a single woman, fit into the picture? Why were the names "corrected" on the hospital records? Who was lying and who was telling the truth? And who was my real birth mother? Was it Rose Ferrucci? Or was it Dorothy Jeanette McDonald? The wait for the answers to my questions only took three weeks.

CHAPTER NINE

The Copa – Tommy – and Trouble

Hello, 52nd Street... Dolly is back!!! That anthem was playing vividly in Dolly's mind as she hauled her suitcase off the subway at Times Square and walked up the stairs to the street. She had been sequestered in a bungalow in Far Rockaway and starved of the nightlife she craved for far too long. She couldn't wait another moment to get back into the swing of Swing Street. It was early Sunday afternoon, August 21, 1944... and the streets of midtown Manhattan were sizzling in the noonday sun as she struggled north up Eighth Avenue to the corner of 46th Street. But Dolly didn't really mind because those streets were also alive with the rhythm and romance she had been lusting for. The final two months of her pregnancy in Far Rockaway seemed like two decades.

"Hi, Buster," she announced as she flung her suitcase down and slid it along the floor of the lobby at 301 West 46th Street. "Did ya miss me?" Startled, the burly man behind the front desk looked up from his newspaper. A big smile lit up his face at the sight of Dolly McDonald back on her home turf. "Geez doll… welcome back. How'd it go with the baby and everything?" he questioned almost matter-of-factly. "How's the old Dolly doing?" Dolly leaned seductively against the counter, tilted her head back and brushed a wisp of hair from her face. She felt at home. "I'll tell you, Buster, it was no cakewalk, I'll tell you that. And I really missed this place. But I got it all over with, and it's just a bad memory, and now I'm back in action," she said with a growing confidence. "What's been happening around here?" Buster, the guy who manned the lobby to keep the riff-raff out of the building, regaled Dolly with the gossip about how Annie in 3-C slipped into Freddy's apartment when Freddy's wife went to work. He told her about the Beaumont twins and how the girls got into a fistfight over a guy who had two-timed both of them. And he told her about Paco's emergency appendectomy.

Once she digested all the dirt, Buster gave her the mail he'd been holding for her and Dolly took the small elevator upstairs to her old apartment. She lived on the fourth floor in the corner of the building overlooking both 46th Street and Eighth Avenue. The hallways were stuffy but not nearly as suffocating as her apartment once she unlocked the door and stepped inside. The windows were closed just as she had left them two months before, creating a musty odor that permeated her 2-room haven. Dolly dropped her purse and the mail on her kitchen table and quickly moved around the stifling apartment opening the windows as wide as she could. The air outside was humid and sticky but Dolly was fortunate to have a corner apartment so she was favored with a wisp of cross-ventilation.

She reached into her purse and pulled a pack of Chesterfields along with a pack of matches, and with a flourish worthy of a silver screen siren, she lit her cigarette, blew out the match, and took a deep, satisfying drag. Dolly was feeling newly-liberated and ready for action as she perched on the window sill overlooking 9th Avenue and stuck her head out to survey the scene below. Smitten anew by the sights and sounds of the big city life, Dolly took another deep drag and exhaled as she shook her head up and down almost imperceptibly as if to be saying "yes, this is it!" She went back to her purse and took out an envelope filled with cash. She opened it and counted the hundred-dollar bills inside. Satisfied that she had accounted for all the money she was due for selling her baby, she opened a cupboard and pulled down a ceramic container in the shape of a cat. The cat's head separated to create a lid for the jar and Dolly dug out several silk scarves that were inside. She put the envelope in, covered it with the scarves, topped it off with the lid, and then put it back in the cupboard. This was the only bank that Dorothy McDonald used. Real banks would require a social security number for an account. Dolly didn't have one. She didn't need one. She was paid in cash. Taxes were never a problem. Taxes were something other people paid.

The stack of mail was surprisingly thin considering Dolly had been away for more than two months. She leafed through the usual bills, some marked "overdue," until she came to a letter from Ossining New York, the home of Sing Sing prison, where her brother Tommy was serving time for armed robbery. It was postmarked nearly a month earlier… on July 25th. She opened it and read: "Hi sis. Hope your well. I am too. I am getting out of here in about a couple of months and I figure to head to the Big City before I go back home. Can you put me up?" Dolly shook her head and smiled as she mumbled out loud, "He'll never change." She made a mental note to write him back and tell him he was welcome to stay with her when he got out.

Dolly was back… and she had plans for her big return to 52nd Street even though it was a Sunday night and not the wildest night of the week. First on the agenda would be a nice, long soaking bath and some pampering before she'd head out for the evening. Her first bout with the bathtub, though, was a bust. When she turned the "hot" water handle it gurgled and then belched out a rust-colored liquid that sputtered several times before it flowed freely and eventually turned to clear, clean water. The stagnant water had apparently rusted the lead pipes in the months that Dolly was gone. And when she turned the other handle, the "cold" water mimicked the hot water in appearance and flow. But once they cleared and Dolly had wiped the residual rust out of the tub she filled it and took a warm, relaxing soak.

After the sun went down, Dolly ventured out to her old haunts where she was greeted with open arms by the club managers, bartenders and the hangers-on at every night spot she frequented. The boys at "Club 52" were especially happy to see her back. "Hey, Leon, look at that!" owner Harry Vance yelled out to the bartender. "Looks like Dolly's back... and Dolly is looking really special." Oblivious to the other people in the club, Dolly hugged Harry firmly and then planted a kiss on his lips. "Oh but it's great to be back here. I missed this joint a lot," Dolly said wistfully. Harry cut her off with feigned disappointment. "Forget about the joint," he asked, "What about Leon and me?" "No offense, baby," Dolly oozed as she gave Harry another little pucker. "You and Leon is what MAKES this joint," she responded as she took his arm in hers and they strolled over to the bar. "Now, how about a drink, Leon?" she cooed seductively. Leon snapped-to and mixed up her usual: a Jack Daniels and water.

Dolly reached into her purse and brought out a pack of Chesterfields but before she could make another move Harry took the pack out of her hands. "Here, let me," he said as she knocked a cigarette out of the pack and placed it in between Dolly's lips. He grabbed a pack of matches off the bar and lit one. Dolly reached up and took Harry's hand in hers as she steadied the match and brought the flame closer. Dolly inhaled deeply and lit her cigarette. She was still holding the match when Harry blew it out and said softly, "It's really good to see you, kiddo. A lotta people been asking about you."

Harry and Dolly sat down together at a small table against the wall. The place was half-empty which was usual for a Sunday night but a fog of cigarette smoke still hung over the room. They talked about the time Dolly spent in Far Rockaway and how she gave birth and came right back to 52nd Street to get back into the groove. But, she told Harry, she wasn't quite ready to "party" yet. She had given birth only about a week and a half ago and she needed some time to rest up and heal. "I'll be back and raring to go soon enough," she reassured Harry with a chuckle. "Hell, I gotta make up for lost time."

And sure enough, several weeks later Dolly was back in action at Club 52. Harry introduced her to Richie and she spent several hours dancing with him, ordering expensive champagne, and showing him a good time. But Richie was hankering to head over to the Copa to hear Louis Prima's band. That was fine with Dolly. It was time to let everybody know she was back in action, she thought… including Jimmy Vincent and the other guys in the band whom she had gotten to know before she got knocked up.

They hopped a cab and Richie took her by the arm as they made a grand entrance into the famous nightclub. The Copa was truly the "in" spot, a real classy supper club that boasted the best entertainment in town. All the big names like Tony Bennett, Ella Fitzgerald and even Frank Sinatra played the Copa. The club oozed elegance and sophistication. It was worlds apart from the clubs on 52nd Street and THE hot destination for a guy with a hefty bank account looking to make a big impression. Dolly spotted her friend Edie in the hat check room and watched Frances making the rounds as the photographer who snapped glamour shots of the customers and their dates. She made a point of saying a big hello to both of them.

Richie was known as a high-roller and a big tipper. It earned him… and Dolly… a table in the front row. When the music started and the lights dazzled across the stage, Dolly stood out among the crowd. "When you're smiling… when you're smiling…," Louis Prima sang, "the whole world smiles with you." And as Louis and the band glanced out into the audience there she was, Dolly McDonald, with a huge smile on her face. Jimmy Vincent caught her eye and she winked a seductive wink that brought a big grin to Jimmy's face. Richie ordered a bottle of champagne and the two snuggled up and held hands as the band wailed and played "pretty for the people", Louis Prima's catch-phrase. When Lily Ann Carol stepped up to the microphone Dolly mouthed the words as Lily Ann sang, "... til you're walking beside me, I'll walk alone." Dolly hoped her lip-syncing would catch Louis' eye and give him a clue that she was ready to stand tall in front of the microphone herself. She was ready. She was eager. And nothing had changed. She still yearned for the day that SHE would be the singer in the band.

She never did step up to the microphone in front of Louis Prima's band but one night Dolly got a chance to sing at "The Three Deuces" on 52nd Street. She wasn't star material but the applause she garnered from the audience proved she wasn't half bad either. It seemed that every time she went out with this new guy named Marty she got invited to sing a set with the house band and Dolly always jumped at the opportunity. She wasn't paid for her talents, at least not for her talents on the stage, but she always hoped some agent or band leader would be in the audience and they would recognize her ability and sign her to a contract. That bubble burst, though, when Marty found a younger girl and gave Dolly the brush-off. It was only after they split that Dolly learned Marty had been bribing the leader of the house band to let her perform. And when the bribes stopped, so too, did the invitations. Dolly was furious that she had been "had" but she didn't dwell on it and never lost sight of her dream. She continued to make it her mission to please the men who frequented the clubs and she kept promoting herself as a singer in the band.

Just as he had written to Dolly months earlier, Tommy McDonald got out of the slammer on November 10, 1944, and headed straight to his sister's place in midtown Manhattan. At 19, he was two years younger than Dolly but he'd been known as "Tommy Trouble" since his early teens. At 16, he was sentenced as an adult for his role in a drug deal that ended in a murder. Tommy didn't pull the trigger but he sure as hell was involved with the guy who did.

Tommy got off the bus from Ossining near Times Square and walked the five blocks to his sister's building carrying the small suitcase with his meager worldly possessions. Buster greeted him in his no-nonsense manner when he entered the lobby. "What can I do for you?" he asked Tommy. "Dolly... I'm Dolly's brother, Tommy," he fired back. "Oh yeah," Buster said as he reached forward to shake his hand, "she told me you were coming to town. 4-D... That's her apartment. Just take the elevator up to the 4th floor and you'll see it to your left."

After several knocks, Dolly opened the door to see her little brother standing there, a little thinner than she remembered and a lot tougher from his time behind bars. He melted, though, when he saw her smiling face, "Sis... Wow... You sure are a sight for sore eyes. I ain't seen nothin as good-looking as you for more than three years. And you ARE a sight for sore eyes even though you're my sister." "Come on in, honey," Dolly cooed as she threw her arms around him. "And make yourself at home." Tommy walked over to the couch and flung himself onto it. "It feels good to be with family after being stuck in the slammer for so long," he said to her as his eyes darted around the apartment. "Nice place."

"It'll do," Dolly said as she opened a kitchen cabinet and took out a small box. "Here... let me make it even nicer." She sat on the couch next to Tommy and pulled out a joint she had rolled the night before. "It looks like you could use this," she told him as she lit up the joint and passed it to her brother. Marijuana was the drug of choice for the jazz musicians who played "The Street" and Dolly joined in the party anytime she could. She'd also buy a "nickel bag" or a "dime bag" to keep some around her apartment for occasions just like this one. Tommy took the joint eagerly and took two long "hits" on it before passing is back to his sister. They sat together on the couch in the late afternoon hours, passing the joint back and forth, and talked about the days back home in Philadelphia. "I couldn't wait to get outta there," Dolly admitted. "There was just no action in Philly. Oh yeah... action on the streets, but not the kind of classy scene like we got going here on 52nd Street. Now THAT'S what was missing back home."

The pot was kicking in and Tommy was feeling buzzed and more relaxed than he had in years. "Yeah, I guess you got a point there, sis," he agreed. "That's why I always got into trouble. And hell, Dad didn't actually help either. He always acted so tough. He was working his deals... working the streets. But he always kept his cool... and he always managed to stay clean." "Well, he paid off half the cops in Philly," Dolly reminded him. "But I was always surprised that he didn't do more to help you out when you got into a jam. I always figured he let you down when he coulda made things right for you

Once the sun set, Dolly took Tommy to her favorite haunts for an evening of drinking and introductions. Dolly's friend, Mary, had seen pictures of Tommy and always wanted to get up close and personal with Dolly's brother... and that night she did... again and again.

Tommy spent several weeks hanging around with Dolly during the afternoons and with Mary every night before he began to long for his friends and family back home in Philly. A phone call added a sense of urgency to his travel plans. "Tommy, your dad's been shot," said the voice on the other end of the line. "He's gonna be okay, but he took two bullets from a creep who was trying to muscle into his territory by knocking him out of commission." Tommy's father, known to all as Angus, was a Ward Boss in Philadelphia. He was an enforcer in a district known for its nasty politics as much as its back door bribes. Angus was no newcomer to the rough and tumble life of political power plays. And yes, he'd used a little "muscle" in the past to get what he wanted. But it never went as far as gunfire... and that's what got Tommy fired up. The rules had apparently changed and he could see that some people were now willing to do anything to knock Angus down a few notches. Tommy hopped on the next bus headed for Philly.

Angus survived and returned home from the hospital with the bullets still inside him. They were near some nerves in Angus' lower back and the doctors felt it was safer to leave them where they were rather than taking the chance of severing the nerves and crippling him. And funny thing... no one ever saw the guy who pulled the trigger again. That was Tommy's doing. He was hardened by his prison sentence and wasn't about to let some low-life punk use his father for target practice. He spent days prying information out of the street thugs who knew everyone and everybody's business. One night, he tracked down the triggerman, put a bullet clean between his eyes and dumped the body in a landfill.

Tommy also parlayed his bad boy image into cash. He netted many thousands of dollars over the years just by keeping business owners "safe" from the "bad" elements in town. He wasn't piggy, though, and he never took too much.

But Tommy's luck would finally run out in the Spring of 1949 when he stopped into Sal's Pizza for the first time to try to get a feel on how Sal would react to his shake-down. Tommy strolled up to the counter as Sal was slipping a large wooden spatula under a pizza to ease it out of the oven. He swung around to place the pie into an open box when their eyes met. Sal knew all about Tommy's reputation but he wasn't about to cough up cash for any two-bit thug that came along. So before Tommy could open his mouth, Sal made his feelings clear. "Get outta here," he told Tommy as he pointed his finger to the door. But Tommy knew that a bold, disrespectful refusal like that could ruin his reputation as a guy you didn't want to mess with, and he wasn't about to back down. He just stood there glaring at Sal. "Get out before I throw you out," Sal threatened.

That threat was a mistake. The tone of Sal's voice sent Tommy into a rage. He snapped. Tommy jumped over the counter in one swift movement and began punching Sal squarely in the face. "Get outta here??!!" he screamed at Sal, "get outta here?!! Is that what you told me?" Sal tried to fight back and he did land a couple of punches but he was no match for Tommy's terrible temper. "You want me outta here??!!", Tommy growled as he grabbed the front of Sal's apron and shoved him hard against the pizza oven. The back of Sal's head slammed into the corner of the open oven door. His eyes sprang open wide as his jaw dropped. Then his body seemed to wither like a deflating balloon as he collapsed to the floor. Tommy stood over him, panting in a rage. Blood gushed from the back of Sal's head and formed a pool on the linoleum-covered floor. Tommy took a deep breath, straightened his clothes, and walked around the counter and out the door calmly, leaving Sal's lifeless body crumpled on the floor.

Detectives investigating the crime scene didn't have much to go on at first. No one was talking because Tommy had a reputation on the streets as someone you didn't want to double-cross. The cops tried to convince reluctant witnesses that they could offer protection but it wasn't until Sal's widow put up a $2,000 reward that the detectives made any real progress. Eager for the reward money, two witnesses fingered Tommy and placed him at the scene. Their eyewitness accounts helped prosecutors make a strong case. Tommy's lawyer, though, convinced the court that Tommy didn't mean to actually kill Sal, and in the end, the judge found Tommy guilty of Manslaughter instead of Murder. But the judge took into account Tommy's previous run-ins with the law and sentenced him to 20 years in prison.

CHAPTER TEN

The Actor
Muffs His Lines

The early 1980's were odd times for me, personally and professionally. My career as an actor began to take root in Dinner Theatre and Regional Theatre productions. I even had a stint on the soap opera "The Doctors." Producers and Casting Directors reassured me I had talent but they always had a problem type-casting me. At one point I was being considered for the role of a Jewish doctor on the soap opera "Ryan's Hope." Several months later I auditioned for the role of a "Ryan cousin", an Irishman from Chicago. I guess I didn't look Jewish enough or Irish enough. I didn't get either role. Then, Katherine Hepburn was heading to Broadway with the show "West Side Waltz." I auditioned for the role of a Jewish lawyer but the Producer thought I was too "young-looking" and I just didn't fit his perception of what a "Jewish lawyer" looked like.

So it turns out, I was passionately focused on finding out who I really was through my investigation at the same time Casting Directors were trying to figure out the ethnicity of the characters I could effectively portray. The only thing they were certain of is that I was not "P and G." That's the code for a blond-haired, blue-eyed actor who is "Proctor and Gamble," in other words someone who is not ethnic... someone who looks very middle-American.

Three weeks had passed since I sent out the last batch of letters to the Ferruccis and I was memorizing lines for a play I was rehearsing when the phone rang. My mind was on the lines from the script and I shouldn't have answered it but I did. "Are you the guy who's looking for Rocco Ferrucci?" a gruff voice on the other end of the phone asked. I was stunned. I was speechless. I was having problems putting my thoughts together. I had never figured on a phone call. I stammered, "I... uh... I... think my father is looking for Rocco... he's a friend... a friend of my father I think. I don't know... er.. I don't know what he wants.. uh... my father, that is.. what he wants with Rocco...." I was losing it and I knew it. I was becoming unglued. The man said that he was calling "for" Rocco but I sensed it was Rocco himself. Panic-stricken, I told myself: I AM TALKING TO MY BIRTH FATHER!!! I was so caught off guard that I didn't know what to say.

I told him I would ask my father what he wanted with Rocco and the man said he would call back the next day... a Saturday... at 2 o'clock. I hung up the phone and was panting hysterically. Then I began sobbing. I had blown it! After many months of working and waiting I wasn't prepared for that call and I knew I sounded like a buffoon. I just didn't expect a phone call. I never included a phone number in any of my letters though I DID have a "listed" number. I just didn't prepare myself for that possibility. I was so close to contacting Rocco Ferrucci, I thought... and now he will never call back.

I paced around my house for an hour... raging against my feeble performance... and beating up on myself emotionally. But after my hysteria subsided I began to analyze what had happened and began to formulate a plan. If the man does call back, I thought to myself, I would apologize for the story... say that I was shocked and surprised by his call... and tell him what I really wanted. I figured that I had nothing to lose at that point. If he didn't call back I knew I would never forgive myself.

I awoke at 5 o'clock the next morning, my mind swirling with anticipation. I got up and paced around the house thinking about what I would say if the phone rang again and how I would say it. And I then realized I would not be able to take notes of our conversation quickly enough. So I decided to record the call. I went to Radio Shack and invested $1.99 in a telephone microphone. It contained a small suction cup which I attached to the receiver of the phone and plugged into my small tape recorder. I was all set to go at 2 o'clock when the caller said he would call again. I sat at my desk, tape recorder ready.

The minutes passed but the phone didn't ring. I sat and stared at the clock as it became 2:15... then 2:30. By 2:45, I was certain that the caller, who I truly believed was Rocco Ferrucci, was not calling back. Then at 3 o'clock... the phone rang. I started the tape recorder and picked up the phone as casually as I could.

"Hello," I said meekly. "Yes, hello again. I called yesterday," a man's voice replied. "Oh listen," I said as my heart started racing, "I was really shocked when you called yesterday and I didn't know what to say. I made up that stuff about my father. It's me... It's me... I'm the one who's trying to reach Rocco Ferrucci." There was a pause and then the voice said, "Well, I'm Rocco. I'm the guy you're trying to reach. What's this all about?" I told him the story... that I was born in St. Joseph's Hospital on August 11, 1944... and that I was adopted, and that his name appeared on my birth records. There was a long pause... a very long pause. Then Rocco broke the silence with the words that remain with me to this day: "I always knew this day would come," he said. "I knew one day you would find me." I was stunned! I truly didn't know what to say. But he continued, "You found me." I was struggling with my thoughts and trying to figure out what to ask next but could only manage the blunt question, "Are you my father?" "No," he sighed, "but I wanted to be."

Now I was the one to take a long pause. I didn't understand what he was trying to tell me. "Wanted to be, but aren't?" I finally questioned. Then…another pause. Rocco explained that he and his wife had lost two children in childbirth and could not have any others. They vacationed every summer in Far Rockaway and he recalled vaguely that he learned of Dorothy through his brother-in-law… or his wife had met Dorothy on the beach. In any case, he said that Dorothy shared a house with two people he called "show girls" and their Hungarian mother. Dorothy was pregnant with a child that she didn't want to keep and she was out of money. She told them that she was a singer with Louis Prima's band and that she had been "involved" with a member of the band but did not want to marry him. They reached an agreement with Dorothy and signed papers to take her baby. In return, they paid her medical bills, the hospital bills, and even took her to the hospital the day she gave birth. He checked her in as "Rose Ferrucci" so they could just go home with me as their child without having to go through any legal adoption proceedings. As far as anyone would know I was born to Rose and would be named "Ferrucci" so there would be no questions once they left the hospital and returned to their neighborhood in Brooklyn.

It was the perfect plan, he said… until Dorothy apparently had a change of heart. When they went to pick me up from the hospital they were told that Dorothy had already checked out and had taken me with her.

Rocco knew that Dorothy had been living in what he called "a hotel in the West 50's" in New York City and that's where he had taken her some money before I was born. So he went back there to track her down and force her to face up to the terrible thing that she had done. The desk clerk, though, told him that Dorothy had left town. Neither he nor his wife ever saw Dorothy again.

All at once, it clicked. In a flash I now understood why the names were changed on the hospital records… why my mother's name went from "Rose Ferrucci" to "Dorothy McDonald"… and how I went from "Baby Boy Ferrucci" to "Baby Boy McDonald."

But Rocco's revelation also made me aware that I was the center of a heartless, horrible deception that dashed the dreams of a young couple desperate to have a child they could call their own. The Ferruccis were overjoyed as they anticipated having a baby boy to fill the void in their lives but they were played for fools and left with a pile of unused diapers and an empty crib. I apologized to Rocco profusely for I now realized that I wasn't the only one who suffered over the years. I was dumbfounded, though, and incapable of thoroughly understanding the cruelty of my birth mother's despicable actions… and I told Rocco so.

Before we hung up Rocco made a vow that he would help me find my birth parents. And he promised that he would call me back again soon.

Just six hours later, at 9 o'clock that night, the phone rang again. And again, it was Rocco. I could tell he was calling from a pay phone again because he had to feed coins into it every so often. This time he put his wife on. "Alan? Is this Alan?" a sweet voice asked. "Yes, it's me. I'm so glad you decided to call me," I responded. I was feeling a warmth, a kinship with these people who had been so heartlessly "burned" by my birth mother. We talked more about what happened and how it all unfolded. Like Rocco, she was a little fuzzy about how she first learned about Dorothy and her pregnancy plight. She remembered that Rocco's brother-in-law was a musician and friends with some guys in Louis Prima's band. He had heard about this girl who got pregnant "by a fellow in the band." But then she reversed course and told me she recalled first meeting Dorothy in Far Rockaway. If I noticed any discrepancy in her story I was too wrapped up in it to question her. I just let her talk. She echoed all the other details of Rocco's account and went on to say that shortly after Dorothy left them empty-handed, they adopted two girls. The love and devotion they showered on their young children helped them overcome their bitterness and allowed them to put Dorothy and her horrible scheme out of their minds. In the end, Rose told me, it all worked out for them.

We talked for about an hour and she promised they would be back in touch. I mentioned several times that they should call me "collect" as they shouldn't have to pay the phone bill themselves. But this was no mere act of altruism on my part. I knew that the calling number for "collect calls" would appear on my next phone bill and that would make it easy for me to locate them even if they called from a pay phone.

Three days later, Rocco called again and this time he called collect. Gotcha! I thought I was so clever. But Rocco was no slouch. "I'm calling from my home now," Rocco said proudly, "now you'll know how to find me." "What do you mean by that?" I asked innocently as I asked myself how Rocco could have known I was setting him up. "You know," said Rocco wisely, "you'll have my phone number on your next bill. That shows you that I trust you." And I truly believed that he did trust me. I felt that a door was opening that would eventually lead me to the end of my Search. Rocco brimmed with confidence. He had the unbridled nerve that I lacked.

"We're going to get to the bottom of this, Alan," he said reassuringly. "I think I remember that Lily Ann Carol was singing with the Louis Prima band around that time and I think Dorothy sang with the band after Lily Ann but before Keely Smith." I told him that I had heard of Keely Smith but that I had never heard the name Lily Ann Carol. "Why don't you try to track her down with the musician's union," he advised me. "I'm going to ask some friends of mine if they know where she might be." I told him that I would work on it and see what I could find out. Rocco told me that he would call me back again. "Collect," I said. He replied knowingly: "Okay, collect."

Rocco seemed like such a great connection and seemed so motivated that I got caught up in his spirit of optimism. I surmised that a band singer like Lily Ann Carol would have been a member of the American Guild of Variety Artists and I got on the phone to AGVA immediately. It proved to be another dead end, though. The nice lady who answered the phone looked her up but said there was no listing for a Lily Ann Carol.

Rocco called two other times that week. In each phone call he told me that he was determined to find out what happened to Dorothy and who my birth father was. I was impressed by his determination but a little puzzled by it at the same time. I could see that he and his wife felt a connection to me even now, nearly forty years after my birth but I didn't know why. I was more focused on what Rocco could find out for me, though, rather than trying to understand his motivation. He kept reminding me that he had connections in the music business and promised he wouldn't rest until he had the answers. He also told me that he had some medical conditions that forced him to retire at a fairly young age so he said he had a lot of time on his hands to dig for answers. He said he'd be back in touch within a week.

Meanwhile, I decided to pursue the Keely Smith angle. In a bizarre coincidence, I had worked with Keely Smith in my first sojourn into Summer Stock. It was 1963 and I was the Technical Director at Storrowton Music Fair in West Springfield, Massachusetts. Keely was starring in "Showboat" along with Andy Devine. She had even given me an autographed picture of herself. I remembered that she and Louis Prima had broken up just a year or two before and that she was out on her own. But I also knew that back in 1958 she and Louis Prima had a hit with their recording of "Old Black Magic." I had heard that song played on the radio again and again during my early high school years. It was hugely popular and earned Louis Prima a "Grammy" that year, the first year Grammys were awarded.

But how could I track Keely down? I knew that she had been based out of Las Vegas and figured that she might even have a home there so I called my friend, Mario. Mario was a hair stylist who lived in Vegas and had many influential clients. Certainly, I thought, he would know how to track down Keely. But a phone call to him brought the news that she hadn't played Vegas for some time. Mario did mention someone else though, Sam Butera, Louis Prima's saxophone player. Mario knew that Sam lived in Vegas and he told me that he could get Sam's address from a showgirl he knew named "Bambi." He also suggested that I write directly to Keely in care of the American Guild of Variety Artists.

While I waited for Mario to get me the information on Sam Butera, I took his advice about Keely Smith. I used my Polaroid camera to take a shot of the autographed picture Keely had given me in 1963 and enclosed it with a letter asking if she had ever heard of a singer in Louis Prima's band named Dorothy Jeanette McDonald. I also asked her for the names of musicians in Louis Prima's band in 1943. By enclosing the picture and mentioning that we had worked together I hoped that it might evoke a sense of theatrical kinship and alleviate any concern she might have that I could be a crazed fan or a stalker. I didn't have Keely's home address so I called AGVA to confirm that the union would indeed forward my letter. The woman who answered the phone told me that the Guild routinely sends letters on to members and to print the words "Please Forward" on the envelope. I can't be certain if Keely ever got my letter but I suspect that she did as it was never returned to me. After many months without a response, though, I eventually gave up hope.

I trusted that Rocco was having more success than I had. After all, he seemed so much more confident and was so much more aggressive than I could be in these circumstances. But I was in a bind. I had to wait for him to call me because I hadn't gotten my next phone bill yet with the Collect calls that would list his phone number. As the days passed, though, I decided not to wait for Rocco any longer but to launch my own search for members of Louis Prima's band back in 1943. A "Big Band" would employ as many as twenty musicians, mostly men. I figured that if one of those guys knocked up the singer in the band, the word would get out and everyone would know about it. These guys were on the road a lot. They ate together. They drank together. Surely, I thought, every one of those band members would know who my birth mother and father were. I just had to find out who played in the band and then locate them. But this was 1981. There was no Internet and certainly no Google search engine.

Before I could come up with a plan, though, my May, 1981 phone bill arrived. Ma Bell listed three collect calls from Amityville, New York, at times that coincided with the calls from Rocco and Rose. The phone number was 516-555-3215. A trip to the public library and a search of the Nassau County, New York phone book yielded a listing for: Rocco Ferrucci, 130 Fern Street, Amityville, New York.

I didn't know why weeks had passed without Rocco calling me again so I summoned up the courage and called his number. After five rings, an answering machine clicked into action and I instantly recognized Rocco's voice. I left word that I was anxious to know if he had found anything and I asked him to call. Days passed and I still heard nothing. So I tried again. I got the answering machine again and left word again. Then I waited a week before calling again. But this time, Rose answered. "Hello, Mrs. Ferrucci," I said in a puzzled voice, "I hope everything is all right..." "Oh," she said haltingly. "Because," I went on, "I have left several messages and I haven't heard anything." Rose paused awkwardly again, then said, "Rocco hasn't been feeling well. I... uh... know he has been trying to help you... and... he has... um... made several phone calls for you, but he... just isn't up to it right now." I sensed the unease in her voice and felt that something had changed in our relationship. "I hope Rocco will be all right," I told her, "I hope I am not causing you any trouble because that's the last thing I want to do. I hope you understand that." "I do, I do," she responded in a way that was too quick and too defensive. I could really tell now that something was up. She tried faking it but wasn't up to the task. "Give Rocco some time," she told me as reassuringly as she could, "He'll help you once he feels better."

I thanked her as pleasantly as I could but when I hung up I kept having a nagging feeling that this was more than Rocco's health. Something had happened with Rocco, and whatever it was, it stirred up those feelings of rejection in me once again. Rocco, I was certain, was blowing me off though I had no idea why.

For days, I pondered what I could have done or said that would have sparked such a radical change in the Ferruccis. There had never been any awkwardness in our talks, no inkling that I was upsetting them after all these years. If anything, Rocco's reaction was reassuring and upbeat. And so many years had passed since Dorothy duped and devastated them both that I sensed he and his wife finally wanted closure. They wanted to know themselves what happened to make Dorothy abandon them and who my birthfather really was. Was he indeed a "member of Louis Prima's band?" They told me that they themselves had been tormented by those questions for years. So I couldn't fathom why Rocco was distancing himself from me now. What had I done? No matter what the answer, I realized I had been abandoned, and I was on my own again.

CHAPTER ELEVEN

We're NOT in the Money

Dolly McDonald was one of the lucky ones. She didn't succumb to the lure of hard drugs that would have gotten her hooked and shortened her working years as a "hostess." She was a drinker and she smoked some marijuana from time to time but she was also a survivor and knew from her teenage years in Philadelphia that heroin and cocaine were shortcuts to hell. So while many of the younger girls spent their nights snorting or shooting-up, Dolly remained relatively clean and kept her good looks and statuesque body far longer than she had a right to.

It may have been the dream of stardom that kept her motivated or just a lack of other viable options, but whatever it was, Dolly was able to reinvent herself time after time as she adapted to the changing face of "Swing Street." The decline was imperceptible at first, but by the late 1940's strip clubs were more numerous than jazz clubs and the clientele reflected that change. The denizens of "The Street That Never Sleeps" came more for titillation than good music and 52nd Street lost the aura of the "good times" that it exuded over the years. The clubs that once catered to the well-heeled struggled to compete with the girlie shows and the backroom gambling but the music in the jazz joints that survived still flowed into the wee hours. The big names and what was left of the Big Bands, though, gradually took their music elsewhere, leaving the lesser-known musicians to fill the void. As the smaller bands took up residence at Club 52 there were more opportunities for Dolly to highlight her musical abilities. She also remained a favorite of the customers into the 1960's when she was in her early 40's. The customers didn't spend as much as they once did but they still were attracted to Dolly's vibrant personality if not her irresistible sex appeal.

It was the Fall of 1964 when Dolly got another call from her brother, Tommy. He had gotten out of Sing Sing a year earlier after another long stretch in The Joint and had headed back home to Philly where he tried to stay out of trouble. "Hey kiddo," he practically shouted into the phone excitedly. "I got someone that you gotta meet. And I'm coming back to your place to introduce the two of you... and I'm gonna be there next week...." Dolly cut him off. "Whoa, slow down Tommy. I can't follow what you're saying. Tell me again... slowly... what you're talking about?" Tommy took it down a notch and told her about his best buddy from prison, Blackie Cafferty. Blackie was a great guy, he said, and was getting out of the slammer after a ten-year sentence. Tommy wanted to set the two of them up. "Okay, okay kiddo. If it means so much to you I'll think about going out with him. But don't get your pants in an uproar," she cautioned. "I've been set up with the best of them. Besides, what's in it for me?" "Maybe he'll get YOUR pants in an uproar," Tommy responded playfully. They both had a good laugh before Tommy continued convincingly, "Besides, I think the two of you could be good for each other. And hell, you're not getting any younger, sis."

Dolly finally agreed to spend an evening on the town with Blackie but only after Tommy gave her a reason that appealed to her monetary instincts: Blackie had sworn to him that he had a box of cash stashed away from a hold-up years before. That cash would be enough for Blackie AND Dolly to live their lives on Easy Street. At least that's what Blackie claimed. "He's looking better and better all the time," Dolly told her brother.

Everything went as planned. Tommy traveled to New York from Philadelphia two weeks before Christmas and was waiting at Dolly's place when Blackie knocked. Tommy opened the door to Dolly's apartment and welcomed his old friend Blackie with a solid hand shake and a shoulder bump. Blackie was a tall, good-looking guy in his 40's with a rock-hard body developed by daily work-outs in Sing Sing. He unbuttoned his heavy jacket and looked around with a huge grin on his face, a grin that telegraphed the relief of being back in a welcoming environment after being locked up for years. Dolly strolled out of her bedroom, her dyed red hair falling lushly over her shoulders, looking radiant. She sized up Blackie and vice versa. And as they did, the temperature in the apartment seemed to soar. Dolly walked over and shook his hand seductively. "You must be Blackie," she cooed. "I've heard so much about you but Tommy didn't do you justice." Nearly speechless, Blackie bantered back, "You too, doll."

Blackie Cafferty was smooth. Even a ten-year stretch in Sing Sing didn't dull his edge with the ladies and he knew how to play Dolly like a Baby Grand. "It's gonna take me a couple a weeks to get my hands on some cash," he told her with a cool indifference, "and I'd like to show you a good time. D'ya think you can spring for some dough 'til I can pay you back? Hell, I'm fresh out of the pen and clean out of cash." "Hey, what do ya take me for... some cheap floozie?" Dolly shot back coyly. Blackie, though, was prepared for her half-hearted objection and turned up the charm. He put his hands on her shoulders, gave a little squeeze and then looked squarely into her eyes. "I'll make it up to you... I promise," he purred.

With the images of Blackie's cash swirling around in her head, she agreed to "front" him some of her savings to help cultivate a long-term relationship. He represented everything Dolly had ever longed for. He was the antithesis of the bad-tempered, bad-breath, beer-belly customer that she was obligated to entertain at Club 52. Blackie was a good-looking guy with a well-developed body and all the smooth moves. Dolly wanted to be seen strutting down the street with him on her arm. She also wanted him to "scratch her itch." Besides... there WAS that cash he had hidden away.

The Good Times ruled over the next several months. Tommy had gone back to Philly to celebrate Christmas with friends and family and decided to stay on while Dolly and Blackie became an item all over town... on Dolly's dime. Dolly bought Blackie a sharp, new, eye-popping wardrobe and took him to her favorite haunts on 52nd Street where she introduced him to all her acquaintances and boasted of their solid relationship. They were a striking pair and created quite a buzz among the customers at the clubs AND among the other working girls who longed for a guy like Blackie for themselves.

In exchange for the dollars Dolly showered on him, Blackie showed Dolly what it was like to feel like a woman... a woman who was fawned over by a man who could have any woman he wanted. They had glorious sex together but Dolly always made sure they used protection. She wasn't about to go the pregnancy route again for any guy.

But the one glitch that kept nagging at Dolly was the money. They were spending HER money every time they went out on the town. And whenever they were on a date it meant that she wasn't working and wasn't able to be the bread-winner. She'd make mention of the stash Blackie claimed he had but he'd respond with, "Just give me some time, Doll. I got it where it's tough for anyone to get at it, including me. So the timing has to be right." He always said it with such finality that Dolly would let it be for several weeks then bring it up again. "Ya know, Blackie, I'm gonna run low on cash pretty soon if we don't start tapping into what you got hidden away," she'd complain. But Blackie kept up the same story and Dolly always backed down. She was living a charmed life with a lover who made her feel like a real woman and Dolly wasn't going to let him go.

Their relationship blossomed into a full-fledged courtship but it was hard to know who was courting who. Blackie wanted Dolly for her looks, her still somewhat-shapely body, and her cash. Dolly, though, was satisfied just to have Blackie's body. No man had ever treated her as well. No man had ever spent so much time lavishing her with affection. Dolly thought, understandably, that this was the real thing. Blackie made it real when he proposed. They were both lying on their backs in Dolly's bed enjoying a satisfying post-coital cigarette when he turned to her and blurted out, "What'd ya say we make this a permanent thing? I never had it so good as I got it with you, Doll... What'd ya say?" Dolly had just inhaled a lungful of smoke and began a hacking cough as his words sunk in. She had only known Blackie for several months, and here he was, asking her to be his wife. "Oh... Blackie," she said as the tickle in her throat subsided, "I'm crazy for you. Sure. Sure I'll marry you. I thought you'd never ask." Blackie responded with a satisfied smile.

Dorothy McDonald became Dorothy Cafferty on March 3rd, 1965. That's the day they went to the courthouse and got their marriage license and tied the knot in front of a Justice of the Peace. They didn't bother with a church wedding. Despite Dolly's Catholic upbringing and Blackie's stint in a Catholic boarding school as a teenager, neither of them was especially religious. But they sure knew how to celebrate. They made the rounds all over town and they toasted each other with champagne at each stop.

Though the passion remained, Dolly's money became more of an issue. Despite the temptations over the years, she had managed to save the bulk of the cash she got from the Ferruccis and the Gerstels more than twenty years earlier. But her fling with Blackie had cost her dearly. Her savings were now running dry and she cautioned Blackie that they'd have to give up their frequent nights on the town if he didn't come through with his stolen cash. Blackie also chafed at the thought of his wife continuing her job as a "hostess" at a jazz club so when Dolly turned up the heat he said he'd try to get the cash and then disappear for several days. He returned empty-handed with a lame excuse: "I just couldn't get to it right now. Too many people snooping around. Too many eyes to see what I'm doing."

By the beginning of May, just two months after they tied the knot, Dorothy Jeanette McDonald was nearly broke. And that meant that Blackie Cafferty was also nearly broke. Dolly was cursing the relationship that cleaned out the thousands of dollars she never could bring herself spend before, the money that remained as a painful reminder of the nine months ripped out of her life and the unwanted baby she traded it for. If it weren't for her pregnancy, she still believed after these many years, she might have had a shot at making it to the big time as a singer. "I sold that kid too cheap," she'd say to herself in desperation as she dwelled on her fate. "I coulda gotten more. I shoulda gotten more." But even without the cash she hoarded for several decades she knew that she and Blackie wouldn't starve. She could always put in many more hours at Club 52. And she feared that was her inevitable fate because Blackie didn't seem willing or able to deliver on the promise of many thousands of ill-gotten dollars.

Dolly had a long-time friend in Harry Vance at Club 52. Harry had always come through for her before and she needed to turn to him again. But this time, Harry had some reservations. He had seen Dolly and Blackie's impassioned commitment to each other during their many evenings celebrating at his club and was very aware of Blackie's possessive nature. "Are you sure this is gonna work out with your new hubby?" Harry asked Dolly. "No sweat, Harry, he'll be okay with it cause he has no choice," Dolly responded. "Hey, that's okay with me. I just don't want no trouble," Harry cautioned. Dolly tilted her head slightly downward seductively and with an unmistakable bravado said, "You're talking to Dolly here, Harry. I'll take care of everything like I always do. You leave Blackie to me. There won't be no trouble." Harry smiled a smug smile of understanding. He knew she was still in control.

Late the following afternoon, Dolly took a bath, pulled out her most seductive dress, and got all dolled-up for a night on the town... on somebody else's dime for a change. Blackie was sitting at the kitchen table drinking a beer and playing solitaire with a worn out pack of cards. He hadn't bothered to shave or shower and the sight of him sitting there in a faded white undershirt with his rumpled hair and sweaty body didn't do much to entice Dolly to change her plans and hang around. He looked up and spotted her. "Wow, you look like a million bucks," he said. "Whatcha up to?" Dolly sashayed over to him as she grabbed her purse off the counter. "Somebody's gotta support us. Somebody's gotta buy the food... and your beer," she said with a hint of bitterness in her voice. "Like I told you before, we're outta cash so somebody's gotta go to work." "In them gin joints on 52nd Street?" Blackie asked. Dolly headed for the door as she fired back, "Yeah, if that's what you want to call them." She opened the door and looked back at him as she said with a chilling finality, "We... don't... have... no... choice."

In the weeks and then months that followed, Dolly got back into the old groove. She provided companionship for the solitary drinkers at Club 52 and she showed them a good time even if they weren't the high-rollers of years gone by. She was a tease but she now stopped short of sleeping with any of the customers. After all, she was a married woman and her husband wouldn't stand for it. Even without any sex, though, Blackie didn't much like the fact that she shared her time with other men. And he told her so. But he couldn't make a strong case against it because he wasn't doing anything to help pay the bills. He did his share of squawking, though. "I saw your lipstick was smeared when you came in last night," he said accusingly. "Well, so what?" Dolly fired back. "So a guy tried to kiss me, that's all. It wasn't nothing, so don't make nothing of it. Okay?" Blackie settled down but the feelings of jealousy would still simmer inside.

Dolly and Blackie began living their separate lives as they lived together in the same apartment. She would go to work each night. Blackie would sneak out and go to a poker game in the basement of a building a couple of blocks away. Dolly would slip her earnings into the cat-shaped jar in her kitchen cabinet and Blackie would slip money out of the jar to feed his poker pot. It didn't take Dolly long to figure out what was going on and she was none too happy about it. "What's with the money?" she asked Blackie as she took her jar and placed it on the table in front of him. "What'd ya mean?" he said sheepishly. "I wanna know what's been happening to all my money, the money I bust my ass for," she asked again. "Uh... well I needed a little cash, that's all," he responded. "I'll pay you back." "With what?" she lashed out. "Where are you gonna get the money to pay me back? It's been more than a year and I'm still waiting to see that stash you told me... and you told Tommy... that you had."

Over the weeks that followed the constant bickering intensified and turned to bitterness. Blackie developed a taste for the Jack Daniels Dolly kept in the kitchen cabinet and gave up on beer. Dolly, meanwhile, took out her resentment by having sex with the customers she found attractive and the customers who still found her attractive after downing a couple of bottles of champagne. But she had learned a hard lesson about Blackie and his lack of cash and ambition. So the really big tips she garnered from her favorite customers went into a special hiding place in her closet not into the cat-shaped jar that Blackie was dipping into for his poker games. Dolly was just looking out for herself.

"Ya know, Doll," Blackie chimed up one night, "you're comin' home later and later these last coupla weeks. And that makes me feel like maybe I'm not the only guy that you got your eye on." Dolly shushed him up with a kiss and an attempt at reassurance. "Hey, I can't help it if I gotta spend more time going from club to club," she told him. "I gotta do what I gotta do to support us. And I gotta do it just as long as I can. Besides, I don't see you lifting a finger to do anything except losing MY money in YOUR poker games." "Well, I win sometimes," Blackie said defensively. "I come home with plenty of money. Sometimes I'm rolling in it."

CHAPTER TWELVE

Basin Street Blues

Rocco Ferrucci turned out to be my latest disappointment. He promised he would uncover the identity of my birth father. But after his initial support turned to stubborn silence, I begrudgingly came to the conclusion that I would have to forge ahead without his help.

Rocco and Rose had provided one valuable, but perhaps doubtful piece of information: My birth father was "a fellow in Louis Prima's band." It wasn't much to go on but I felt it was worth a try. So I checked out several vintage record stores in New York hoping to find Louis Prima recordings from the 1940's. The jackets, I theorized, would have information about band members and perhaps even biographies of the singers with the band. But that theory fizzled when I found the recordings from the 1940's were all 78's with precious little information on the records themselves and literally no information on the record jackets.

I still had a phonograph at home that could play the old 78's so, even though they lacked any real information, I bought several Louis Prima recordings and listened to them intently hoping in some bizarre way that I could divine the answers to my questions through a sort of musical cosmic connection. I loved the Big Band music but it frustrated me even more to listen to the recordings and wonder if one of the musicians making such sweet music was my birth father.

Whenever I became frustrated, which was an ongoing and fairly routine occurrence, I would go through my notes hoping to generate a spark, a piece of new information that could fill in the blanks or tie names and places together. Now that I knew my birth mother's name I thought back to the person who seemed to remember so much about her: Rabbi Schwartz. I figured her name might jog his memory so I called him. "Dorothy McDonald... yes Dorothy McDonald... that rings a bell... that, I believe, was her name," Rabbi Schwartz told me. "Yes, I'm certain of it now."

It gave me a great sense of relief to know that, at the very least, I now had a confirmation of my birth mother's name. Not that I had any real doubts after seeing the hospital records and my birth records in the New York Public Library. But in a Search as convoluted as mine had become, I learned the confirmation of any information is always welcome. "But did she ever talk to you about my birth father, Rabbi? Did she ever even make a reference to the man who was the father of her baby?" I pressed on. "Alan, I wish I could help you," the rabbi told me plaintively, "but I was only involved in your adoption process for less than two weeks. With all my heart, Alan, I wish I could remember more." "I understand, Rabbi, I really do. But please let me ask you just one more question," I begged him. "Did you ever hear the name Louis Prima mentioned? Did that name ever come up in my adoption?" There was a pause before he answered, "No, Alan, I can't say that I ever heard that name talked about. I ... no... that name never came up." "Maybe someone in Louis Prima's band?" I asked again. "Could someone have talked about Louis Prima's band?" "No, there was no mention that I recall about your birth father, Alan... only that he was a musician in a band... maybe he was the leader of the band. I'm really not sure anymore."

I felt that Rabbi Schwartz was being honest with me and that I had gone as far as I could with my line of questioning so I ended by saying, "Thank you for all your help, Rabbi. And call me anytime... please... if you think of anything else." "You have my word, Alan, if I think of anything I won't hesitate to give you a call," he said warmly, "And please keep me informed of your progress. I would love to know what you find out." I assured him that I would.

It had taken several months but my friend Mario called me from Las Vegas with Sam Butera's address: 1707 Westwind Drive. So, on July 4th, 1981, I wrote to Sam Butera to ask him for his help. Two weeks later, I received this reply written on a half-torn piece of paper:

"Dear Alan,

I wish I could help you but I'm afraid that's impossible. I did not join Louis Prima until December 26th, 1954. Prior to that, I have no knowledge of the Prima band.

Sincerely, Sam Butera."

It was another dead end but at least Sam Butera had given me the courtesy of a response.

I hadn't had any success with earlier efforts but the recent series of dead ends fired up my frustration and prompted me to take another stab at letter-writing. This time, I sent form letters to all the McDonalds in the Nassau County phone book. It was another massive undertaking but I believed that someone named McDonald, somewhere in or near New York City, would know something about Dorothy and could lead me to her. But just as my earlier exercise with the McDonalds in the Boroughs of Brooklyn and Queens, the hundreds of letters I sent out proved to be an exercise in futility.

Even as I was trying to locate my birth mother, though, I remained convinced that I had to track down members of Louis Prima's band to find the man responsible for my birth. Someone told me about a vintage record shop not far from my home called "The Record Studio" in Ridgewood, New Jersey. I headed there in search of more Prima recordings and I was successful in finding several 33 LP's that actually had pictures of the Prima band on the jackets along with a little biographical information. As I was paying for the albums, the clerk started making small talk and asked me if I was a big Louis Prima fan. I told him that I had just discovered his music and that I liked it a lot. "Then you have to meet Bob Pentatore," he was eager to tell me. "Bob is the biggest Louis Prima fan in the world. In fact, I think he even met Prima in person and he lives just minutes away in Fair Lawn." The clerk described Bob as a "character" but he had Bob's phone number and gave it to me.

This could be the break I was looking for, I thought, as I left the record store. So when I got home I formulated my approach to Bob. I wouldn't bring up my adoption. I would just tell him that I am a fan who wants to learn everything he can about this great musician named Louis Prima and his band back in the 1940's. I would also find a way to slip in the name Dorothy McDonald. And that's just how it played out on the phone. Bob sounded like a quirky kind of guy but he was absolutely obsessed with Louis Prima. He was quick to tell me, though, that he was married with three kids. "Don't think I like him in 'that' sort of way," he said pointedly to reassure me that he wasn't homosexual and didn't look upon Louis as any kind of sex object. "I just love his music and the way he had with his audience." Hearing his gruff voice, it never occurred to me that Bob was sexually attracted to Louis Prima so when he brought up that fact that he wasn't, I understood why some people might think of Bob as a "character."

Bob's passion for Louis Prima's music and the stories behind his music became more evident as he talked on about the entertainer. He was a walking encyclopedia of "everything Prima"... from Prima's roots in New Orleans to his ascension to fame in New York City to his legendary fear of flying. There was nothing Bob Pentatore didn't know about Louis Prima. So when I said that I had heard that a "Dorothy McDonald" had been a singer in Prima's band he set me straight with a certainty. "Never," he said emphatically, "no one named Dorothy McDonald ever sang with Louis. In 1943 and 1944, Lily Ann Carol sang with the band and she stayed on until 1947. There was never a "Dorothy" he told me again emphatically.

Bob even told me that Louis Prima died August 24, 1978 as a result of a brain tumor. And he knew the details: Louis' tumor was causing severe headaches. He decided to risk surgery in 1975 even though he was told that his chances of success were slim. And in fact, when the surgeon began to enter Louis' brain, Louis began to hemorrhage. The operation ended with Louis in a coma... that lasted for three years until his death. Bob had even visited Louis in the hospital. He was THAT big a fan and THAT close to the Prima family! Bob was a pleasant guy and told me to call him anytime I wanted to know more about Louis Prima. I thanked him for his kindness and told him I would get back to him.

I trusted Bob's assessment but I had to make certain that Bob hadn't missed something. Maybe there was just one time when Dorothy sang with Prima's band and Bob didn't know about it. So over the next several months I spent literally hundreds of hours pouring over microfilms and microfiches at various locations in New York City. I was looking for birth records, death records, voting records, marriage records... anything that would link Dorothy Jeanette McDonald with me or with anyone in Louis Prima's band. The tedium was excruciating. The results proved negative.

I tried calling Mr. Andre at St. Anthony's Hospital again to see if he had come across any new information. He told me about a "delivery room log" that might be helpful but said that he wasn't able to locate it. He also told me that Rocco had called him and the two of them had talked at length about my birth records. "Why did Rocco say he was calling you?" I asked Mr. Andre. "Did he say he was trying to help me?"

Mr. Andre was very clear in his response, "Yes, Alan, he told me that the two of you had talked and he was interested in exactly what your birth records said. And I knew I wasn't talking to any phony person because he told me his address in Brooklyn that was on the hospital records." "I just don't understand what Rocco is up to," I confided. "He talked to me several times and now he won't answer the phone or return my phone calls." There was a pause before Mr. Andre told me, "It's funny that you should say that about his behavior… because he said something to me what I found to be quite puzzling. I don't remember his exact words, though." "It's okay, Mr. Andre," I said as I urged him on, "just tell me whatever you remember." "Again, I don't remember it exactly," he said, "but after I told him about everything in your birth records, he said something like you would never find your birth father… because he was dead… and that there was some kind of disease."

Since Bob Pentatore had told me about Louis' brain tumor and how it led to his death, I found Rocco's comments pretty strange and I told Mr. Andre so. "I thought it was very odd too, Alan," he responded. "How would he know… or how would he even be able to make a reference… to anything about your father… or to the fact that your father was dead? I think it is very strange that he would know anything like that."

I too was puzzled… truly puzzled by Rocco's comments and I thought I had nothing to lose but to pick up the phone and call. Rocco had withdrawn from me anyway so I figured I couldn't do any more damage. Rocco answered the phone and the conversation was pleasant but Rocco remained evasive. He made many excuses for not contacting me, claiming that he was in poor health, and saying that his brother-in-law, who was a musician, had just died unexpectedly. "I'm just having so many problems myself, Alan, that I haven't been able to help you as much as I wanted," he told me with his voice aching for sympathy. I wasn't buying it but I couldn't bring myself to challenge him outright after he shared his story of sickness and grief. I just knew something had changed. He and his wife were joyful and so upbeat when we first spoke and they convinced me that they were on my side and would help. People don't just make that kind of abrupt turnaround without some other factor entering the picture.

My focus snapped back to Louis Prima and his band when I spotted an ad in the Bergen Evening Record, the newspaper that served all of north Jersey. Sam Butera would be playing at a club called the "European Market" in a show called "A Tribute To Louis Prima." There was no question. I knew I had to see it. I thought back to Sam's response to my letter and remembered that I was impressed and heartened that he responded at all. Even though he claimed not to know anything about Prima's band prior to 1954, I believed that a personal conversation might jog some memories. Ronni and I called for reservations.

The "European Market" was actually a catering hall in a predominantly Italian section of Ridgefield Park, New Jersey, a short trip from our home. It was packed the night Sam was playing with a group billed as "The Witnesses." The show was a killer! Sam Butera, I was to later learn was Louis' number one "side man." He played a mean saxophone, and he sang too. Many of the songs were peppered with Italian references. Most had a distinct Dixieland sound. And the audience just ate it up. The music was solid and so infectious it was hard not to get swept up in it.

After the show, Ronni and I approached Sam. I thanked him for responding to my letter and said that I was still searching for my birth mother. He was gracious and friendly but had nothing new to add. He continued to maintain that he didn't join Louis Prima's band until ten years after I was born and he was unaware of anything that happened at the time.

I remained hungry for any small pieces of information I could get so I stopped in a bookstore on one of my many trips to the Big Apple and bought a book called "The Big Bands" by George T. Simon. He was a musician and music critic who began to write for "Metronome" magazine in 1935. This man was the definitive authority on the jazz scene and his book was a wonderful encyclopedia of just about every musician who made a name for himself (or herself) in the Big Band era of the 1930's and 40's. The section on Louis Prima included a picture and George Simon's critique from June of 1945. Looking back, he notes "the bands he led were generally fairly good ones, always colorful, with plenty of zany vocals from Prima, plus duets first with Lily Ann Carol and later with Keely Smith." No mention of Dorothy McDonald.

The lack of Dorothy's name continued to puzzle me. Bob Pentatore was adamant that no Dorothy McDonald ever sang with the Prima band and now George T. Simon didn't mention her name in his book. Yet, Dorothy claimed, according to Rocco and Rose Ferrucci, that she was a singer in Louis Prima's band. So why was there no mention of her name? I needed more confirmation so I got creative and wrote to George Simon in care of the book's publisher. I told him precisely who I was looking for and why I was looking. Since he wasn't personally involved in any way I thought that honesty would be best this time.

It worked… because one week later I got this response: "I wish I could be of some assistance, but I can find no trace of the singer to whom you refer, and whose stage name sounds like a "nom de plume" to me. There were quite a number of attractive singers with long, dark hair. Louis Prima did have a rather attractive singer named Lily Ann Carol, but I do not know what has become of her. Sorry not to be more helpful. Good luck to you in your search. George T. Simon." Here was the undisputed expert of the era telling me that my birth mother did not exist as a "singer in the band." The lies and misinformation that surrounded my birth continued to baffle me.

But I learned that not every statement was a lie. My private investigator, Bob Fitzpatrick, made a trip to visit Rocco and found that Rocco was not a well man after all. Rocco had handicapped license plates on his car, and slept in a hospital bed. So his claims that he wasn't feeling well were apparently legitimate. That, I conceded, might explain a fraction of what was going on but I was certainly skeptical of Rocco's motives and the distance he was putting between us. In fact, when he first arrived at Rocco's home, Bob told me that Rocco denied his identity, saying that he wasn't Rocco Ferrucci. But he softened when Bob pulled out pictures of me. The conversation was strained and Rocco even told Bob that he didn't know Dorothy's last name. He said he heard it first from me. That was certainly backtracking because he never indicated to me that he didn't know her name. Here was a man and his wife about to adopt her child and they never bothered to ask her last name? They claim they took her for visits to the doctor and yet they didn't know her last name. Rocco says that after she skipped out of the hospital he tracked her down to a hotel in the "west 40's in Manhattan" where she had been living and he still didn't know her last name?

Whatever happened with Rocco it was clear that no one was going to get any further information from him. Not even a private investigator with pictures of me. I pondered his change of heart for days... and for the weeks ahead. Our first calls had convinced me that Rocco was determined and capable of finding the truth. More or less confined to his home, I knew he had the time and the conviction to learn the identity of my birthparents and perhaps even their whereabouts. So what happened? It occurred to me that my feelings might be more accurate than even I imagined. Perhaps Rocco got close to the truth and somebody paid him off or threatened him to keep his mouth shut. Perhaps there were famous people involved or wealthy people... people who didn't want me to show up and demand a piece of the action. But just as quickly as I came to that conclusion I put my mind in reverse... and questioned my own state of mind. Was I becoming paranoid and having delusional thoughts? Was I going over the edge and plunging into instability? If I did "snap" I realized it would happen because I remained obsessed with trying to figure out what Rocco learned and why he was keeping information from me. I ran the possible scenarios through my head over and over again. But I kept coming back to Rocco's motivation for shutting me out. Here was a sick man probably living on a pension. Paying him ten grand for his silence, I concluded, would be a lot cheaper than having to split a chunk of a rich person's estate with a bastard child. It would be money well spent. And given what Mr. Andre told me about his conversation with Rocco, my conclusion that he was paid off made the most logical sense.

After weeks of speculation about Rocco and no further contact with him, I once again went back over my notes. I had been focused on Brooklyn and Queens when I sent out letters to the McDonalds and Ferruccis in the phone books. I even sent letters to the Bronx where my relatives who summered in Far Rockaway lived year round. But I had overlooked Manhattan. There seemed to be no connection there... until I discovered that the hot music scene during the 1940's was New York City's 52nd Street in the... Borough of Manhattan. Maybe Dorothy actually lived in the City... to be near the swinging music and nightlife. My next step would be to check the old Manhattan phone books.

I was becoming a "regular" at the New York Public Library. By now I could easily navigate its corridors and elevators. And after dozens of trips I knew how to find the research materials I needed. A librarian in the Reference Department told me that the old phone books would soon be transferred to microfilm but they were still in paper form. The Manhattan phone books were arranged according to date and I arbitrarily chose to start with the year of my birth: 1944. I took the book to a nearby desk, opened it to "McDonald" and found this incredible listing: Dorothy McDonald, 301 West 46th Street, Columbus 5-4144. I gasped for breath, paused, and then looked again! I had no way of knowing this was my actual birthmother but it added up. It was only 6 blocks from the music mecca of 52nd Street and it nearly matched Rocco's narrative when he told me that he went to "track her down to a hotel in the West 40's in Manhattan."

I went back to the shelves and checked the Manhattan phone book for every year after 1944. In book after book I found the same listing... through the 1965/66 Book. The listing then disappeared. To be certain, I skipped ahead and checked through 1970/71. Finding no listing, I made the presumption that Dorothy moved out sometime around 1965. Yet, I couldn't be certain yet that THIS Dorothy McDonald was my birth mother.

Next, I checked the phone records for the boroughs of Brooklyn, The Bronx, and Queens for 1965 through 1968 to see if Dorothy had moved to a nearby area. Nothing. When Dorothy McDonald left 301 West 46th Street, she apparently truly "left town." But I had one more avenue to pursue. I called Information for New York City, and asked for a current listing for Dorothy McDonald. Again, nothing. Dorothy McDonald left New York City around 1965 and she wasn't coming back. And, most importantly, I didn't even know if THIS Dorothy McDonald was the woman I was really searching for. Given what Rocco had told me about her whereabouts in the 1940's, it seemed to be a solid assumption but I couldn't be certain. Yet I couldn't ignore it either.

I had been keeping a diary of my Search up to this point and after recording all my steps and missteps it was time for a new one. It was May 22nd, 1981. I labeled it "Search Diary 2" and I began by writing: "Now I come to an event that I would have preferred not happened: I'm beginning my Search Diary #2.... I had hoped that all this research would have paid off but I'm still working at it. I hope and pray that there will NOT be a Search Diary #3. I find my Search very exhausting, both emotionally and physically. At this point, however, I feel I am so close and have spent so many hours on my quest that I feel compelled to continue. I don't care to form any relationships with my birth parents I just want to find out WHO they were and the circumstances surrounding my birth."

To that end, Bob Fitzpatrick and I made the journey to 301 W. 46th street in New York City. Dorothy McDonald hadn't lived there, according to the phone books, for nearly 15 years yet Bob felt that someone still living there might remember her and lead us to her. And they might be able to help us determine if she was the Dorothy McDonald we were looking for.

The building stood at the corner of 46th Street and Eighth Avenue. It was five stories tall with a brick exterior and fire escapes running down two sides. A vegetable market and a bar were situated on the ground floor. The door to the building was on 46th Street as far from Eighth Avenue as it could be. During the 1940's it may have been a clean, well-run apartment building. But 40 years later, it was a woeful eyesore. And that was the impression that Bob and I had from the outside. Once inside, we couldn't see how anyone could still call this building "home."

A small sign on one wall in what was once the Lobby read: "Super 2-B". That's where we headed. As we walked down a narrow hallway to the stairs the stench was overwhelming. The walls were decaying. And as bad as the building looked from the outside, it was far worse on the inside. I did not feel comfortable in these surroundings and was glad that I had Bob Fitzpatrick with me. I never asked him if he had a gun but I certainly hoped he was armed.

We talked with Jesse, the "Super" in 2-B. Jessie was pleasant enough and agreed to ask around to see if anyone knew anything about Dorothy McDonald. Bob slipped him a twenty-dollar bill and said we'd stop back another time to see if he had learned anything.

Before we left, Jesse told us to check with Paco, a man who lived down the hall in 2-F and had lived in the building for many years.

I was anxious to leave but still eager to see what Paco might say so I followed Bob down the hall. He knocked on the door to 2-F. We heard a rustling inside and then the door opened several inches, stopped by a safety chain. "What is it?" asked the man on the other side of the door. Bob fired back, "Are you Paco? Jessie told us to see Paco." We could only see a sliver of the man's face through the narrow opening of the doorway but he admitted that he was Paco. "What do you want with me?" Paco asked nervously. "It's not about you. It's about a woman who lived here and moved out about fourteen years ago," Bob responded. "How long have you lived here?"

Paco confirmed that he had lived in the building for twenty years and he asked who we were looking for. Bob told him we were looking for a woman named Dorothy McDonald. "Oh yeah, Dorothy. Yeah, I remember Dorothy," Paco said proudly. He then went on to describe her as maybe 45 to 48 when she moved out and said she was tall and blonde. He also thought that Dorothy was a waitress on the East Side. But he said she fancied herself as a singer and was always telling people that she was working in a band somewhere. "But she moved to Philadelphia," he said matter-of-factly, "and I heard from somebody that she died."

As I stood behind Bob in the hallway and heard Paco rattle off his commentary, I was convinced that we had indeed located the apartment building where my birth mother lived. I was struck too, by how much information Paco knew or at least claimed he knew. But I admit that I put little credence in, and had little reaction to his comment that my mother had died. I was more focused on what he said about Philadelphia. I had been searching for Dorothy in the five boroughs of New York when I should have been looking for her in the City of Brotherly Love. I felt a newfound rush of optimism sweep over me. Bob left his business card and asked Paco to call if he remembered anything else. Paco barely had time to close the door before I blurted out, "Bob, she went to Philadelphia. No wonder I got no responses from any McDonalds in New York."

What Bob said next deflated my expectation in a heartbeat: "Sorry to disappoint you, Alan, but that's a common story when someone is hiding information. They just say 'she moved out of town.' I wouldn't waste my time or money going that route. And when he said that Dorothy died he was really telling us he didn't know anything else. It was his way of saying he didn't want to be bothered anymore."

Before I had the time to question Bob further, he was walking down the hallway, knocking on other doors. A woman calling herself "Jean" opened the door marked 2-G. She didn't remember Dorothy but suggested we check with the postman. She said the regular guy was Nick but he had only delivered mail to the building for 12 years. But she knew that a mailman named John, who now delivered on 47th Street, had been around for more than 20 years. Bob thanked her for her help and we headed home.

As we drove through the Lincoln Tunnel on our way back to Bob's New Jersey office we formulated a plan: Bob would check with a friend of his at the main post office in Manhattan to see how long they kept forwarding records while I would come back some other day and try to track down the mailman, John on 47th Street. Since Paco remembered that Dorothy was a "waitress on the East Side," Bob would check with the restaurant workers' union to see if it had a record of her employment.

Within days, though, all three elements of our plan proved fruitless. Bob's friend at the post office said that Mail Forwarding records only went back a year or two. Records from 16 years back would certainly have been destroyed. An inquiry at the restaurant workers' union also failed to bear fruit. The clerk there could find no record of a Dorothy McDonald ever working as a waitress in New York City. I, meanwhile, had gone back to West 47th Street to track down John. I walked up and down the street several times from Broadway west to Ninth Avenue. Finally, I saw a mailman entering a building. I waited for him to come out and asked him if he was John. He told me he was, and when I asked, he said he remembered delivering mail to a Dorothy McDonald at 301 West 46th Street. But he said he had never met her, could not describe her, and certainly could not remember where her mail was forwarded 16 years ago.

When I planned the trip into the City to try to locate John, I also planned to visit the library again. This time I would search newspaper records for November, 1943. That was nine months before I was born, the time I would have been conceived. In my mind, I imagined a musician in Louis Prima's band having an affair with my birth mother in her apartment at 301 West 46th Street. And if that was true, I felt that Louis Prima's band was probably playing a gig in the City at the time. Maybe a newspaper article would shed light on the band members and their singer. So I went to the microfilm department and checked the New York Times and the New York Post for the entire month of November, 1943. But I couldn't find any listing or even any reference to Louis Prima performing anywhere in or around the City at the time I would have been conceived.

CHAPTER THIRTEEN

Blackie Pulls A Bank Job

The months of bickering over money forced Blackie to make a decision that would take the pressure off his withering relationship with Dolly. He decided to rob a bank. He placed a call to Tommy in Philadelphia. "Hiya Tommy, how's it goin' in the city of brotherly love?" he asked jokingly. "Not bad, Blackie," Tommy replied. "How're you and Dolly doin?" "Not as good as I'd like," Blackie confessed. He told Tommy about the money problems he was having with Dolly. And he told Tommy he was planning another bank job. "This one is perfect. It's a little bank down in the Bowery."

"I gotta tell you Blackie, you get caught on this one and you know what happens," Tommy cautioned. "Even you yourself said that they'll lock you up for Life." "Yeah, I know," Blackie admitted, "but this is a sure thing, Tommy."

For all his planning, though, Blackie had miscalculated.

Dolly had no idea why Blackie was gone for days. He didn't tell her anything about the bank heist but he had no choice when he called her from jail. "Hi Doll," he said with the bravest voice he could muster. "I got some bad news... real bad news." Dolly was stunned. "Blackie, I want to know. What happened? Where are you?" she asked him almost frantically. "I'm done. I got nabbed trying to rob this bank in the Bowery. They're gonna send me away for Life." And then he added plaintively, "And I did it all for you, Doll. I wanted to get you out of the clubs and have you home and make you happy. And I screwed it all up big time." The phone slipped out of Dolly's hand and smacked hard on the floor as Dolly felt woozy and nearly fainted.

Dolly found a Defense Attorney to take Blackie's case but Blackie was caught in the act, and witness after witness, including the teller and the bank guard, told the same story. And since Blackie had a gun and hundreds of dollars in his pockets when the cops arrived he was convicted in what Prosecutors call a "slam dunk." Bank robbery is a federal crime with stiff penalties and Blackie had been in prison before, so the judge showed no leniency. As expected, he sentenced Blackie to Life. Blackie was shipped back to Sing Sing to serve out his sentence and to die there. Dolly was devastated... and was on her own again.

The transition back to a life without a husband wasn't an easy one for Dorothy McDonald. Oh sure, she had her gentlemen "friends," the old-time customers who still enjoyed Dolly's company. But the money they left behind became more and more of a mental liability. Dolly had started out on 52nd street as a Hostess, a "Party Girl" who wanted to be a singer in a band. And here she was after the passage of so many years, in the same place, entertaining the same tired men with all hope gone of becoming the popular band singer she once aspired to be. It was a huge comedown and it was one that increasingly tortured Dolly night after night. She drank more than she should and as the years passed, it was taking its toll on the way she looked and the way she acted. She drank because she needed to forget, to forget who she was and what she had become.

After one especially unpleasant night with an unruly customer, Dolly returned to 301 West 46th Street and walked down the hall to find a kitten playing with a piece of string. It was rolling around with the string, getting itself wrapped up in one end while trying to snag the other end in its uncoordinated claws. Dolly began to snicker quietly at the sight of this playful little creature but the kitten heard her and jumped up, tangling its hind legs in the twine when it landed. Dolly reached down and picked it up. "There, there, little guy," she said tenderly as she held the kitten, "let me get you all unwrapped." A few twists and turns of the string and the kitten was free from its restraints. But it seemed content in Dolly's arms and made no attempt to escape.

Dolly knocked on several doors down the hallway until Mary in 4-C opened up. "Is this little guy yours, Mary?" Dolly asked as she held the kitten up for inspection. Mary opened her door further to reveal her mama cat and its remaining litter frolicking around. "I don't know how he got out," she told Dolly, "but I sure wish I could find homes for them. They're more than a handful for me." "I wish I could help you," Dolly purred as the little kitten licked her hand, "but I never had a cat before." "Look, he likes you," Mary said eagerly as the kitten continued to lick. "They're really pretty easy to take care of and they don't cause a lot of fuss." Dolly was easily swayed and agreed to give it a try.

Dolly named her kitten "Blackie" and let him have the run of her apartment. Blackie was a cute little warm body and Dolly lavished him with affection. She sat there for hours with Blackie in her lap, stroking the kitten and mourning her loss. She wasn't able to shake the memory of Blackie and the good times they had together but she tried hard by pouring glass after glass of Jack Daniels.

As month after month slipped away, Dolly grew more and more lonely so she made plans to visit Blackie in Sing Sing, hoping he would seduce her with his charms and make her feel like a woman in love again... if only for a moment. She would take a bus to Ossining, New York, on a Sunday morning and meet with her husband for the allotted time in the afternoon before returning to Manhattan that night. The trip seemed almost futile, though. She wouldn't be able to touch Blackie or to hold him and show him how much she missed him. Her only contact would be across a table with a barrier between the two of them. Yet, she was determined to make the trip.

The hour-long bus ride from the 42nd Street Bus Terminal to Ossining was uneventful and unexciting. Dolly sat next to a window and watched the scenery go by but she was still half-hung-over from a Saturday night on the town so much of the journey was just a blur. She was fortunate, though, that the bus dropped her off less than a block from the penitentiary and she was able to walk to the visitor's entrance without working up a sweat. After she was cleared to enter the secure area of the prison, she was taken down a windowless hallway to a room that had rows of tables with a chair on each side and a wood partition about a foot high running the length of the table to separate inmate and visitor.

She was seated at an empty table and told to wait there, and after about ten minutes another guard brought Blackie into the room and sat him down across from her. "You are sure a sight for these tired eyes," Blackie said without missing a beat. "You are looking terrific, Doll. Do ya miss me?" Dolly looked over the partition at the man she once invited into her life. Her throat tightened and she couldn't find the words to say. Blackie looked at her the way he did when he was first introduced to her with that smile and those eyes that twinkled with delight but Dolly could only stare back at him with tears welling up in her eyes. "Of course, I miss you," she finally blurted out. "Why do you think I came all this way to see you?

Cause I wanted to take a bus ride?" Blackie chuckled at her caustic response and then he was the one who had trouble getting the words out. He had trouble making eye contact as he confessed, "I... I musta been crazy to try to pull off that heist. I dunno what I was thinking. And... I sure as shit didn't... want to spend the rest of my life locked up so far away from you."

Dolly and Blackie worked hard at denying reality as they looked hard into each other's eyes and shared their love the only way they could... in a sterile room, across a table, with guards looking on. They talked about the good times. They talked about 52nd Street. And they talked about Dolly's apartment and the kitten that now filled the void that Blackie had left behind... the kitten that was Blackie's namesake.

Blackie, though, had a secret. It wasn't something that he could continue to keep bottled up inside. Not behind the concrete walls of his cell in Sing Sing. Not when he had 24 hours a day to dwell on it. And it wasn't something he could write in a letter or spill out in one of the rare phone calls he was allowed. So he looked at Dolly intensely to confess and unburden himself of his burning guilt. "There's something I gotta tell you, Doll. Something that's been buggin' me... and it's something I just can't hide from you no more," he confessed as he looked at Dolly remorsefully. "There never was any stash. I never had any cash hidden away. It was all bullshit."

Dolly looked across the table at Blackie in silence. Her eyes glazed over as her mind reeled from his confession. Her thoughts were racing back in time to hear Blackie's voice again and again bragging about all the money he had hidden away. Then, in an instant, it all made sense. The stalling, the stupid reasons he gave her for not being able to get to the stash and his apparent indifference to having that money to start a better life together. What had she been thinking, she agonized as she questioned how someone as street-smart as Dolly McDonald had been so thoroughly duped and so blinded by Blackie's charms?

Dolly pushed her chair back and stood up slowly. "I can't ...believe that you... did that... that you lied to me... that you used me for my money," she said as she tried to catch her breath. "And I can't believe I fell for your bullshit." Blackie was quick on the reply, "Dolly, I had to keep it goin'. Aw, I started bragging to your brother when we was cellmates, and hell, I couldn't back down after that. What was I gonna say? I didn't mean to hurt you Doll... I just didn't have no other choice." His eyes begged her to stay but Dolly had heard enough. She hissed at him, "You didn't have to lie to me. You didn't have to piss away MY money while you bragged about your precious stash." And before Blackie could come up with something else to say, Dolly shoved her chair back under the table and in a measured, ominous voice said, "Don't say it... Don't say another word." She turned sharply away from the prisoner who had been the love of her life, straightened her back and held her head up sternly, and took measured steps toward the door that read: "Visitors This Way." A waiting guard opened the door... and without looking back to even acknowledge his presence, Dolly walked through that door... never to set eyes on Blackie Cafferty again.

"Blackie the cat" greeted Dolly when she returned to her apartment. But she needed more than a cute little kitten to numb the pain, so she went right for the bottle of Jack Daniels on the kitchen counter and poured herself a stiff one. Then she plopped herself down on her sofa and stared vacantly at the ceiling. Feelings of loneliness and despair overcame her. Dolly looked around at what she had: an apartment that had seen better days, some fancy worn-out clothes hanging in the closet, and a cat named for the husband she once relied on as the ticket out of the life she had chosen. The good times had passed for Dolly and she never became that singer in the band.

CHAPTER FOURTEEN

The Plot Thickens, Along with the Spaghetti Sauce

I hit so many dead-ends trying to locate Dorothy Jeanette McDonald that my frustration level became unbearable. Each successive disappointment piled on another layer of despair and so, once again, I found myself at a crossroads. I had run up against a brick wall and wasn't able to face any more angst. So I called my investigator, Bob Fitzpatrick, and told him that I was taking a break from my Search because it had turned me into an emotional train wreck. I also thanked him for all his work and asked him to send me a final bill. He said that he understood fully and wished he could have been more help but he said my case was the toughest he'd ever seen and solving it was going to take a lot more time, a lot more money, and more than a few lucky breaks.

The ups and downs had truly worn me out emotionally but they also helped forge an even stronger bond between Ronni and me. She had been by my side through each crisis. She had encouraged me and she had participated directly in so many different facets of the investigation. We had been married for five years and we now felt it was time to switch gears... put the past in the past... and look ahead to start a family. It didn't take us long. Ronni became pregnant with twin boys and I couldn't have been prouder! As I was naively basking in my own virility and thinking ahead to the challenges of raising twins, it quickly became apparent to me that I would have to trade my aspirations as an actor for a steady job with medical benefits. A chance encounter made that happen.

I was introduced to the Studio Engineer at a small cable company in North Jersey. We struck up a conversation and talked for a while before he made the prescient comment, "You have a great voice, Alan. Have you ever thought about doing television news?" It was a defining moment for me, and his question sent my mind into overdrive. I felt like a cartoon character that had a light bulb pop on over his head to indicate a great new idea! Television news... I thought to myself... why didn't I ever think of that before? I told the engineer that I had never considered it and had no real training in news but that I was VERY interested. He told me he would see if his boss would let me volunteer at the station so I could learn the ropes.

A few days later he set up a meeting for me with the General Manager of the station. She was interested in my background and experience but told me that the station's insurance coverage prohibited using volunteers. She recommended instead that if I was willing to take a college course in television journalism she could bring me on as a non-paid college intern. So that's what I did. And it only took a few months before a position opened up and I got a paying job at the television station with the benefits I needed.

Our twin boys, meanwhile, decided to make an early entrance. They were born 8 weeks premature in our local hospital, weighing just

3 pounds-1 ounce and 2 pounds-7 ounces, respectively. They were then rushed to St. Joseph's Hospital… THIS St. Joseph's in nearby Paterson, New Jersey, where they spent several months in the Intensive Care Nursery. The doctors and nurses there looked after them and nurtured them around the clock. Ian and Evan came home from the hospital about two months after they were born. They only weighed about 5 pounds each and required lots of extra care for many months. They were also colicky and never slept through the night, turning Ronni and me into sleep-deprived zombies who focused all our energies on helping our fragile babies thrive. As I settled into the early days of fatherhood I had a revelation: My sons would have no doubt about the identity of THEIR birth parents but I still had no real connection with mine!

When the boys were about 6 months old, we were finally able to leave them with a babysitter one evening and went to a dinner party thrown by our friends Deborah and Paul. The dinner conversation centered on our boys and I casually mentioned that I had given up on my Search because of them. One of the guests, Christian, took a keen interest in my story and asked question after question about the steps I had taken. I told him that I hadn't had any luck with private investigators. But Christian had other ideas. He worked for a large security firm and suggested I contact his boss, who he was certain, could break the case wide open. He was so enthusiastic and had so many success stories to share that he sucked me back into my Search by practically guaranteeing that his boss would locate my birth parents.

After several days of consideration I concluded that it was some sort of "sign" that Christian was invited to the dinner party, so I called and set up an appointment with Christian's boss, Peter MacIntosh. If I had any doubts about the success stories that Christian shared and his boss's abilities they evaporated when I drove up to the address and approached the building. The entire three-story, shiny, aluminum and glass building was home to "Outreach Investigations." I was overwhelmed by the sheer size of the place and felt confident that this company had the resources to level the playing field and finally solve the riddle surrounding my birth.

I told Peter my story in great detail. He took notes and asked me specific questions as I went along. He seemed particularly fascinated with Rocco Ferrucci's story and why Rocco cut me off so abruptly. But it was Rocco's recently-deceased brother-in-law that elicited the most curiosity. Rocco's brother-in-law had been a musician and Peter saw that as an important connection. He wanted me to prepare a list of twelve questions for Rocco so he could prepare a P.S.E., a Psychologist Stress Evaluation. Peter said he would call Rocco and record the answers to the questions. Then Rocco's voice would be evaluated in much the same way as a lie detector. That way, we could determine if we were on the right track.

Peter felt confident about several points: 1) Rocco is my uncle. 2) His brother-in law was my father. 3) And Rocco is trying to protect his sister-in-law from learning the truth. In addition to the P.S.E., Peter told me he would send several agents to the Rockaway Beach neighborhood to snoop around and see what they could find out.

Peter MacIntosh seemed legit. He talked a good talk but I wanted more than just talk. I was eager for some real investigative work that would yield results. When he called me to report in several weeks later I began to realize that he was handing me a line of bullshit. "My investigators had a chance to stop by the old neighborhood in Rockaway Beach," he told me somewhat matter-of-factly. "They spent several hours talking to neighbors along Beach 78th Street but no one remembered anything as far back as 1944." "Who were these people?" I asked, "Were they people who lived close to 170 Beach 78th Street?" He paused for an uncomfortable moment before answering me, "Yes, Alan, some of the people lived right next door but they weren't living there so many years back." "Right... next... door," I said with conviction. "That's funny. My wife and I made a trip to Far

Rockaway a while back and there are no houses on Beach 78th Street. No houses at all. So I have to wonder who your investigators actually spoke with." There was a long silence at the other end of the line then a halting voice saying, "I'll... uh... I'll have to... uh... no houses, you say... uh... I'll have to get more information from my investigators... and... uh... I'll get back to you."

Either he was lying to me or his investigators were incompetent. In either case, I instantly lost all faith in Peter MacIntosh and Outreach Investigations. I was desperate for answers and perhaps that desperation made me vulnerable to Peter's confident spiel. But I could feel that something just wasn't right and I resented being played for a fool... so I terminated our agreement.

I was on my own again and back to spending hours scouring my notes to consider the progress I had made while dwelling on the burning questions that remained. I reviewed my sources of information and my potential sources. And I could see that I was running out of options. I had been trying so hard to be sure that no word of my investigation leaked back to my (adoptive) mother who had moved to Florida after the death of my dad. Although she was living faraway in The Sunshine State, she still had many friends and acquaintances in North Jersey and I feared that she would learn of my Search. Growing up I always felt an uncomfortable awkwardness whenever my mother told me how "very, very much" she loved me and how I was an "only child" because she could only love me and no one else. I worried that her world would somehow be shattered if she learned I needed to know more about my origins. When I was a teenager and old enough to understand our family history, she told me that she had been abandoned by her father back in Hungary when her mother died and she was raised by her aunt. Knowing that she harbored such a deep insecurity filled me with concern that, if she learned of my Search, she would feel that just like her father had, I too was abandoning her.

I got a reprieve from my ongoing concerns about my mother when I saw a newspaper story about the group ALMA, The Adoptees Liberty Movement Association, in my local newspaper. This was the same group that Barbara Sandusky had told me about several years earlier. It was comprised of adoptees who had completed their Search and adoptees still Searching. The article explained that ALMA chapters hold monthly meetings where members gather and share information about beating the system that tries so hard to keep adoptees from learning about their roots. The article shared success stories and even spelled out some simple tips about how to get information.

I called the number in New York City for ALMA and joined for a nominal yearly fee. The person I spoke with said that there were monthly meetings in New Jersey, and if it was all right, she would have someone contact me about the date and time for the next one. I gave her the go-ahead. She also asked me in what state I was adopted. I told her it was New York. "Wow," she said, "did you know that New York State just began an Adoption Information Registry? It's supposed to be a way to learn about your past. But I don't want to get your hopes up because it would be a big departure from the secrecy the state has pursued over the years. Who knows, though? It might be worth a try." I told her that I would try anything that might help so she gave me the address to write for an application.

The New York State Adoption Information Registry turned out to be a first-rate farce perpetrated on adoptees by New York State lawmakers. They were under pressure from adoptees to open adoption records so that adoptees could search for their birth parents. Yet, they apparently wanted to remain true to their conviction that mothers who gave up their children would invariably be embarrassed or hurt if those children tracked them down decades later. So they enacted the Adoption Information Registry to appease the vocal adoptees who had been pressing for reforms.

Here's how it worked: An adoptee would fill out an application that required WRITTEN AUTHORIZATION from the adoptee's birth parents AND the adoptee's adoptive parents and then the Registry would release "Identifying Information" about the adoption. Read that again. The "catch" becomes obvious: Adoptees who are searching for their birth parents couldn't possibly get their birth parents' authorization because they didn't know who their birth parents are!! Those lawmakers had merely added to the frustration of children adopted in the state of New York. Though I had little faith in the Registry I was desperate enough to fill out an application and mail it in. It was clearly a very long shot but in the words of an old Yiddish philosopher: "It couldn't hurt."

It didn't hurt either that I began to talk up my Search among some friends in my home town of Westwood. It elicited a phone call from Howie Reist. Though he was older than me, I had gone to high school with his younger brother and knew him well enough to trust him. I laid out my story and told Howie about Dorothy Jeannette McDonald. Howie, in turn, had a stunning revelation for me: He told me he played with Louis Prima for just a short time in 1945. But he joined the ranks of the others like Bob Pentatore and George T. Simon, who didn't know anything about a girl singer named Dorothy McDonald.

But Howie had an idea. He suggested that I place an ad in the Local 802 Musician's Newsletter asking to hear from anyone who played with Prima back in 1944. Local 802 is the Musician's Union in New York that was "home base" for many musicians all over the country. The big money was in New York and so were the most prestigious gigs. Howie's idea sounded like a great idea to me and he offered to give me the latest copy of the newsletter as a reference. He also told me he would try to dig up an old Directory of all Local 802 musicians and their contact information.

Howie made good on his word and I picked up a newsletter and a 1978 Local 802 Directory. I checked out the newsletter and sent in an ad:

"Trying to locate musicians who played with Louis Prima 1943-45. Please contact Alan Gerstel, (201) 666-0142." But it was the 1978 Directory that piqued my interest. I leafed through it looking for familiar names and came across a listing in Louisiana for Louis Prima. This was now 1984, six years after the Directory was printed, but I hoped that I could reach Louis Prima's widow at that address or that my letter would be forwarded. I was troubled, though, about what I should write. Honesty, I found, was not the best policy when it came to my adoption so I thought about using the birth of my sons, their premature delivery, and their health problems as the reason for my Search. I was hoping that no one would deny me critical information that could help save my children. I wrote:

Dear Mrs. Prima,

I am writing to you with a very special problem that I was hoping you would be able to help me with - - - I was born on August 11, 1944, and was adopted when I was ten days old. My wife recently gave birth to premature twin boys who have medical problems.

The doctors have been asking about my family medical history but, as I am adopted, I do not know. So I have been trying to locate my biological mother and father to find out.

I know that my biological mother went under the name of Dorothy Jeanette McDonald and she claimed to be a singer in the Louis Prima band. My father was said to be a leader of the band (that would have been in the Fall of 1943). Now you can see why I am writing to you.

Would you have any knowledge of any of the musicians or singers that were with Louis in 1943? And would you be willing to help me in any way? I would most sincerely appreciate any assistance you can give me, for the health of my sons is at stake.

If you can help me, please either write, or call me COLLECT at (201) 666-0142. Perhaps you have some of Louis' old papers, or maybe you can put me in touch with other musicians, or booking agents, or anyone who might help.

Thank you very much for your help.

Sincerely, Alan Gerstel.

I mailed the letter to the Post Office Box listed in Covington, Louisiana for Louis Prima.

I never got a reply... and later learned that she never received it.

My membership in ALMA, though, brought a measure of hope. I got a call from a lady who identified herself as Nancy Davis about an ALMA meeting the following week. Nancy told me that the meeting would be held in her house and she gave me her address and phone number. I told her I would be there.

The ALMA meeting was part support group... part peer counseling on how to conduct a Search. About eight of us sat around Nancy's kitchen table and talked about the Search process. Some of the people in attendance had found their birth parents and were eager to help others. Some, like me, were in varying stages of investigation. Everyone was upbeat and positive. The people who were still searching told their stories and hoped the veterans around the table could suggest avenues to search that they hadn't thought of. I told my story and was immediately advised to write to the Surrogate's Court in the Borough of Queens for my Order of Adoption and final Decree of Adoption. Even though these were normally sealed records, one veteran told me that sometimes mistakes are made and that occasionally a letter will reach a sympathetic person in the Surrogate Court's office who will release the information. Likewise, I was urged to write to the New York State Health Department for a birth certificate for Dorothy McDonald. That might have information that could lead me to her. So I composed another two letters. The first went to the Surrogate's Court for Queens

County on February 28, 1984. I thought a reference to a legal matter might sway the Clerk to release the documents, so I wrote:

Dear sir or madam,

I would like certified copies of my Order of Adoption and my Final Decree of Adoption to replace the original ones that were stolen in a robbery of my father's store. (That part was true.)

My name is Alan David Gerstel, born August 11, 1944, in St. Joseph's Hospital, Far Rockaway (Queens), New York. My birth certificate number is 9740.

I have enclosed a $20.00 money order to cover the costs. Thank you very much for your assistance as I need these documents in a legal case brought by my father's relatives who are challenging my rights. (That part was pure fiction.)

Sincerely, Alan Gerstel

The reply came on March 8, 1984, just eight days later:

Dear Mr. Gerstel,

Adoption files are sealed and cannot be opened without an order of the court. Accordingly, it is impossible for us to furnish copies of any documents in the files without court order.

If you need these documents in a case which is pending in any court, I suggest you petition this court to have the files opened, specifying the exact documents which are needed, the court in which the case is pending and the name and file number of the case. If your petition is granted, we will send the necessary documents to the court in which the case is pending.

I suggest that you engage an attorney to assist you in this matter, if you decide to petition the court.

We are herewith returning your money order in the amount of $20.00.

Very truly yours, Patricia F. Gilmartin, Chief Clerk

Apparently, she had heard all the lines before because Patricia Gilmartin's letter sounded like she was very savvy. My letter to the New York State Health Department also proved fruitless. No one named Dorothy Jeanette McDonald was born in New York State on December 31, 1922. Since the hospital records identified Dorothy as my birth mother, I'd made a presumption that she lived in New York somewhere. After all, she once had an apartment in Manhattan and had worked there. Somewhere in the throes of my Search I made the assumption that she had been born in the state. The Health Department apparently proved me wrong.

I had little time to ponder. The next day the postman came to my door with a certified envelope from the New Jersey Division of Taxation. I signed for it, although it unnerved me, and made me wonder if I had made a mistake on my State Income Tax form. Quite the contrary; I was being informed that I had a winning $50 lottery ticket which was selected to be placed in a pool. The winner of the pool would receive one million dollars. It also stated that the million-dollar drawing would be held at the Golden Nugget casino in Atlantic City, New Jersey. Included in the packet of information was a slick, color brochure from the Golden Nugget. When I opened the brochure I saw that Lily Ann Carol, Louis Prima's singer in the 1940's, was performing in the Lounge! I had a chance to win a million dollars and a chance to talk with Lily Ann Carol personally. Ronni and I made plans to go to Atlantic City for the drawing later that week.

We didn't win the million dollars but we did see Lily Ann Carol perform. The Lounge at the Golden Nugget consisted of a bar and about three-dozen small tables. Only about a dozen tables were occupied for the "set" we sat in on. But the place should have been packed. Lily Ann was wonderful. She still had the little-girlish quality to her voice I had heard in Louis Prima recordings from the 1940's but her voice also had a huskiness that added a richness and warmth to her sound. Ronni and I sat there, enraptured by this woman who had been such a big name during

World War Two so many years ago. When Lily Ann finished I approached her with a 78 rpm record that I had bought. It was on the "Hit" record label and was titled: "I'll Walk Alone, Louis Prima and his Orchestra, vocal refrain by Lily Ann Carol."

Lily Ann was in disbelief! "You're much too young to remember this song," she said to me, "I can't believe you even found this recording." I told her that my wife and I were huge fans as I gestured to the table where Ronni was still sitting and I asked her to autograph the record for me. Lily Ann graciously came to our table and sat down. I produced a white crayon for her to autograph the dark-colored record. She wrote: "To Ronni and Alan with all my love… God bless you, Lily ann Carol."

When she finished signing the record I began my spiel. "I am more than just a fan. I also have a favor to ask you," I told her. "Honey, ask away and I'll do what I can," she replied warmly. So I went into my story and told her how I was looking for Dorothy Jeanette McDonald who claimed to be a singer in Louis Prima's band. "I was the only one," she said firmly, "I was the only singer in Prima's band from 1940 to 1947. Anyone who tells you otherwise is just telling tales." She also said she didn't recognize the name Dorothy McDonald and couldn't recall ever hearing of a Frank McDonald. "I sympathize with you," she told me, "but I just can't help you. Somebody is making up stories that just aren't true. There just wasn't any Dorothy McDonald or any other girl singer with Prima during those years and I should know. I was there."

I had focused on the Louis Prima band since Rocco and Rose Ferrucci first told me about the alleged connection. I believed Rocco and Rose when they told me Dorothy was a singer in Louis Prima's band. I believed Rabbi Schwartz when he told me Dorothy was a "singer in a band" and my father was "the leader of the band." How could they both be so wrong? Yet, Lily Ann would know. But unlike Bob Pentatore and George T. Simon, she could take it one step further by telling me, "Honey, I was there." And she had been so kind and open to Ronni and me, and seemed to have nothing to gain by fabricating the truth, that neither of us believed she would be telling a lie. So, who WAS Dorothy really? And why did two different sources believe that she was a singer in Louis Prima's band while others were adamant that she was not? And now Lily Ann weighed in and put an absolute end to a possible connection, leaving little hope that I would find my birth parents in Louis Prima's orchestra.

My head was reeling and my frustration was at a fever pitch. My search had taken nearly nine years and I believed I was on the right track until Lily Ann Carol made it absolutely clear. Dorothy McDonald was NOT a singer in Louis Prima's band. Lily Ann WAS. Period. So now I was questioning everything that I thought was true about my birth parents. I wondered who was lying and who was telling the truth. I questioned motives. I reconsidered what I thought was rock-solid information. My mind went into a dizzying spin as I thought about and rehashed all the bits of information that had led me to this point.

I had a lot to talk about when I attended another ALMA meeting the following month. My fellow members were stumped also but they tried to keep me focused. If my adoption was legal, and everyone presumed that it was, then they said a lawyer must have been involved. They suggested I try to track down attorneys in Far Rockaway who might have handled my adoption. It was a long shot but I didn't have any other avenues to explore.

As the meeting broke up, the hostess, Nancy Davis, asked me to stick around. I said "good night" to the others as they left while Nancy poured me another cup of coffee. "What's up?" I asked once the others had left and closed the door behind them. Nancy laid it out. "There's another group. It's called Origins. And maybe its members can help you," she said stealthily. "I can see your frustration," she went on, "and I want your Search to be successful. It's pretty clear from listening to your story that you're not going to find your birth parents through normal channels. You need some special help." Then she went on to tell me about Origins and how it has a source that can obtain original birth certificates for anyone born in New York City. She cautioned me that it was costly... between one and two thousand dollars. But that original birth certificate would have both my parents' names on it and I could then be certain. She also told me not to mention anything about this to the other ALMA members because this group, Origins, was very hush-hush and it didn't want any notoriety since it was operating outside the law in getting these birth certificates which were sealed by order of the Court. She told me to contact a Marsha Rudolph at the phone number she provided.

I left her house fired-up over this new possibility. The thought of paying someone off and breaking an antiquated law to gain access to my records was no big deal in my mind. After all, I had already bribed Mr. Andre at St. Anthony's for information. And after so many years of butting heads with the laws of secrecy surrounding my adoption, I was more than willing to work outside the system to produce results when working within the system couldn't.

Marsha Rudolph was a talker. When I called her I had trouble injecting a word into the conversation. She talked about how she has helped so many other adoptees, how she has "sources" that can get documents under court seal, and how she could essentially make things happen. Her enthusiasm was infectious! I felt that I was finally talking to someone on the inside, someone with connections who wasn't afraid to break the rules to pry information out of the hands of unwilling bureaucrats.

"First of all, Alan," she told me, "I need you to send me all the information you have or anything you have uncovered up to this point. But I also need something else. I need you to promise that you will not discuss our relationship with anyone. That is the most important thing." I responded reassuringly, "You can trust me, Marsha. The steps I've taken during my Search have taught me how important it is to keep my mouth shut. I wouldn't dream of burning anyone."

She seemed reassured and told me she could obtain my original birth certificate for 500-dollars. "No problem," I responded. "And when I get all your Search documents I'll be sharing your information with a guy who is a super-snoop," she told me with a sense of pride. "He's a master at getting information." Marsha also had another idea. She recommended that I find out what laws Rocco and Rose may have broken back in 1944 when they checked Dorothy into the hospital as "Rose Ferrucci." She thought maybe they could serve the Ferruccis with phony subpoenas and threaten them with prosecution if they didn't talk about everything they knew. I was blown away by her legal approach, one that has never crossed my mind. Marsha Rudolph sounded like someone who had "been there-done that." I was truly impressed by her savvy.

CHAPTER FIFTEEN

Heading Home to Philly

The years of late-night partying and draining the limitless lineup of liquor bottles had finally caught up with Dorothy McDonald. She plumped up and her skin was beginning to take on a pasty patina while it sagged from the ravages of her ongoing bouts with the bottle. Here it was, less than two years after she married Blackie and Dolly was alone with no job and very little money. The clubs on 52nd Street had crumbled into poor imitations of their former glory and even though the nation was at war again, this time in Vietnam, the mood on "The Street" was far different. The country was ambivalent about this war and there was no celebration of the American spirit in the clubs that supported the G.I.s and their families so wholeheartedly during the War Years in the 1940's. "Swing Street" wasn't jumpin' and jivin' anymore. It was merely limping along.

The mood of the country in 1967 was a fitting match for the mood of Dolly McDonald. But Dolly's options were limited. She was too old to work the faded Club Scene anymore but her life on 52nd Street was the only life she had really known. Without the excitement she craved, Dolly drank more and became even more despondent. That's when she decided to head back home to Philadelphia.

When Dolly packed her clothes into a big suitcase and left New York, she left Blackie behind in his prison cell and never troubled herself with the formalities of a Separation or Divorce. Why bother? Blackie was locked up for Life with no possibility for parole. He would die behind bars and she would never see him again. Besides, a divorce would generate legal fees. And money was something that Dolly was sorely lacking.

Dolly called Tommy to tell him that she was coming home. During her lengthy absence her mother, Rita Shelfein, had died and her father had re-married, this time to a black woman named Madeline Jackson. Dolly wasn't particularly close with her father or her new stepmother but they were the only family she had aside from Tommy. She was hoping they would put her up until she could straighten out the mess she had made of her life. She wanted to put her past IN the past and decided on a symbolic name change to start anew. She would no longer be known as Dolly. She returned to her birth name: Dorothy.

Angus McDonald was a man filled with anger and resentment toward his daughter and that's how he greeted her when she knocked on the front door of his row house in Philadelphia's south side. "I see you finally decided to come home," he said with a healthy dose of hostility. "I guess you must be desperate if you have to stoop to this." Dolly had lived in New York for more than 20 years and didn't make any effort to include her father in her life. She'd been just as distant from her mother while her mother was still alive. Angus never forgave her for not coming home for her mother's funeral. "Not now, Angus," Dorothy scowled. "I don't need a lecture right now. So cut me a break, okay?" Angus backed down and gestured for her to come in. Dorothy WAS his daughter and he didn't want to be accused of shutting her out of his life the way she had shut him out of hers.

"So what is it that you want?" Angus asked her. "What do you plan on doing?" Dorothy put her suitcase down and made her case. "I've been having a tough time of it, Angus," she said plaintively. "I need a place to stay until I can get my life back together. Yeah, I know that maybe I shoulda' done things and maybe stayed more in touch... but that's over now I promise. I promise it'll be different." She reached into her purse for a Chesterfield while Angus had his say. "I figured things had to be real bad for you to come home like this," he said, "and you're still family so I'm willing to give it a go. But you're gonna have to pay your way. There won't be any freebies around here." "I promise," Dorothy said earnestly, "I promise I won't be any trouble. I'll do my part around here." Angus held up his hand and pointed a menacing finger directly at her face. "You'd better. This is the last chance I'm giving you here."

Dorothy settled into an empty bedroom on the third floor fully intent on changing her ways. But all those years of partying and alcohol-induced stupors made it hard. She frequently took refuge in her quiet bedroom with the endless supply of Jack Daniels she kept stashed there. And she became a nasty drunk. She blamed everyone who didn't appreciate her talent... and that nagging resentment haunted her every waking hour. But it got especially nasty after the sun went down when she knew the music was playing in clubs all over the country and she wasn't a part of it. What had happened to her life? Where did the time go? And what would she do now?

Though Angus barely tolerated the daughter who had abandoned him so many years ago and was now strung out on booze in his own house, Dorothy's stepmother had a kinder, more understanding heart. Madeline Jackson offered sympathy and tried to get Dolly to open up and talk about the demons that possessed her. Dolly had watched life pass her by and was now trapped in circumstances that she could no longer control. But most of the time Dorothy resented Madeline's prying and wanted no part of her advice. Madeline would make a suggestion only to have Dorothy rant and rave at her in a drunken rage. "You don't know nothing about what's bothering me," she'd lash out at Madeline. "And you never will…. You NEVER WILL!!" Madeline was a wise woman and she knew when to back off and let Dorothy unburden herself of the anger that was locked inside.

There were those other times, though, when they sat down and shared a drink and Dorothy lost her inhibitions in the process. Madeline was no stranger to the bottle herself but she never let it rule her life like Dorothy did. Madeline functioned. She cleaned the house and cooked the meals and only resorted to a "snort" when her work was done. Dorothy, on the other hand, was out of control. She got job after job as a waitress or a restaurant hostess only to lose it when she would go on a bender and get so drunk she would show up late for work or not at all. And every time she got canned Angus had something to say about it. "What is it about you, Dorothy?" he would chide. "How come you can't even do something simple… like keeping a steady job? Is that asking too much… that you keep a job so you can start paying some money for rent? Or is that asking too much of a fifty-year-old woman?" Dolly would get offended, storm off to her room and have a fit. But still, she couldn't seem to get a grip on her behavior.

Madeline thought of her friend Connie Henley who had cared for her younger brother for many years. Connie's brother was mentally disabled but Connie wouldn't let him vegetate in some mental facility. She had the patience and caring nature that wouldn't allow it. Connie became a beacon of light to all her friends as they watched her struggle to meet her brother's needs over the years. She gained the admiration of countless others who understood and appreciated her sacrifice.

"You know, honey," Madeline told Dorothy as they sat at the kitchen table nursing their drinks one night, "I got an idea that could be just the trick for you. Now don't get all upset with me. Hear me out on this... okay?" Dorothy nodded her head as she reached for a cigarette. Madeline went on, "I got a friend, Connie. She's living in Atlantic City. I think you may have met her once.... anyway... she got a good job there as a waitress... and I think you might wanna look into that. And Connie could help you out getting a job and finding a place of your own... so's you could get outta your daddy's hair and back into being on your own again."

Dorothy blew off the suggestion by saying, "Well... I dunno about that.... I gotta figure out what I'm gonna do... Maybe I'll look into that some day." Madeline, though, wasn't about to be dissuaded. She knew that Connie would be a good influence on Dorothy so she persisted. "Hey, maybe we'll take a ride there one day and check it out," Madeline said. "I wanna see Connie anyway and it's only a little more than an hour's drive." Dorothy wasn't easily convinced, though. "Well... we'll see..... We'll see what happens," she responded as she knocked back her drink and drained the glass.

CHAPTER SIXTEEN

The Legal Dis-Connection

It was several weeks before Marsha Rudolph called back. She reviewed all my papers and figured that since mine was a Gray Market adoption, a lawyer or several lawyers were involved. That seemed likely, I thought, since I had heard the same comment at the previous ALMA meeting I attended. Marsha wanted me to pursue any lawyers who might have been practicing in Far Rockaway at the time and she wanted to know if my adoptive father used an attorney. I could only remember one name from the past: Robert Minsky. My father had mentioned him a number of times over the years, telling me that Mr. Minsky oversaw the purchase of our house and of the two-story building in the heart of the business district in Westwood, New Jersey, where my father had his jewelry store. I never met Robert Minsky and never recalled hearing him mentioned in the present tense so I assumed that he died long ago. Still, it was worth checking it out. Marsha also told me she thought that the name I found for my birth mother, Dorothy Jeannette McDonald, was a legitimate name since she said people don't usually use a middle name when they're giving a phony name. When I pressed her on how well her "inside man" was doing with my birth certificate, she admitted that he was able to get my amended birth certificate but not the original. But, she said, he was still trying. In the meantime, she suggested I try to locate Robert Minsky and any lawyers in Far Rockaway.

At the next monthly ALMA meeting another adoptee told me of the "Newark Business Library," in Newark, New Jersey, and said I would find City Directories there that might lead me to Robert Minsky. I had made the assumption that Robert Minsky practiced in New Jersey because of the way my father had spoken of him years ago. It was nothing solid, just a hunch. I had success with the City Directories in Manhattan to locate Rocco Ferrucci so I was quite certain I could also find Robert Minsky.

Several days later I got a very suspicious phone call. A man named "Gary" was on the line. He claimed to be a writer for "New Orleans" magazine and said he was responding to my ad in the Local 802 musician's newsletter for musicians who played with Louis Prima. He was writing an article on Prima and asked me what my involvement was.

I hesitated but then figured that I had nothing to lose by telling him all about myself. He was fascinated and asked me the full gamut of questions to validate my identity. He seemed convinced and told me he would make inquiries for me. And then he gave me his phone number and told me to call him any time. Okay, I figured... this guy is legit.

The next day I got another call in response to the ad in the Local 802 musician's newsletter. It was from the wife of Jimmy Vincent. Jimmy had played drums in Louis' band for many years and was a close friend of Louis Prima. She, too, was taken with the story of my adoption. But when I asked about Dorothy McDonald and someone named Frank (my birth name) she couldn't help me. She told me that Jimmy didn't know anyone by those names and confirmed again that Dorothy McDonald was never a singer with Louis Prima's band. Again, I felt that I was on the wrong track and that somehow Rabbi Schwartz and Rocco and Rose Ferrucci didn't get the story straight about my birth mother. Maybe Dorothy lied to them or maybe they just weren't clear about what she told them. In any case, Mrs. Vincent seemed to be a nice person but she was also someone who, once again, made me question my years of research.

My next step was a trip to Newark Business Library and the City Directories. It didn't take long to find what I was looking for. The 1944 Bergen-Passaic County Directory has this listing: Minsky, Robert ATTNY. 271 B'way, WEstwood 4-1733. Res. 655 E. 27th Pat. SHerwd 2-7557. What that spelled out for me was that an attorney named Robert Minsky had an office at 271 Broadway in Westwood, New Jersey, where my parents lived and worked. Mr. Minsky lived at 655 E. 27th Street in Paterson, New Jersey... about a half-hour away... in the same city as the St. Joseph's Hospital that cared for our baby boys. His home phone number was SHerwood 2-7557.

His business listing in Westwood remained in the Directories for 1945-46... 1953-54... and 1957-58. But the listing disappeared in 1959-60. My Search, though, had taught me to be thorough so I checked the shelves and found there was also a 1956 Paterson City Directory. In 1956, it listed Minsky, Robert (Rachel) lwyr. Westwood, h. 655 E.27th. That was the same listing I had found in the Bergen-Passaic County Directory. I continued to search the phone books and City Directories but Robert Minsky's name dropped out of all of them in 1959. I did find continuous listings, though, for Rachel Minsky... whose name was in parentheses in the Paterson City Directory, indicating that she was Robert Minsky's wife. She moved from time to time but always within the boundaries of the Bergen County, New Jersey phone directory. The most current listing for her was 22 Rosemont Road, Clifton, New Jersey. I decided to call.

"Hello," said a sweet voice on the other end of the phone. "Is this Mrs. Minsky?" I asked. "Yes it is," she replied. "Mrs. Minsky, my name is Alan Gerstel. I believe you and your husband know my parents, Herman and Selma Gerstel," I said eagerly. "Oh, Alan, of course, I know your parents. Such lovely people. We go back so many years," she said nostalgically. I then launched into a mini version of my Search. I told her that I had young twin boys with medical problems and was trying to find out about my medical history. Mrs.Minsky understood perfectly. But what she told me next... dashed my hopes in a heartbeat: Her husband was dead. And in a truly bizarre turn of events, he died over the Labor Day weekend in 1957... as he and Mrs. Minsky were returning from the New Jersey Shore to attend my Bar Mitzvah! Robert and Rachel Minsky were slated to be honored guests. But sadly, Mr. Minsky died of a heart attack just hours before they were due to attend.

Mrs. Minsky had even more disappointing news for me: Robert kept all his records in his office and they were all gone. But she didn't think he was actively involved in my adoption although he might have known something about it. We ended the conversation by saying that we would keep in touch and that she would call me if she remembered anything about my adoption.

After we hung up, another groundswell of frustration erupted from deep inside. I had been methodical in my Search. I had been determined. I had managed to uncover the names and identities of people who had intimate knowledge of my adoption. But their stonewalling or faded memories raised even more questions. And now THIS... the death of Robert Minsky, who I knew was a confidant of my father. He died on the way to my Bar Mitzvah!!! Was that a cosmic sign that God decreed that I should never know the truth? I wanted to walk away from my Search and put it out of my mind as I had wanted to do so many times before. But once again, I was incapable of turning my back on the pain that haunted me. No matter where I was or what I was doing my mind would drift back to the nagging questions about all that I had learned about my past.

I tried over and over again to process all of the facts I had uncovered but those efforts would spawn new avenues of attack and new questions. On one such occasion, I remembered that during my teenage years, before my nose job at the age of 21, the people I worked with in Summer Stock would tell me that I looked like someone they knew… that I reminded them of someone else. "Do you have a brother?" I would hear time and again and each time I would answer "no." I was an "only child." But the same question was repeated again and again by people who worked in the same theatrical settings. At the time, no one could figure out who I reminded them of… but a dozen people or more were convinced that they had seen someone who looked just like me… that I had a "double" somewhere. The possibility that I could have brothers or sisters somewhere gave me even more reason to press on with my Search.

Each ALMA meeting seemed to bring fresh ideas and that's what brought me back every month. Most of those ideas led nowhere but some ideas bore fruit. We were sitting around Nancy Davis' kitchen table again when a woman who completed her Search put some facts together. "You were born in a Catholic hospital, right?" She questioned rhetorically. "That would mean you had to have been baptized." So she suggested that I write to Catholic churches near St. Joseph's Hospital in Far Rockaway and any that would be near Beach 78th Street. "Write to them as Frank McDonald, born to Dorothy McDonald on August 11, 1944, and ask for your Baptismal certificate. If your birth mother named you then you were likely baptized."

The next day, I called the Chancellery of the Archdiocese and asked for the names and addresses of the churches in Far Rockaway. There were only two: St. Mary's Church on New Haven Avenue, and St. Gertrude's Church on Beach 38th Street. With fresh hope, I wrote them both only to get two gracious, though negative replies.

The advice I heard over and over again at every ALMA meeting was to turn to family members for help. "Someone will know something," my fellow adoptees told me, "and they will likely put you on the right track." I always hesitated, though. I was raised with more than my fair share of Jewish guilt. Each time I considered talking to a family member I worried that if word of my Search leaked back to my mother, it would hurt her terribly. That, in turn, would add a mountain of guilt to the dizzying emotions already churning inside me. But as time passed and my desperation grew I became increasingly bolder and less fearful that my mother would find out what I was doing.

The mental sparring that pitted my mother's well-being against my need to know the truth was put on "hold" one day when the phone rang. I picked it up and said "hello." It was followed by silence. I said "hello" again… and then heard a soft sigh and a breathy "oh, no." There was another pause so I said "hello" a third time. Then I heard a click and the line went dead. Had I just heard from my birth mother, I questioned frantically as I felt my heart pounding harder? Had she somehow learned that I was trying to find her and she called… but then couldn't go through with it? Just the possibility that my birth mother had called and then hung up… was almost too heavy a burden to bear.

A little more than a week later the phone rang again. This time Ronni answered it. She heard only breathing on the other end. Several seconds passed before she asked, "Is this Alan's Mother?" I heard her comment and ran into the kitchen to pick up the extension… just as that person hung up again. Ronni and I both became convinced that my birth mother was reaching out to me. We felt helpless, though, because she never spoke a word.

It seemed obvious to both me and Ronni that we were getting close to the truth. Someone I had contacted must have reached out to my birth mother, I thought, and that lead to the phone calls. There was no "Caller

ID" back in 1984, though, and no simple way to trace the origin of those calls. But since whoever made those calls never called back again, I had to put those calls aside... and refocus on who to contact in my family.

After giving it a lot of thought, I concluded that the person I felt most comfortable talking to was my cousin Alan Katof. Alan is four months older than me and I remembered that we spent time in Far Rockaway together when we were eleven or twelve. His grandmother Ruth Paul was my adopted mother's older sister. There was that extra generation in his family because his mother Miriam had married young and had given birth to Alan soon after. That made Alan and me contemporaries. Both Alan's mother and grandmother had "summered" for many years in the bungalows of Far Rockaway.

When I called, Alan was very helpful and assured me that I could trust him to be discreet and keep my mother from learning of my Search. The only tidbit he remembered hearing when he was growing up... was that my birth parents were in "show business." That comment about my birth parents came up in conversations among his family members, he said, when they talked about my decision to go to college to study Theatre. As we talked, he remembered that his family had always stayed in a bungalow on Beach 79th Street every summer. The information certainly fit with what I knew about my birth mother's summer address in Far Rockaway and I could see the pieces of the puzzle beginning to fit. "I'll talk to my mother," he told me, "she may remember more details... and I know you can trust her."

The next day, Alan called me back with a torrent of information! He said that his mother was very comfortable talking about the circumstances of my adoption, "and don't worry. She wants to help you and would never want to hurt your mother. So she will be very tight-lipped about your inquiry." Then the floodgates opened. Alan told me that everyone involved "summered" on Beach 78th Street in 1944. My birth mother was staying with another Hungarian woman, Margaret Welch, a neighbor from the Bronx. His mother, Miriam, had struck up a friendship with my birth mother and specifically asked her where she was going to go after I was born. But she wouldn't say. Miriam recalled that my birth mother was a singer in a Big Band. Margaret Welch's daughters, Miriam said, worked in nightclubs but were not showgirls although she said they often looked like they were. Their mother was a baker, and years later, my mother's younger sister, Fritzi, ran across her after she opened a restaurant in Los Angeles. My cousin Alan didn't think my birth mother sang with Louis Prima's band because his mother said something about the bandleader's hair color that he didn't quite understand. Miriam was very close with the Welch sisters as well as my birth mother, but after I was born my father laid down the law and made his demands known to all the family members in Far Rockaway: He did not want Miriam... in fact, he FORBADE Miriam... to associate with my birth mother or either of Margaret Welch's daughters ever again.

Two days later, my Aunt Miriam called me directly... as my cousin Alan said she would. We talked for an hour and fifteen minutes but Miriam's recollections, other than what she had told my cousin, were not as vivid as I had hoped. She couldn't remember my birthmother's name but said "Dorothy" sounded familiar. "McDonald", though, didn't ring any bells at all. She said that my birthmother had dark black hair. But when I questioned her further she admitted that Dorothy could have colored her hair as many women did during those times. I told her that I found official records that indicated I was named Frank McDonald at birth. But Miriam could not recollect anyone named Frank and so she couldn't tell me if I was named after my birthfather, a relative, or maybe even as an offhand tribute to Frank Sinatra. Miriam also told me that my birthmother would never reveal my birthfather's identity except to claim that he was a band leader with light hair and blue eyes. She thinks he might have played the trumpet. And when I told her about my hospital records, she said she never heard of the Ferruccis. It became clear to me during our conversation that my Aunt Miriam had a very spotty memory of what happened so many years ago. She was trying hard to help me but I realized that I had to weigh all the things she told me very carefully.

Her memories of Margaret Welch and her two daughters seemed very credible, though. I took the name "Margaret Welch" at face value because she seemed so certain and was also familiar with the family from her neighborhood in the Bronx. So it was time for another trip to the New York Public Library. I used telephone directories and old City Directories to research the name of all the "Welch's" living in the New York metropolitan area and in Los Angeles, where she said my Aunt Fritzi had seen her many years after my birth. I also checked the Yellow Pages and made a list of all Hungarian Restaurants in Los Angeles (that might have employed a "baker"). I then wrote to all the "Welch's" still living in Far Rockaway and Queens and also to all the "Welch's" living in Los Angeles.

I wrote:

Dear Mr. or Mrs. Welch,

I am trying to locate a Mrs. Welch, who is Hungarian and a baker by profession. She and her two daughters lived on Beach 78th Street in Far Rockaway during the summer of 1944. Years later they operated a Hungarian Restaurant in Los Angeles. My aunt and uncle, who I haven't seen in years, lived in the same building, and I am hoping Mrs. Welch or her daughters will remember them and will help me locate them. It is extremely important to me that I locate them and I pray that if you have any information you will call me COLLECT at (201) 666-0142. Thank you very much for your cooperation.

Sincerely, Alan Gerstel

Weeks passed… and no one responded.

Meanwhile, my Aunt Miriam called again to say, "Alan, sweetheart, I have been thinking and thinking and I am so sorry that I can't remember everything. I wish I could remember enough to really help you." She went on to suggest that I check out a Frank McDonald with the musician's union. She also thought my birth father was Irish but she couldn't be sure. It was maddening to me that she couldn't remember the really important details that would lead me to my birth parents but she was being so wonderful by just trying to help me that I didn't have the heart to complain about her memory lapse. "Honey, I remember visiting your mother in the hospital. I remember that we went for walks in the evening on the boardwalk. 'My' Alan was just a few months old and while my mother watched him at night after he was asleep, your mother and I would walk as far as Rockaway's Playland and then walk back. We never went on the rides but we would buy a nosh to eat on our walk and we would talk. And I can tell you sweetheart, that there was no bitterness. Your mother just accepted her fate." At that moment, I was stunned and more than a little frustrated that my aunt was so close with my birth mother that they went on evening walks together, yet she couldn't recall more specific information. She was apparently not just Dorothy's acquaintance but also a friend who shared intimate thoughts about her pregnancy.

While I was wallowing in my frustration, Miriam went into more detail about my Aunt Fritzi's chance encounter with Margaret Welch in Los Angeles: "Mrs. Welch… the Mrs. Welch from Rockaway, was a friend of Fritzi's also from The Bronx… and Fritzi ran across her when she was out on a drive after she moved to Los Angeles sometime in the late 1960's. Fritzi was surprised to see her… and she told my mother and me that Mrs. Welch owned a little restaurant near her home in the Fairfax district." That would have been about 16 years earlier, coincidentally, about the same time that I lived in Los Angeles. I continued to question her about details but she just couldn't come up with any other facts. "Let me ask my mother," she said, "I'll be sneaky and won't tell her anything about you. I'll just bring it up in conversation like I was just thinking about it and was curious about what happened. I'll bet my mother has some answers." I cautioned her again about my mother. I knew it would be particularly hurtful to my mother if she knew I was making inquiries among her own family members. Miriam assured me that she would handle it very tactfully.

The trail kept leading to Los Angeles and this Mrs. Welch, the Hungarian baker, who was somehow at the center of my adoption. I became increasingly convinced that finding this Mrs. Welch would unlock the puzzle surrounding my birth. I could only hope that some other family member still lived in the New York area so I expanded my mailing list beyond the Borough of Queens and I fired off more letters to the "Welch" families living in Nassau and Suffolk Counties of Long Island. But shortly after I got those letters into the mail I began thinking about Mrs. "Welch." Perhaps her name was spelled "Welsh?" Or maybe it was "Welsch." So I wrote more letters to people with those alternate spellings living in the New York City area and also in Los Angeles. But again, my frustration level increased because I didn't get any response.

I also decided to focus on Hungarian restaurants in Los Angeles. Fortunately, there were only three: Tokay Hungarian Restaurant, Paprika Restaurant, and Hungarian Budapest Restaurant. Since the list was so short I called each one rather than writing. In each case I asked for a Mrs. Welch. I would also ask if a Mrs. Welch ever owned the restaurant or if she was the baker for the restaurant. All my questions turned up negative responses. No one had heard of her. But there was little doubt in my mind that Mrs. Welch was Hungarian. My parents were Hungarian. So too were my aunts and uncles and I knew they liked to stick together. I was also fairly certain that Miriam knew what she was talking about when she said Mrs. Welch was a baker and that my aunt Fritzi had run across her at her restaurant in L.A. Those were coincidences that would be unforgettable.

Miriam called back after talking to her mother. "It all went well, Alan," she assured me, "my mother just thinks it was an interesting conversation and nothing more. I'm sure she will never say anything to your mother." Miriam then told me the woman's name was Margaret Welch who was divorced. She did not know the spelling of her last name. But Ruth had told Miriam that Margaret Welch was dead. One of Margaret's daughters, she said, still lived in California but the other had moved back East. "My mother also told me that she had always been puzzled why your mother never told you anything about your birth parents, Alan," Miriam said warmly. "She never understood why it was such a secret. And she said to me, what could possibly be so bad? What could be so bad that Alan shouldn't know?"

What my Aunt Miriam told me next truly sent me reeling!!! "Alan, do you remember when you lived in Los Angeles?" Miriam asked me rhetorically. "Darling, my mother remembers that you were a customer in Mrs. Welch's restaurant many times during the three years you lived there. I don't know if you remember or not... but my mother says Fritzi took you there the first time... but, of course, nobody said anything about what happened back in Far Rockaway." I was speechless. Miriam filled the void by continuing, "And Fritzi said that you went back to that restaurant many times... because it was around the corner... or it was near CBS... where you worked... at least that's what she said." Miriam and I talked a little more before saying goodbye but my mind was clearly in "rewind" mode and I had difficulty engaging in any other conversation.

I focused almost frantically on my days in Los Angeles as I tried to create an image in my mind of some restaurant near CBS Television City where I had "eaten many times." But... nothing. I had no recollection at all. As much as I tried I could not envision this restaurant or its location. How odd was that? How could I not remember? And how unfair was it that my Aunt Fritzi knew about my connection to Mrs. Welch and even took me into the restaurant to show Mrs. Welch the young man whose adoption she helped facilitate so many years before? They had intimate knowledge about my adoption but my Aunt Fritzi had passed away in the years since I lived in Los Angeles… and Margaret Welch, I was just told, had also died.

Howie Reist, meanwhile, the local musician who had played with Louis Prima briefly in 1945, made some discreet inquiries of his own. He told my story to the owner of a local music store, who in turn, gave me a call. Owen Michaels couldn't help me directly but he referred me to his friend, an adoptee who located her own birth parents. He thought that Barbara Cohen might be able to help. Barbara was very determined and a very savvy woman who told me, "You have a real problem, Alan. Your adoption was handled on the sly. You probably won't find any records. And even if you do, they will likely contain lies. You need an expert in tracking people down, someone who is unconventional and knows how to play the game." She recommended a private investigator, the same guy who helped her. "His name is Lou LoScialpo," she said, "and Lou can sound intimidating on the phone. But he is the very best. He's about 40 years old and a former cop. And he's an adoptee himself who successfully completed his own Search so he knows exactly what you are going through." She gave me Lou's phone number and address and urged me to call him. "You are really in a bind here, Alan," she told me bluntly, "and as I see it, your only way out is Lou."

But I had used private investigators before. Bob Fitzpatrick was a nice guy and certainly competent, but not any real help. Peter MacIntosh had either ripped me off or his investigators were incompetent. And the secretive investigator with the group Origins, for all the talk about how he was a "miracle worker," hadn't worked any miracles for me yet. I got the impression that his specialty was gathering information and figured that he was probably a whiz with the emerging computer technology. But my case was different. There was precious little factual "information" to go on, and what little I had been able to uncover didn't lead anywhere. So my options were very limited. Barbara Cohen had been so upbeat and so positive that Lou LoScialpo could help me that I took her advice and called him to set up a meeting.

Lou had a second-floor office in the business district of a working-class north Jersey neighborhood. I parked my car as my eyes darted up and down the street at the faded three and four story brick buildings that lined both sides. Nothing fancy about this place, I thought. I grabbed my briefcase off the front seat that I had filled with notes and letters and even the tapes of my phone calls with the Ferruccis, and headed across the street to Lou's building. The peeling paint in the tiny lobby reinforced my initial reaction to the neighborhood. I walked up the creaky stairs to the second floor and walked down the hallway with the cracked linoleum groaning under my feet. The door at the end read: "Eagle Investigations." I felt like I was in a black and white Humphrey Bogart movie and couldn't help but fantasize that I was a client coming to see the legendary detective Sam Spade. I turned the handle and opened the door but my fantasy didn't end there. About ten feet in front of me in the small office with buckling wood paneling and worn out carpeting was Lou LoScialpo. Lou was sitting behind his plain wooden desk smoking a cigarette. He was a tough-looking guy with a solid body and a full head of slicked-back, shiny, dark hair. "Hey, good to see you," he said in the most resonant, raspy voice I think I have ever heard. I could understand now why some people would find Lou intimidating. He stood up and shook my hand, exhaling cigarette smoke as he spoke. "Yeah, Alan, Barbara Cohen told me all about you. Let's see if I can help," he said as he began to sit. "Take a seat... and lemme hear your story with as many details as you can remember."

"Before we get started," I asked haltingly, "how much is this going to cost me?" Lou never flinched, never missed a beat. "We'll see," he responded matter-of-factly, "but you gotta know that I'm not in this for the money. I was adopted myself and I found my own birth parents. And it wasn't easy. So if I can help you, I will. We'll talk about the money when I know more about your case. Let it rip."

As the sunlight streaked into the small room and mixed with Lou's cigarette smoke to create a beam of textured haze, I unburdened myself once again. I must have talked for an hour, listing detail after detail of my torturous investigation, prodded occasionally by questions from Lou. When I got to the end of my story Lou took another drag from his cigarette and then exhaled slowly. He snuffed it out in an ashtray piled high with cigarette butts and ashes and then responded, "You've done a helluva job there, Alan. Lots of headway. I'm impressed. You clearly are committed to this... and because of your commitment, I'm going to help you."

He asked me to leave the tapes of my conversations with Rocco and Rose Ferrucci with him so he could listen to them and see what he could figure out. There was something no-nonsense about Lou LoScialpo, something that seemed right. I got a feeling of confidence from him that I never got from the other private eyes. He wasn't high-tech and he wouldn't be using any fancy gadgetry. I was convinced that this guy was going to find my birth parents through sheer determination and investigative skill.

As I left his office and headed down the stairs I found that I was smiling. Somehow I knew this guy was going to be the key that would unlock the door to my past. Lou was going to do the impossible. I was certain of it!

CHAPTER SEVENTEEN

The Knock-Up

After just a few months back home in Philadelphia, Dorothy McDonald had become the Poster Girl for angry, bitter drunks. Madeline Jackson would share a drink or two with Dorothy just about every night, hoping she could get Dorothy to open up and spill her guts about what was apparently eating away at her. She knew Dorothy had an ugly life, one that didn't turn out like she wanted, but it was hard to fathom what could have gone so wrong to turn her into a hopeless, deadbeat drunk. "You always say something's eating at you," she'd tell Dorothy, "but you never say anything about what's hurting you so." It would take some time and Dorothy would usually drain another glass of Jack Daniels before she'd open up a bit. "I never got a chance to make my dream come true," she'd tell Madeline. "I never got to be a band singer like I always wanted. Never happened... even though I did everything I knew how to do."

Madeline tended to the house during the day and shared the bottle with Dorothy just about every night. But as the weeks passed, Angus grew increasingly impatient with his "no good lush of a daughter" lounging around the house all day, half in the bag… or passed out on the sofa at night. He also didn't much like the idea that he was supporting his middle-age daughter who couldn't hold down a job. Madeline could see Angus' growing resentment and knew she'd have to help Dorothy get back on her feet and out on her own before Angus reached the breaking point and threw Dorothy out of the house.

The one person Madeline knew who had the patience to deal with Dorothy was Connie Henley. If Connie could take care of her disabled brother for all those years, she thought, surely she'd be able to handle Dorothy. Madeline knew that Connie could be the positive force Dorothy needed. She held down a job as a waitress and could help Dorothy get a job too. No, Dorothy wouldn't be the hot young "Hostess" she used to be but Madeline figured Dorothy still had the looks and personality that could get her some decent tips. Every time Madeline brought up the idea, though, Dorothy blew her off and the inebriated debates between these two strong-willed women often deteriorated into screaming matches. "You can't tell me what to do…you…!!" Dorothy would vent. "I don't have to listen to this shit. You just want me out of the house… that's all you want me to do." Madeline shrugged off the insult and would fire back, "Well, at least I ain't pissing my life away with no place to go and no one to care for me. I don't have to take no crap from you, honey. If it wasn't for me, your daddy would toss you out on the street… so don't you play no big shot with me!"

The women would eventually retreat to their respective bedrooms only to wake up the next morning to apologize and start the pattern of substance abuse all over again.

One night, as Dorothy was telling stories about the good times on 52nd Street and how she once sang with a Big Band at Club 52, she suddenly became quiet and stared down into the glass of whiskey she was caressing. "That damn kid……" she muttered then paused to take a healthy swig of sour mash. "That damn kid really fucked me over." She stopped again…

paused... and knocked back another mouthful. An uncomfortable silence fell over the room. Dorothy reached for a cigarette and lit up. She took a deep drag and exhaled, watching the smoke rise. But still, she didn't say anything. Madeline waited to hear more but Dorothy seemed lost in her thoughts. Madeline gently questioned, "Hey honey, what about that kid... what kid are you talking 'bout?" Again, the room was silent as Dorothy looked down into her glass and then up at the ceiling as she sighed and took another drag on her cigarette. It felt like hours passed until she finally spit out the words: "The damn baby I had after I got pregnant."

The silence in the room was now so intense that Madeline could hear the throbbing of the blood surging through her inner ear as her mind spun wildly with burning questions. Madeline sensed that the words Dorothy uttered were the chink in the emotional armor Dorothy had surrounded herself with all those years. She watched uneasily as Dorothy stared into her glass again and took another mouthful of the satisfying elixir. Madeline finally broke the silence. "Honey... oh child... you never said nothing before about no baby," she said as tenderly and compassionately as anyone could. "That must've been tough on you... and you never told anyone all this time? You never told your daddy... or me." Dorothy looked Madeline straight in the eye and said firmly, "I don't like to talk about that baby.... But I.... I can't help it.... I... that baby messed up my life... He killed any chance I had of singing in a band..... I was so close to getting in front of the microphone... and then... that baby really fucked me over."

Madeline reached over the table and poured another fistful of whiskey into Dorothy's glass and then reached over and took her hand. "That explains a whole lot, honey," she said reassuringly. "You know... that's explains a lot."

Dorothy was hurting but she seemed touched by Madeline's genuine show of affection and support. "I guess I should tell you the whole story," she sighed. Then after another pause, she continued, ".... ah.... What the hell.... Why not?" Madeline responded as she squeezed Dorothy's hand, "Yeah go ahead... why not?" The years of bottled-up emotions spilled out as Dorothy retold and relived her story. "Mama, I had only been in New York for a little while and I was working on 52nd Street at the clubs there. But the real reason I was there was 'cause of the bands," Dorothy admitted. She began to smile as she thought back to the glory days when she was barely 21 and a "wanted" commodity. "Hell, Madeline, I coulda had just about any guy I wanted... and I knew it. But I was putting all my attention on the guys who played in the bands.... Cause I figured that could get me in good with the bandleaders and maybe get me a gig in front of the microphone." Then her smile faded and Dorothy seemed to look off into the distance. She took another drink, took a final drag on her cigarette, and snubbed it out in the dirty ashtray that was half-full of butts.

"Sounds like you had a plan, honey," Madeline said encouragingly with a slight chuckle. "Sounds like you had a real good plan..... and I seen pictures of you back then... and mmm-mmm... honey, yes... you had a good plan... and you had the goods to make it happen."

The compliment worked to snap Dorothy out of her haze as she remembered how good she felt as a sexy, 21-year-old Hostess. "Madeline... oh mama... you don't know the half of it," she said lustily. "I got real tight with some of the fellas in Lou Prima's band... I mean REAL tight. I was hanging around them all the time... and I would sing a little tune here and there... ya know... just by myself... just so's they could hear what kind of good voice I had. And we had some good times... We had some REAL good times." Madeline was clearly impressed with Dorothy's story and her relationship with Louis Prima's band members. "Louis Prima? Louis Prima? That's the guy you was hanging around?" she questioned with a hint of jealousy in her voice. "THE Louis Prima? That's the guy you was hanging with?"

Dorothy leaned back away from the table still holding her glass. She was resting on the back of the chair now in an easy, relaxed position. Clearly, she had broken through her emotional wall and was relishing the memories of the old days... and she was enjoying Madeline's response.

She continued, "Well, I wasn't hangin' with Louis himself at first. I was just friends with the drummer, Jimmy Vincent, and a couple a other guys. But eventually I started getting tight with Louis. I wanted soooo bad to sing with his band. He was such a funny guy... a great trumpet player... with great lips... if ya know what I mean... hah!" Madeline and Dorothy shared a wink, a nod. Dorothy went on, "That guy was the sexiest guy I think I ever saw. He was just something. Every night, women would go crazy. I don't care who they was or where they was from. He drove them bananas. Yeah... and he drove ME bananas too." Dorothy fidgeted with the pack of cigarettes in front of her, grabbed a Chesterfield, and lit it.

"But there was this problem with me and his band. He already had a singer," Dorothy said with a sneer, "this mousy woman... Lily Ann Carol." Then she repeated the name with more emphasis, spewing, "Lily - Ann - Carol... A NOTHING. No sex appeal. No voice. No nothing.... And there she was... singing in front of the band..... Well, mama... I KNEW I could do better. I just had to convince Louis that I should be the one singing there and not her. So I fixed myself up real nice and turned up the heat."

Madeline was fascinated by the story unfolding at her kitchen table. She never met anyone as famous as Louis Prima so Dorothy' story played out like some scene out of a Hollywood movie. "So honey... what happened then? How'd you get him to notice you?" she quizzed Dorothy a little more impatiently, "Not that you didn't have the goods..." "Well, for one thing," Dorothy said as she relished every word, "Whenever Louis and the guys played Club 52 where I worked I made sure to wear my lowest-cut dress so he would notice me. And I always managed to give him a wink when I walked by. Hell, I knew the guy's reputation.... Yeah... EVERYBODY knew the guy's reputation.... Oh, he was married... hitched to some broad who lived back in Hollywood... an actress, I think.... But that didn't stop ol' Louis... He had a real eye for the ladies... and oh, oh, oh... the ladies had an eye for him."

Dorothy continued to weave her tale and she relived each moment with gusto. She had been keeping the story of her pregnancy a secret from her family for so many years but tonight something was different. She couldn't help herself. Once she began talking about Louis she weakened. "Louis didn't actually come on to me right away," Dorothy sighed, "and I didn't get it at first..... uh.... maybe he had another girlfriend at the time... I dunno... but he didn't take the bait.... UNTIL one night when he came up to me at the bar after a "set"... and he asked me real nice... if I wanted to hang around with the band when they went on the road for a couple-a weeks." "HAH!" Madeline practically snorted, "I knew it... I knew you'd get to him." They toasted the moment by clicking their glasses together and taking a sip.

"Oh, but it didn't end there," Dorothy went on. "He got real close to me and rubbed the back of his hand against my bosom as he leaned in and whispered that he couldn't wait til we was alone... cause he said he had a real thing for me. The next thing I knew I was on a train leaving Penn Station... going to San Francisco. Louis hated to fly... I ... Come to think of it... I don't think he ever was on a plane. He didn't like planes at all. So we all went by train... But I knew I was striking gold with Louis... I knew he wanted me... and I figured I could get him so hepped-up that he'd get rid of that bitch... Lily Ann whatever... and put me up there in front of the microphone... I was riding the train to Heaven."

"Mama," Dorothy went on, her chest heaving with a sigh, "that man was the best lover I ever had. After he had done show after show he finally came up to my room in the middle of the night with a bottle of bourbon and two glasses. We talked... and we talked... and I told him that I could be the best singer he ever had in his band... and he actually said he'd give me a try-out some night when that Lily Ann woman wasn't there... Oh...

he knew how to put the moves on... and he was just so smooth... and so... so sexy... that he coulda had me any which way he wanted. We got in the sack and we went at it... like... like I had never felt before... and when it was over, I couldn't wait 'til the next time.... But there was never any 'next time.' He just told me that he was real busy and we'd get together again soon enough. The days, they kept going by and he always seemed to be busy... and I started seeing my dream slipping away....." Dorothy' voice trailed off again and she stubbed out her cigarette without taking another drag on it. This time Madeline gave her a little breather. She could tell that Dorothy was getting closer to what was really hurting her.

"Lemme get you another drink," Madeline said in a soothing voice and she poured another stiff one for Dorothy and just a little more for herself. "That's quite some story you got there, honey... and I think we BOTH need to get fortified after that." They both had another taste... and after the burn in her throat eased Dorothy continued to tell her tale. "Yeah... yeah mama, it's one helluva story... but this one didn't have the kind of fairy tale ending I was hoping for. I figured we'd get back to New York and Louis might get hot for me again... and he would sorta work me into singing some songs with the band. But Louis and the guys had a bunch of other gigs planned... and they was bouncing in and out of The City for weeks.... Playing clubs in Jersey... and here in Philly... and then in Scranton... and all over the place.... And Louis couldn't take me along cause they usually traveled by bus and there wasn't enough room... and I think he didn't want to make a big deal outta the two of us being together... cause he WAS married... and we WAS seen together enough as it was... and those gossip reporters would just have a field day if they got wind about Louis and me. But I was praying that one time... just one time... he'd give me a try-out with the band... and I'd show 'em what they was missing." Dorothy stopped and took a deep drag on her cigarette before continuing, "But I.... I wasn't counting.... on getting pregnant."

"Pregnant... oh mercy, honey!" Madeline said, shaking her head in disbelief. "How'd that happen, honey? Didn't you use protection?" An exasperated Dorothy fired back, "OF COURSE we used protection... You don't think I'm dumb, do you? I'd never be doing it with a guy who didn't have protection.... That's why I could never... ever... figure out how it happened. Hell, I could be drunk as a skunk and I would always check to see every guy was wearing a rubber... That's why I got the heeby-jeebies when that time of the month came around and nothing happened.... It was just before Christmas... and I was praying for a Christmas "present", if you know what I mean... but it never came... Instead... I started getting up in the morning and puking... and it wasn't from what I drank the night before.... I went to a doctor who told me I was pregnant."

"Oh, Lordy... ," Madeline responded, "that musta come as a real shock... considering all that you went through. Did you tell Louis?" "I had to... what else could I do?" Dorothy went on. "But when I told him... I didn't wanna blow my chances with his band.... So I said to him that I knew the baby was his... even though we just had one incredible night in the sack... but I wasn't gonna make any stink... I wasn't gonna tell anyone... It was gonna be our secret... and nobody else's... And you know what?..... he was okay with that.... He didn't blow me off... he nodded a lot... and seemed like he cared about me... and he said that he would always be there for me after the baby was born... and not to ever forget what a terrific time we had together... and shit... he even said stuff like he was maybe gonna divorce his wife 'cause he and she didn't see eye to eye anyway... and maybe... ya know... maybe he and me could be an item... and he said he'd give me some money to get me through it."

"Sounds like a decent enough kinda guy," was the only response Madeline could muster. "Oh yeah... it seemed like that to me too," Dorothy told her. "except that he started traveling again... a lot... while I kept working at the Club... and we would only see each other once in a while... but he was always nice to me when we did meet... and he did give me some money to help out... but that kid.... That kid...." Dorothy choked up and couldn't speak. She took a deep breath... then a sip from her glass... and then another. Madeline reached across the table and took her hand again tenderly. "Yeah... it musta been tough on you," she said. "You was what?... only 20 when that happened?" "21," Dorothy corrected her, "21... and looking real fine.... Not like I look now.... And I was ready for anything.... But not THAT... And then I had to take off from work cause I was "showing"... and no one wanted to see some plump pregnant lady around the clubs... so I had to just stay at home... while I grew fat and ugly."

Madeline prodded Dorothy once again. "So you... did... have the baby?" she questioned uncomfortably. "Oh... yeah...," Dorothy answered while rolling her eyes. "I had the baby... a boy... at some hospital near the beach in Far Rockaway... that's near Brooklyn.... And I gave the baby up for adoption. But Louis could never come to see me... cause he was a big star... and he couldn't be seen with some pregnant woman... a married man with a pregnant woman?... nah.. he couldn't do that... the newspapers would ask too many questions.... But one of the guys in the band actually came to see me in the hospital and asked me to marry him... can you believe that?" Madeline was hanging on every word. "And.... And?" she questioned, "and did you do it?" Dorothy put her glass down on the table sharply. "I couldn't," she said with disgust. "I couldn't get married and stay at home with a kid.... Mama, I was just 21... I wanted more... I wanted so much more... I wanted to be a star... not a housewife... so... nah... I told him no..."

Madeline was too wrapped up in the story to let it end there so she had to ask, "Tell me, honey, what ever happened to the baby?" The ugly feelings Dorothy had been repressing for many years were now kicking in and she responded almost casually, "Oh, I made a few bucks by selling the kid to some family in Jersey… screw it…. I never saw that kid again… never wanted to… That kid killed any chance I had to make it in show business… he killed my dreams… he killed my future…. After I had that kid…. I…. I…. my life was never the same again…… never." She held her glass up as if she was toasting and said with a determined sense of finality, "And that's the end of the story." Dorothy knocked back the remains of her glass of Jack Daniels in one gaping mouthful. Tears welled up in her eyes as she swallowed and felt the burn once again. Then, she fell silent.

In the weeks that followed, Dorothy repeated the story to Madeline again and again. Each time she told it she felt more at peace with herself. She went to a hair salon and got a new "look," which did far more to complement her robust figure than the hairdo she had sported for years. She cleaned herself up and was feeling the need to drink less often. The makeover didn't go unnoticed by Madeline. Something in Dorothy just seemed to click and she had put a stop to her downward spiral. Maybe it was sharing her lifelong frustrations with someone who understood or merely recounting the story of her pregnancy and her baby. Whatever it was, Madeline sensed that the time was right.

"I want you to come with me tomorrow when I go visit Connie," Madeline said out of the blue as she and Dorothy were sipping their morning coffee. "It's only an hour or so to Atlantic City and Connie will show us around. Sounds good, doesn't it?" Dorothy hesitated for a moment then let out a sigh of resignation and said, "Okay… what the hell. What've I got to lose?" "That's the spirit, honey," Madeline encouraged her, "you got nothing to lose and you might actually like it."

The next morning Dorothy and Madeline got into the 1962 Buick that Angus kept around for out of town trips and headed to Atlantic City. The drive took them over the Delaware River into New Jersey… and then roughly east to Atlantic City on the Jersey shore. It was a pretty uneventful drive and Madeline was filled with the anticipation that Dorothy would be attracted to the beach, the boardwalk, and the salt sea air. The seaside resort town has fallen on hard times but there was talk the town was on the verge of a come-back and that it would soon be an "in spot," the kind of place Dorothy would want to call home.

Connie Henley was expecting them. She and Madeline had known each other for years, sparked by a friendship among their individual families that went back decades. Madeline had called Connie and told her all about Dorothy and her problems, except of course, about Dorothy's secret pregnancy and the baby's father. That deep, dark information, she felt, was best left unsaid in light of the intense emotional pain it had caused Dorothy. If anyone was going to tell Connie that story Madeline felt it had better be Dorothy herself.

Connie Henley had a heart of gold and would do anything to help family members and friends in need. But just like the McDonald family, Connie's family was also involved in questionable activities. She had several uncles and cousins who were numbers runners and her older sister did assorted "errands" for the local book-makers. Connie steered clear of those illegal entanglements, though. She was afraid that if she were ever arrested there would be no one to take care of her disabled brother and she was just too involved in his care to let that happen.

"Oh, Lordy, Lordy, it's so good to see you," Connie said as she threw her arms around Madeline's shoulders in a big hug. "It seems like forever, don't it?" Madeline beamed back at Connie as she took her hands and squeezed them lovingly. "It sure has, honey," she responded as she smiled warmly. "It's been way too long.... But lookee here. This is Dorothy. This is my STEP-daughter if you can believe that." The two black women had a chuckle as Connie turned to Dorothy. Dorothy held out her hand but Connie would have none of that. "Put those hands down, child," she said as if she was indeed talking to a child. "That's not how it's gonna be 'round here." Connie reached out and gave Dorothy a big hug. That gesture broke the ice and brought a big smile to Dorothy's face. She felt immediately at ease with this stranger she had just met.

"Come on in, girls," Connie said as she welcomed them into her modest apartment. "You must be parched from the drive. What can I fix you? ... Sit down, sit down." Connie headed to the kitchen and said matter-of-factly, "Sit down. Take a load off them tootsies." Madeline and Dorothy took their cue and settled into Connie's tattered couch that was covered with a colorful, red blanket. "Coffee sounds good," Madeline shouted to Connie who had already disappeared into the kitchen. "That is, if it isn't too much trouble." Connie shouted back, "No trouble at all. I got a fresh pot already brewed."

As Connie prepared coffee for three, Dorothy reached into her purse and pulled out a pack of Chesterfields. Madeline looked at Dorothy and whispered, "Well, what d'ya think? She's a real treasure, ain't she?" Dorothy was in the process of lighting her cigarette so she shook her head in agreement as she was inhaling. "You weren't kidding me about Connie," she said as she exhaled, "I don't think I ever met anyone like her. She's a real doll." "I'm glad you're taking a liking to her," Madeline said reassuringly. "She can be your best friend if you let her. She can really show you the ropes in this town... cause this is where she's been living for years now... and she's got a good job here too."

Connie came out of the kitchen with three coffee cups on a small tray along with a sugar bowl and a small pitcher of cream. "This is how we serve coffee when guests are around," she said with an impish grin as she put the tray down on the coffee table in front of the couch. "But don't be expecting this all the time." All three of them shared a chuckle at Connie's joke and then fixed their coffee to their own liking as they talked about Dorothy... her life in New York City for those many years... and the possibility that she might want to move to Atlantic City to find work.

"Child, you just ain't gonna believe what this town is about to become... and it's got everybody talking," Connie said proudly. "Nobody knows exactly what's coming... but if it's legal gambling like some folks is saying... it'll make for a lot of opportunities for the people who's here who wanna stay on the up and up. In fact, I gotta take you over to the boardwalk to see what the fuss is all about.... Yup... you gonna like it here, I'm sure of that." Dorothy took another drag on her cigarette and seemed to relax even more. "What's gonna be different than what it always was?" she asked pointedly. "I mean... I remember comin' here as a kid... and the salt water taffy... and the cotton candy... and the arcades along the boardwalk. And it was a lot of fun... but is legal gambling gonna make that much of a difference?" "Why don't we all finish our coffee...and you come with me and we'll go take a look?" Connie beckoned. Dorothy was curious. "Okay, you got my interest," Dorothy responded. So, the three ladies jumped into Angus's car for the short ride to the boardwalk.

The Atlantic City of the early 1970's was a rundown empty shell of its former glory but the boardwalk was still a draw as well as the beach and ocean breeze. Several former first-class hotels still stood tall up and down the beach but they were near-vacant testaments to their days of glory. Tourists still roamed the boardwalk and shops along the wooden walkway still sold souvenirs but this was clearly a city in need of help. The old-timers who frequented the remaining shops, restaurants and bars all chatted about the rumors of legal gambling and how that could be the magical potion that could revitalize the city. It could be even better than Las Vegas many of them believed, because Las Vegas didn't have the ocean as a backdrop. "This here is gonna be swinging again... mark my words, child... swinging again," Connie said like a proud mother talking about the future of her baby. "It's looking downright nasty-looking right now... but... it's gonna get a lot better."

Dorothy, Madeline and Connie strolled the boardwalk and Connie continued to "sell" the city to Dorothy and even promised to help her find a job. "All you gotta do is come to live here, child. The rents is cheap and the people... real nice. It's gotta be your move. You gotta make up your mind and just go for it," Connie proclaimed. "And I'll do what I can... whatever I can... to help you get started. I can probably get you into my place... there it is down there... The Haddon Hall Hotel. I work in the restaurant there. They know me real good. And anything I can do for a friend, I am happy to do it." Dorothy was genuinely impressed by Connie's offer and told her how grateful she was.

In the late afternoon, Madeline and Dorothy left Atlantic City and Connie behind but Dorothy promised to keep in touch and told Connie she would make a decision about moving there in the coming weeks.

That decision, though, didn't take much time at all. It was made for her. Because when they got back to Philadelphia they found that Angus had packed Dorothy's bags and left them on the front stoop. "What's you doing, Angus?" Madeline questioned as she opened the front door and dragged the two bags back inside. But Angus wasn't about to answer any questions. He was the one asking them. "Where did you go today... you and this daughter of mine?" he began grilling them. He didn't wait for an answer. He pointed his finger as if warning them not to dare answer as he circled Dorothy, looking her up and down in disgust. "And you... how long do you think you're gonna stay here and mooch off me like I was some rich guy?" he questioned derisively.

Neither Madeline nor Dorothy knew exactly what had set Angus off, but whether it was warranted or not, he unleashed a tirade against his daughter that had apparently been stewing inside for years: "You think you are such hot stuff. You think you're better than me 'cause you don't have to go out and work to support yourself. You always acted like you was better than your mother and me. You was such a big shot New Yorker that you couldn't even come home to see your mother being put into a hole in the ground.... No, not you! You had your own life.... And now... now you think you can mooch offa me... Well Dorothy... or Dolly... or whatever your name is... the free ride is over... you just take your stuff... and you find someone else to live off of... cause you ain't gonna be living off me anymore." Then, having unleashed his pent-up anger, Angus stormed up the stairs toward his bedroom. But just before he reached the top step he turned and fired off one last salvo, "I'm gonna take a little rest... and when I come outta my bedroom... I want you gone... gone... got it?" He then made a beeline for his bedroom and slammed the door without waiting for an answer.

Dorothy stood there, stunned and wounded by her father's hostility. She had just returned from a day-long outing with Madeline and was finally having some positive feelings about her future only to be blindsided by her father's bile.

Madeline broke the ice. "Maybe it was a real good thing that we went to Atlantic City today. Maybe that's the best place for you to end up... right now." Dorothy's mind was still in a pandemonium of panic as her thoughts darted from one idea to another but those thoughts seem to crystallize with Madeline's suggestion. "Yeah, sometimes things kinda work out that way," she said. "But that ain't gonna do me no good right now. My bags are sitting right inside the front door. What am I gonna do now? Where am I gonna stay tonight?"

"You're gonna stay with Connie Henley... that's what you're gonna do," Madeline responded as she got up and walked over to the phone table in the corner of the room. She picked up the phone book from the bottom shelf and started leafing through it. "Are you okay with that... if I can get you on a bus tonight?" She kept flipping, looking for a listing for "Greyhound." Dorothy nodded her head, amazed at how quickly Madeline had come up with a solution. "Sure... sure...," she mumbled, "but what about Connie? What's she gonna say about all this?" Madeline found the number for the bus company and dialed as she responded, "Connie? I'll call Connie next… but I'm sure it's not gonna be a problem with Connie. We just gotta get you on a bus before Angus gets up from his nap… cause I dunno what he's gonna do next."

Dorothy was in luck. A bus was leaving at 9:15 bound for Atlantic City. It would arrive there shortly after 11PM. They had about an hour and a half leeway. The next step was to call Connie and hope that she would agree to put Dorothy up for the night. "Hi Connie… This is Madeline… I'll bet you never expected to hear from me so soon?" Madeline said sweetly into the phone. "But we got a problem, honey… and we got a favor to ask."

CHAPTER EIGHTEEN

The Good, The Bad and The Unreliable

I didn't have to wait long for Lou LoScialpo to get back to me. He called me just one day after our first meeting in his office to tell me he had listened to the tape of Rocco's first phone call. It apparently lit a fire under him. He said he would go to the Brooklyn Board of Elections the next day and then to 343 Vernon Avenue where Rocco had lived. He would try to get voting records for Rocco but his main goal was to find someone who still lived on Vernon Avenue who might know Rocco, someone who might fill in the blanks. He wasn't optimistic given the picture I painted of Vernon Avenue, but he still felt he might find someone down the street or around the corner, someone who he could pump for information. As the months passed, I learned that this was Lou's gift... talking to people, catching them off-guard, and then prying information out of them. Whether on the phone or face to face, Lou could put on a very unassuming manner and people would respond. They might not even realize that they were divulging valuable information. They just warmed up to the guy and would let their guard down.

Now that Lou was committed and actively pursuing leads, I went back and laid out my xerox copies of pages from the New York City phone books that contained the names: Welch, Welsh and Welsch. I then called my Aunt Miriam once again hoping to jog her memory and learn the first names of the "Welch girls" who lived with their mother, Margaret Welch. I ran down the names from the phone books, reciting every name and asked Miriam if any of them sounded familiar. She apologized that she didn't recognize any of them. But she had some good news. She had gotten more information from her mother. Her mother told her that my birth mother had married a very wealthy man and had three children. That meant I had brothers or sisters! And that might explain those comments from people I worked with in Summer Stock who claimed they'd seen someone who looked like me or reminded them of me. It was hard to fathom but certainly not out of the question that a blood brother would have similar interests in the Theatre. We might be traveling in the same "circles" and might even have met without knowing our genetic connection. The possibilities were staggering for an "only-child" searching for his biological roots.

I quizzed my aunt over and over again to find out how her mother knew all this information about my birth mother. But Miriam didn't know her mother's source. She told me she didn't want to press her mother too much, fearing that her mother would become suspicious. She said she kept their conversation more like idle gossip so her mother didn't begin to question why Miriam wanted to know so much. But in the course of their conversation, Ruth also told Miriam that the Welch's were Jewish and that my birth mother was Italian!! That's when I became suspicious. My birth mother was Italian? "Dorothy McDonald" was Italian? That seemed incredulous to me... but Miriam was certain that's what her mother told her.

Lou, meanwhile, had gotten Rocco and Rose Ferrucci's voting records from 1944 but they didn't reveal any new information. They did confirm that the Ferruccis lived at 343 Vernon Avenue but even Lou was dumbfounded when he went to that neighborhood. "I think it's even more of a dump than you told me, Alan," he said with a solemn little chuckle. "I thought you had to be exaggerating when you described the place. But now, I'll know to take your word in the future. What a wasted trip!" Lou wanted more time to listen to all of the tapes of the Ferrucci phone calls, so we said we'd talk again soon.

Several days later, I got a surprise phone call from the sleuth at Origins. I had written him off because I hadn't heard from him in months and I had moved on and begun working with Lou. Apparently, he was still on my case and was trying some interesting ideas of his own. He had one of his operatives call Rocco Ferrucci using the name "Angela." Angela told Rocco she had gotten a letter from me and that she remembered Rocco and Rose from Far Rockaway and that she looked them up in the phone book. Angela apparently made them feel like they were renewing an old friendship and he told her why he broke off contact with me: He feared that "I" thought he was my birth father and so he didn't want to get more deeply involved. He went on to tell her he and his wife lived in Far Rockaway a few doors down from "the Romanian lady." They said they learned that Dorothy had sold me to my parents for 2000-dollars but said they would have paid more for me.

As I held the phone I was gripped by the pain of the truth: I HAD been bought and sold!! And I now knew my "sticker price." It was no longer just a suspicion based on the way my father had made me feel. It was now confirmed. I was merchandise sold to the highest bidder.

"Angela" also found out from Rocco that his brother-in-law had been a musician. His name was Joe Grant. Then, this so-called "super sleuth" put an end to our association. He admitted to me that he had done just about as much as he could. "It's going to take a lot of time... which unfortunately I don't have... to get somebody to get really hands-on with your Search, Alan," he told me flatly, "and even then, I don't see a lot of hope. I don't want to bum you out. But I have never seen a case as complicated as yours. I got a feeling there's a lot more going on here and I wish you a lot of luck." That brush-off left me downhearted but certainly not desolate. After all, I had Lou working for me now and Lou gave me all the confidence I needed.

My next step was an easy one, so easy that I was surprised that my former "super sleuth" didn't look into it. I checked the 1980 Directory for Musician's Local 802. It listed Joseph Grantonio (Joe Grant), 212 Chestnut Drive, Kings Park, N.Y. Could Joe Grant be Rocco's connection to the music business? Maybe Joe Grant was Rocco's source. I even considered that Joe Grant might be my birth father. I called Lou immediately to share the information. We were both convinced that this was a connection that was too close to home to overlook. Lou said he would make plans to visit Joe Grant as soon as he could.

The phone rang at 10:15 on a Wednesday night. I had gotten into the habit of having my tape recorder hooked up to the phone and hitting the "record" button before I picked up, and that's what I did this time too. A "Mrs. Welch" from Queens was on the line. She had received one of my letters. "I have an aunt, a Margaret Welch, who was a baker," she said, "and she lived in... no not all the time, but in the summers, she lived in a bungalow in Rockaway... ah... Far Rockaway." This is more than just coincidence, I thought, as I tried to formulate a line of questioning.

"Was she Hungarian?" I asked.

"I don't know. I don't think so. But she had two daughters and I know they moved to Los Angeles."

"My aunt told me recently that she had passed away and that her daughters were alive and married."

"How old do you think they are?"

"Oh... let's see... maybe around 60."

"You're a cousin or a nephew?"

"No, I'm a cousin of a Miriam Katof who was friends with the daughters. And I am trying to reach my Aunt Miriam and hope that the Welch girls will know where she is."

"Why did you send a letter to me in Long Island?"

"I sent out many letters to many Welch families. I was told that one daughter stayed in Los Angeles and the other moved back to Long Island."

"Are you a lawyer... or a detective?"

"No. I am just someone who is looking for the Welch family and hoping... to find... my Aunt Miriam."

"I don't think it's the same... or the same family. Did you ever think of hiring a professional... a private investigator to help you?"

"I did. But I still don't know the first names of the two girls."

Then there was a pause and I sensed this "Mrs. Welch" was trying to back away. As she did, I became more nervous, more impassioned, more panicked to keep her on the line. So, I tried to level with her:

"Look... I'm adopted. I am trying to find my birth mother. And the only way I can do that is to find the Welch girls who would have known her. I just need to reach them for information. Will you please help me?" "Sometimes it's maybe not so good to know. Maybe it could be a bad thing to know," the voice on the phone cautioned. "I'm trying to be tactful," I told her. "I am trying so hard not to hurt anyone. You can see that I am trying so hard not to come barging back into someone's life. But it's just so coincidental that your aunt, Margaret Welch, was a baker with two daughters....." "And two sons," she added.

"Oh... I didn't... I don't know anything about sons..."I admitted curiously. "But... maybe... is there anyone else in your family that you could talk to... somebody who might have more information?" "Actually,

I have another aunt who might know. But she is ill and I can't talk to her for another couple of days. But I will. And I wish you luck."

"Will you call me back?" I asked. She seemed sincere when she told me, "If I find out anything new, Alan, I will call you back... I promise you." Then I pressed a little harder by asking, "Will you tell me who you are?" "I'm a little leery...," she responded. "Maybe it's not the same family. So I don't want to get involved with someone else. But I'll call you if I hear of anything."

I found myself pleading... begging her not to leave me hanging: "It's not the Welch girls who are involved... it's... it's... that they knew my birth mother... and maybe... they still know where to find her. I'm not trying to upset anyone. I... you see... I have... been trying to be tactful... careful about what I say." "I understand, Alan. I will do my best. I will try... And if I have any information at all I promise I will call you back."

Then she hung up, leaving my mind racing and my fists clenched in frustration as I reviewed our conversation. The more I thought about what she said the more I grew convinced that she was the connection who could lead me to the Welch sisters. But would she call back? And how long will it be until she calls back? (Whoever she was, she never called back.)

I took the tape of our conversation to Lou the very next day. We sat and listened to it and determined the name sounded like "Welch" not "Welsh," and that the woman who had called me was from Nassau County, not Queens County because she had asked me, "Why did you send a letter to me in Long Island?" Lou would start calling all the "Welch's" in Nassau County and, if he were successful, he would use his charm to try to get more information out of her. At the very least, he hoped to be able to determine whether she did have a connection to a baker named Margaret Welch. Lou also planned to visit Jewish cemeteries on Long Island to see if he could find a gravesite for a Margaret Welch. He would also go and talk to Rocco Ferrucci himself.

The day after Lou's visit with Rocco, I met with Lou at his office. We talked for more than two and a half hours. "Rocco is a pit bull," Lou said pointedly, "despite whatever health problems he has, he is one tough cookie." Lou said Rocco was evasive and even-tempered but said Rocco over-reacted when he brought up Joe Grant's name. "You leave the soul of my dead brother-in-law alone," Rocco threatened, "You and Alan... I'll break your knuckles if you go after my family." Lou and I agreed that maybe he had hit a nerve there. Maybe there was something that connects my birth to Joe Grant... to the "late" Joe Grant. Maybe Joe knew something that Rocco didn't want me to know. Maybe Joe Grant WAS my birth father and Rocco was trying to protect the family. Given Rocco's reaction it seemed reasonable that any of those options were possibilities.

Lou told me that one of Rocco's brothers was there for much of the conversation and when Rocco left the room briefly, he told Lou that he thought Rocco over-reacted to the mention of Joe Grant and he didn't understand Rocco's motivation. Lou and I tossed around possible scenarios for some time but could only guess at why Joe Grant's name hit such a raw nerve. And there was more bad news. Lou checked a number of cemeteries and couldn't find the death and burial of any Margaret Welch.

The confusion mounted with another phone call from my cousin Alan. He had called our cousin Muriel in California to follow up on the phone call his mother had with her. Muriel was worried about the health of our boys and said she wanted to help me find my birth parents because their medical information could help my children. But she was very close to my mother, so understandably, she wanted to protect her from any knowledge of the search that was underway. She told Alan that, years before, she heard that Dorothy was married to a soldier overseas and that my father was a drummer in a band. She thought the two Welch girls were "show girls" and she seemed positive that Mrs. Welch had died. How, I wondered, would she know that? I considered calling Muriel myself and involving her in my Search. But even though we shared a warm relationship, I was hesitant to involve any other family members in the secret quest I was trying so hard to keep from my mother.

It was now New Year's Eve, December 31, 1984. Lou ignored Rocco's threats and drove to the Long Island home of Mrs. Joe Grantonio, Rocco's brother-in-law. But first, Lou stopped in Rocco's neighborhood and caught up with the local postman. Rose had given December 31, 1922 as her birth date on the hospital records. That was New Year's Eve. Lou had a scheme to determine if Rose was indeed born on New Year's eve in 1922, which might indicate that she was my birth mother even though Rocco might not be my birth father. "Hey, I'm Rose Ferrucci's cousin. And boy am I in the family dog house," Lou said charmingly to the postman. "I forgot if her birthday is today or next Monday. Boy, what a dummy." The postman seemed perplexed until Lou added, "Can you see if you have any birthday cards for her today? That way I'll know whether I'd better run to the bakery right now and get her a cake." The postman fell for Lou's sincere-sounding ploy and eagerly checked his bag. There were no birthday cards for Rose Ferrucci on this New Year's Eve. "Hey, I am so relieved now," Lou told the postman. "I didn't blow it with my cousin. But I'd better get busy and get her a present for her birthday next week. Thanks a lot for helping a guy out." As he walked away Lou was even more convinced now that the Ferrucci's were who they said they were. They told a legitimate story. And neither one was my birth parent.

That matter settled, Lou continued his trip to Mrs. Grantonio's house. Lorraine Grantonio was a warm, caring person and she was eager to help. She said that Rocco was very pig-headed and stubborn and that he wouldn't co-operate at all. In fact, she said, she didn't ever remember Rocco being this obstinate about anything before. Lorraine proved to be just the opposite. She provided a picture of her late husband which bore absolutely no resemblance to me. And she willingly signed a release for his medical records. Lou took the signed release to the local hospital where Joe died but the hospital would only release Joe Grant's blood type to an attorney representing the family. Lou wasn't deterred. He spoke with an attorney friend of his who wrote a letter requesting medical information including Joe Grant's blood type. We didn't know it, but we would wait many months for a reply.

While Lou focused on Rocco and his sister-in-law, Lorraine Grantonio, I remained determined to solve the puzzle of my apparent patronage of Mrs. Welch's restaurant when I lived in Los Angeles 14 years earlier. I would play out various scenarios in my mind as I took virtual trips around the neighborhood near CBS Television City where I had worked hoping to visualize it. I even tried self-hypnosis relaxation techniques, hoping for a glimmer of recognition. Yet I remained stumped. "If I ate there so many times why can't I remember that restaurant?" I asked myself over and over again. "Why can't I recreate a picture of it in my mind?" It was that thought of a picture... a photograph... that triggered the idea that a visual reference might help. So I called my friend Yanco, who lives in Los Angeles in the same general neighborhood. I asked him to take pictures of all the streets near Television City and to particularly to focus on restaurants in the area. "Take as many shots as you want," I told him, "this is important stuff and I'm not worried about the cost."

Several days later, three rolls of film arrived. I rushed them to the local One-Hour Photo Lab, got them back, and began to study them intently. My expectations quickly turned to disappointment, though, when I couldn't recall going into ANY of the restaurants in the pictures. Nothing looked familiar no matter how long I stared at the street scenes, nor how much I tried to envision myself walking into one of the storefronts.

It was time to regroup. Lou's visit to Rocco convinced him that despite Rocco's early enthusiasm, Rocco had dried up as a source of assistance. Lorraine Grantonio wasn't able to provide any more information, and even though we didn't yet have her husband's blood type we no longer truly suspected that he was my birth father. So it was back to Margaret Welch. Lou and I both felt strongly about the need to find the "Hungarian baker and her two showgirl daughters." Lou made it very clear. "Alan, we gotta go to Los Angeles," he said in his no-nonsense manner. "Margaret Welch and her daughters moved to California. We've heard that. We accept that. The trail has led us to California, and that's where we have to go." It was a big step and not one that I embraced readily. "What will we do once we get there," I asked somewhat incredulously. "We'll cross that bridge when we come to it," Lou said, looking me straight in the eyes. "You don't have to pay me for it either, Alan. Just pay my air fare and expenses. I won't charge you for my time. I am THAT certain that we have to do this."

It was a huge crap-shoot but I got up at 5AM on Wednesday, February 6, 1985 to head to L.A. I gave Ronni a long hug and said goodbye to our three-year-old twins… then drove the 45 minutes to Newark International Airport, where I met up with Lou. We hopped on American Airlines flight #46 non-stop to L.A. It arrived at 10:45AM Pacific Standard Time. My friend Yanco met us at the airport and drove us to our motel on Fairfax Avenue near Television City, where we checked in and dropped off our bags in the room. We then embarked on a slow drive, criss-crossing the neighborhood near Television City, looking for a Hungarian restaurant or in fact any restaurant that I would have gone to with my Aunt Fritzi. Yanco had photographed it all for me but we thought a first-hand look might jog my memory. Still, nothing clicked. We parked in the Farmer's Market parking lot next door to CBS Television City. Lou talked to merchants and even went into a bakery to ask if anyone knew of a Margaret Welch from New York, a Hungarian woman who was a baker. Nothing.

Yanco offered us his car and said that we could use it as long as was necessary. So we dropped him off at his apartment and headed to the Chamber of Commerce and the Board of Health. Again, we found no listing anywhere for a Margaret Welch. The next day, we drove to the Los Angeles Hall of Records where we looked at Death Records (for Margaret Welch) and Marriage Records (for her two daughters who might have been married there.) But once again we came up empty-handed.

After four hours of painstakingly checking every public record available to us, my frustration morphed into the realization that this cross-country "shot in the dark" was likely to end as a bleak exercise in futility. Lou and I looked at each other bleary-eyed. "Well, what do we do now, partner?" I asked Lou numbly. "I... I just don't know, Alan," Lou responded sheepishly, "but we gotta figure something out. This Margaret Welch and her daughters didn't just disappear. We know Margaret was here when you were working here. There's gotta be some lead somewhere." Lou and I walked out of the Hall of Records in silence and back to Yanco's car parked in a metered space on the street, each of us thrashing around ideas in our minds.

I couldn't bear the thought of returning home without any answers so I considered turning to my family once again and taking a chance that my secret Search would remain safe from my mother. It had been emotionally difficult for me to even reach out to my cousin Alan and his mother, Miriam. The thought of discussing my adoption with close relatives who were in frequent contact with my mother had been distressing enough. But if I could again summon the courage to overcome my crippling fear of rejection I could face one more option. It was my final option: my cousin Muriel. She had been initially reluctant to discuss my adoption with my cousin Alan, which made the thought of facing her even more difficult.

But my course of action became clear when I weighed Muriel's possible negative reaction against the definite crushing defeat of leaving Los Angeles the next day empty-handed. "We can try one more thing," I said to Lou stoically. "Maybe I can talk to my cousin Muriel." Lou quickly picked up his cue. "We got nothing to lose... and we need somebody to cut us a break," he said convincingly. "Maybe your cousin knows more than she's been willing to let on... but maybe she'll let loose if you talk to her face to face. Besides, we got nothing else to go on, Alan." I pulled out my address book and called Muriel. Her daughter, Susie, answered and told me her mother would be home after 4 o'clock. I told Susie that I would call back later.

We drove to Manhattan Beach and walked down to the sand, all the time fidgeting as we waited until 4 o'clock. We found a pay phone and called. No answer. We tried again at 4:30. Again, no answer. And once again at 5. But at 5:30, Muriel's husband, Bill, finally answered the phone. "Hi, Bill," I said as matter-of-factly as I could under the circumstances, "I'm here in the neighborhood with my friend Lou and we would love to stop in and see you and Muriel." "Well, this is a surprise," Bill responded, "I didn't expect... I didn't even know you were in California. But... hey, come on over... why not about 6:30. Maybe Muriel will be home by then."

Lou and I drove around for about an hour and then took Bill up on his offer. Muriel still wasn't home yet so the three of us sat at the kitchen table and made small talk. Just a few minutes passed before Muriel finally arrived. She was surprised, of course, to see me and another guy... but we hugged and I introduced her to Lou. "I'm sorry I didn't call earlier," I told her. "My friend Lou here is helping me try to find a lady named Margaret Welch.... I, uh... well someone told me that Margaret Welch was a Hungarian baker and she lived in Far Rockaway.... And... uh... she knew something about my adoption."

The room got very silent as Muriel became visibly upset. There was no stopping now but I could see that I needed to reassure Muriel about my motive. "This has nothing to do with my mother," I told her. "It doesn't change anything about how I feel about her. That could never change. It's my kids I worry about and I want their doctors to have all the help I can give them by finding out if there's anything in their medical background they need to know about." It wasn't the complete explanation for my Search but what I told her was true. Muriel had even told my cousin Alan of her concern about my boys. "I really need to get a medical history for the doctors and my mother cannot bring herself to talk about this," I said in a voice laden with emotion, "I don't know where else to turn."

Lou sat back and let me do the talking. Occasionally, he would throw in a reinforcing comment but he knew that it was up to me to get through to Muriel. At first, Muriel denied knowing much, but my pleading softened her heart and she gradually revealed that the Welch girls, the "showgirls" as she called them, lived on Morris Avenue or Walton Avenue in the Bronx in the same neighborhood where several of my relatives also lived. She went to a closet to pull out some old scrapbooks and found her mother, Fritzi's, phone book. Her mother had died years before but Muriel kept many mementos to keep her memory alive. The phone book had entries in red ink. We began to leaf through the worn pages at the hand-written names and phone numbers from so long ago. When we got to "G", we even found MY old address on Havenhurst Drive from the time I had spent in L.A. almost 15 years earlier. We continued to turn page after page until we came to an entry that read: WELCH... 829 NFF... 653-0020.

My mouth dropped open! I could feel my throat constrict and my chest throb with excitement!! It was just a brief entry in this small book, but to me, it spoke volumes. "NFF" could only be "North Fairfax Avenue," a neighborhood near CBS Television City. I also recognized the "653" exchange as the same exchange that my Aunt Fritzi had when she lived just one block from North Fairfax Avenue so many years ago. It all added up. There was no doubt that we had finally found Margaret Welch.

"This is absolutely amazing, Muriel," I said to her as I tried to maintain control. "This must be the woman Lou and I have been looking for. You have no idea how much you have helped." Muriel had a puzzled look on her face. "But this book must be 15 years old... okay, maybe it's 10 years...

who knows?" she said incredulously, "So how do you know Margaret Welch is still living there? She could have moved years ago." I told her that we obviously didn't know for certain but we would check out the address. Then I added warmly, "I feel that you have helped us get on the right track again, Muriel... and I can't thank you enough for helping me. I want you to know again that I am never saying anything to my mother about this... but you have really done a Mitzvah here for my boys. You never know... if they will need the medical information I hope to find for them." Muriel and I hugged and I told her that I wouldn't trouble her anymore.

It was dark as Lou and I drove back to our motel and too late to effectively check out the address on North Fairfax. But given this solid lead on Margaret Welch we decided we had to stay one more day. I called Ronni to tell her how we had gone from hopelessness to a sense of optimism and told her that we planned to extend our trip. As always, she was supportive and encouraging. She told me she missed me but she understood why Lou and I needed to stay on. I also called the airline to cancel our flight the next day and rebook it for one day later. Muriel's information had bought us another 24 hours but no more. Given the fact that I wasn't paying Lou for his efforts here in the City of the Angels, I was keenly aware that we were running out of time.

The next morning, Lou and I rose early and had breakfast at Cantor's, the famous Jewish Deli on Fairfax Avenue only about a block from where my Aunt Fritzi used to live. We left the restaurant at precisely 9 AM and drove about a dozen blocks to the address in my Aunt Fritzi's phone book: 829 North Fairfax. It was a 2-story garden apartment building with about 20 units. We found a door out front marked "Office" and went inside. We told the manager that we were looking for a Mrs. Welch who we believe had lived in the building about 15 years ago. We made that assumption on the time-frame based on the fact that Fritzi had MY old address in her book and figured that Mrs. Welch's number would have been placed in her book somewhere about the same time. The manager said he was new to the area and had just gotten the job a few months earlier. He was also curious about why we wanted to locate this Mrs. Welch. Lou went for the straightforward approach and told him, "Look... we are trying to find Alan's mother and we know that years ago Mrs. Welch knew her well... so we were trying to reach Mrs. Welch... So, we need a break here... Hell, we flew here all the way from New Jersey to try to find her. Won't you please help us?"

Lou's approach obviously hit a nerve because the manager not only agreed to help us he went to a filing cabinet and pulled out several rent receipt books from years before. We began looking through the books for a reference to Margaret Welch, which proved to be a tedious chore. All the entries were listed in longhand and a very sloppy longhand at that. There was no master list so we had to go page by page. Lou was losing his patience and getting antsy and the next thing I knew, he just disappeared... even as the manager and I continued the task before us. Some 20 minutes passed and still there was no reference to Margaret Welch as having been a tenant. While the manager pulled out another rent receipt book I walked outside to see where Lou was and what he was doing.

As I stepped into the daylight, Lou was just emerging through the shrubs from the building behind 829 North Fairfax. He had a big smile on his face. The manager followed me out of the office but before either of us could speak, Lou told him, "Thank you for all your help. You have really been wonderful trying to help us out. But I think I found some information that will lead us to Mrs. Welch. You've been a great help." With that, Lou said his goodbyes to the now-bewildered manager and ushered me back out to the street.

Lou could hardly contain himself as we walked. When we were out of the manager's earshot, Lou blurted out, "I found Margaret Welch's daughter. No shit... and I found her because I never saw a lemon tree before." Okay, he certainly had my attention at this point. Lou explained that he began walking back behind the office toward the apartments when he noticed a tree that was different from any he had ever seen before. He approached an older gentleman who was sitting nearby and struck up a conversation… only to learn that the tree was a lemon tree. "I'm from New Jersey," Lou told the man, "and I never saw anything like that before…. A lemon tree…? That's really pretty amazing." Lou was genuinely curious about this new sight but he also used the opportunity to ask about Margaret Welch. The man told Lou that he remembered Margaret but said that his neighbor, Malvina Tannenbaum knew even more because Malvina and Margaret were friends. Lou knocked on Mrs. Tannenbaum's door to find a woman with a remarkable memory. She not only remembered Margaret Welch but that her daughter had married an optometrist, HER optometrist, Doctor Irving Yasney. She even had his phone number. This was classic Lou LoScialpo!

Maybe Margaret Welch had died as my Aunt Ruth said, but Lou had found her daughter anyway. We spotted a pay phone nearby and Lou reached into his pocket for change, put a quarter into the phone, and dialed. The phone rang a few times and Lou questioned, "Hello, is Doctor Yasney available?" The receptionist told Lou that the doctor was off that day and wouldn't be back in until tomorrow. Once again, Lou would not be dissuaded. "It's very important that I talk to him… actually to his wife. Is there any way you can reach him?" Lou said in his most heartfelt voice. "We have come from New Jersey and it is so very important that we reach Mrs. Yasney. I'm with a young man who is looking for his mother and I know Mrs. Yasney can help us find her. But we have to return to New Jersey tomorrow and we can't wait. Won't you please help us?"

Lou's magic worked. The receptionist told Lou that she would call Dr. Yasney at home and have him call us. Lou indicated he was at a pay phone and he rattled off the number. "Thank you so much for what you're doing," Lou said, piling on even more gratitude. "You have been incredibly helpful."

Then we waited. We were standing on a wide stretch of sidewalk on busy Fairfax Avenue at about 10 o'clock in the morning. The sky was as blue as it could be through the Los Angeles smog and the sun was shining brightly. Cars whizzed by and we waited as the minutes passed. We felt helpless, knowing our fate was in the hands of Dr. Yasney's receptionist. I paced back and forth and Lou did too but he didn't saunter far from the pay phone. He wanted to be certain that no one else would use it. Time seemed to pass at a snail's pace but in reality, our wait was over in a little more than 5 minutes. The phone rang.

Lou answered it in a heartbeat! It was Dr. Irving Yasney... and he had a lot of questions for Lou. One by one, Lou fielded them and reassured the doctor that we were legitimate. Dr. Yasney then handed the phone to his wife, Frances. Lou was on his game. "Mrs. Yasney, my name is Lou LoScialpo. I'm a private detective from New Jersey and I am here with a young man who is looking for his birth mother and I think you can help us." Then without seeming to take a breath he went on, "He was born in Far Rockaway and we were told that your mother was friends with his adoptive mother's relatives from the Bronx. They were all Hungarian and I am told that your mother was Hungarian too."

Frances Yasney was overwhelmed!! It had been so many years, she told Lou... and yes, her mother had been involved in the adoption of a baby boy. She confirmed to Lou that her mother was the Margaret Welch we had been looking for. "It's so puzzling to us," said Lou, "that we were never able to locate any records for her and that's why we had to fly here from New Jersey because we had been told your mother moved to L.A." Frances asked how we spelled the family named. Lou told her that we had checked "W-e-l-c-h", "W-e-l-s-h", and even "W-e-l-s-c-h." "But you didn't think to check "Weltsch", did you?" Frances asked. "That's my maiden name. Frances Weltsch... W-E-L-T-S-C-H." Lou looked at me and spelled out... "W-E-L-T-S-C-H...." while he admitted sheepishly into the phone that we hadn't even considered another spelling, particularly not the one that Frances rattled off. I could only kick myself for all the time I had wasted writing letters.

"We need to talk to you face-to-face," said Lou urgently. "We came all the way from New Jersey. Won't you please help us now that we found you? It would mean the world to Alan to meet you and to ask you some questions about his past." It didn't take much convincing for Frances to agree. She said she would call us in about a half-hour to set up a meeting place. We gave her the phone number at our motel and headed back there to wait. It was 10:15. It had taken us one hour and fifteen minutes to find Frances Yasney from the time we arrived at the address on North Fairfax Avenue!

A half-hour later, as promised, Frances Yasney phoned our motel room. She agreed to meet us at noon in the lobby of the new Sheraton Premiere Hotel right next to the Sheraton Universal hotel at Universal City. Her husband would be with her.

Lou and I arrived about 15 minutes early so we sat in the lobby and waited nervously. The minutes ticked away as we checked our watches and wondered if they would show up. We really had no way to contact them except through that office phone number. At 12:15, I decided to walk over to the nearby Sheraton Universal hotel, thinking that maybe there had been a mix-up in our meeting place. When I didn't find anyone there I walked back and rejoined Lou at the Sheraton Premiere hotel as he was heading to a bank of pay phones to call the doctor's office again. It was almost 12:30.

Just then, a man and a woman approached us and said, "I think you may be looking for us." Lou smiled that warm smile of his and responded, "If you are Doctor and Mrs. Yasney, then you are indeed the ones we're looking for." Doctor Yasney was a fit, good-looking man in his 60's with curly salt and pepper hair. His wife was a petite, very attractive woman with short pixie-ish hair and a twinkle in her eyes. "Thank you for agreeing to meet us here, "Lou said sincerely. "I'm Lou Loscialpo. I spoke to you on the phone. And this is Alan Gerstel." We sized each other up cautiously with Dr. Yasney and Lou being the first to shake hands. When Frances reached out to take my hand I could feel her radiance and was aware that she was "kvelling" (a Yiddish word that means "gushing" or being "extraordinarily proud.") As she held my hand in hers she straightened her back and stood just a little taller while she glowed with satisfaction. Lou suggested we go to the coffee shop in the lobby and sit down over a cup of coffee. But Frances chimed in, "I don't need coffee! I need a drink!" That comment broke the ice and we all crossed the lobby to the lounge in agreement... We ALL needed that drink! We also needed privacy, so we sat at a table for four across the room from everyone else.

As we waited for our drinks to arrive I talked about how I had spent time in Los Angeles years before, working at Television City and we chatted about the Los Angeles smog and how it never seems to change. Then, with our drinks in front of us and the waitress gone, I began my story. I told Frances about being born at St. Joseph's Hospital in Far Rockaway in the summer of 1944 and being adopted by my parents in New Jersey. I told her that my relatives, who also summered in Far Rockaway, had told me about a Margaret Welch and her two daughters. They said my birth mother stayed with Margaret Welch in a bungalow at 170 Beach 78th Street.

"After all these years," Frances said nostalgically, "after all these years to see you back in my life again. You don't have to tell me anymore about your birth or your adoption, Alan. I know it all. I was there." Frances was excited and eager to share. "Your birth mother and I were next door neighbors back in the 1940's. We were very close. We worked in the clubs on 52nd Street as hat check girls or cigarette girls or ushers and we were just teenagers. No one bothered to check our ages back then." She seemed so matter-of-fact about what she was sharing with me... while I hung on every word, becoming enchanted by her revelations. She knew my birth mother! They were next-door neighbors! I wanted to ask so much more about my birth mother but I also had a burning desire to know the identity of my birth father... and I was afraid that Frances' enthusiasm might wane.

"I have to also ask you about my birth father," I blurted out almost breathlessly, "I have no idea who he is... uh... uh... there are no records..." I was stammering and growing anxious about asking the question. I had so much riding on her answer yet I harbored an inner fear that she might not tell me. My timidity, though, was overcome by a groundswell of emotion that erupted inside of me and I asked very pointedly, "Do you know who my birth father is?" Almost immediately, Frances answered "Yes"... but in a mysterious, almost awkward way. I tried to divine what her answer meant. Was she toying with me? Was she not going to tell me? Did she even know for certain? I took another breath and asked even more directly, "Would you please... tell me who he is?"

Frances looked me squarely in the eyes and said in a firm, unequivocal, unwavering voice: "Your birth father is Louis Prima."

I took a deep breath as my mind processed what she had said. But Lou wanted to be absolutely certain so he asked in as non-threatening a voice as he could, "How can you be sure? How do you know for certain it was Louis Prima?" Frances then explained her relationship with Dorothy McDonald in detail. She knew Dorothy from the Avon Apartment on 43rd or 44th Street in New York City. They were close friends... very close friends. Dorothy had, in fact, given Frances her first marijuana "joint" to smoke. Frances was married when she was only 15. She came home late one night and discovered her husband in bed with another woman. She quietly went next door to Dorothy's apartment and asked Dorothy to be her witness. Then they both went back to Frances' apartment where Frances confronted her husband... and her husband and his girlfriend got dressed and stormed out. In the minutes that followed that ugly early-morning encounter, Dorothy became an even closer friend when she shared Frances' tears...

the tears of a woman scorned. Dorothy not only offered a shoulder to cry on, she appeared in court and testified to the infidelity she had witnessed. Dorothy's testimony led to Frances' divorce at age 16. Oh yes… Dorothy and Frances were very close.

Dorothy became pregnant in the fall of 1943. As the Spring of 1944 approached and she was clearly "with child," she stopped working in the clubs. Since her due date was late summer, Frances suggested that Dorothy would be more comfortable in the ocean breezes of Far Rockaway than in midtown Manhattan. Dorothy would also be disappearing from the "scene" and other people from whom she might want to hide her pregnancy. Frances' mother, Margaret, had room to spare in her bungalow. So when the temperatures started to rise and the humidity became too uncomfortable, Dorothy packed a bag and headed to the seashore.

I still needed more assurance. "But how can you be sure that Dorothy wasn't just telling you a little white lie? Are you truly certain that Louis Prima is my birth father?" I asked Frances again with even more urgency. "Alan, I cannot prove any of this to you. But I was there. I spent hours and hours in your mother's company. I have never felt a closer bond with anyone in my life. She helped me through my divorce. She was always there for me. And she spent months with my mother in Far Rockaway before she gave birth to you. She would never tell anyone else who your father was… at least not that I knew… but she would never lie to me about your father. No, Alan, I am certain that Dolly was completely truthful." "Who" I asked curiously, "is Dolly?" "Oh, Dorothy… she liked to be called Dolly… Dolly McDonald," Frances bantered. "And that's what everyone called her on 52nd Street. I knew her as Dorothy from the time she spent with my mother in Far Rockaway." "Dolly McDonald?" I repeated as I looked at Lou. It's no wonder people like Lily Ann Carol didn't recognize her name, I thought. Nobody knew her as Dorothy. She was "Dolly"!!

We sat for several hours and talked about the 1940's and how The Mob ran the Jazz Joints on 52nd Street. Everyone was paid in cash. The booze flowed nightly and the club-goers partied until the early morning hours. Doctor Yasney remained fairly quiet during all this. It turns out that he was Fran's third husband and he didn't know anything about her distant past in New York City. Much of her former lifestyle 40 years earlier came as a shock to him but he remained supportive throughout our talk. I expected that Irv would have many more questions for Fran once they went home!

Though Fran Yasney knew Dorothy well and spent several years as her neighbor, friend, and confidant, she knew precious little about Dorothy's past. She didn't know her date of birth (no woman wanted to talk about her age back then), and she didn't remember if she ever knew Dorothy's hometown. But she confirmed that her mother helped set up my adoption and she told Lou and me that her mother was still alive but that she was in and out of a coma. Frances was hoping that her mother might improve so she could ask her if she had any recollections about Dorothy.

But Frances vividly remembered the day in 1944 that I came home from the hospital. Dorothy brought me to their bungalow where Mrs. Weltsch had created a make-shift crib out of a dresser drawer. She lined the drawer with towels and Dorothy placed me there. As she was preparing to leave, Frances remembered that Dorothy began to cry. It was a highly emotional moment. Frances went to her and put her arm around her shoulder and said, "I know it must be tough, leaving your child like this. But it's the best thing for your baby and the best thing for you." Dorothy stiffened. "I'm not crying because I'm sad about leaving him," Dorothy said caustically, "I'm crying because of the nine months he took out of my career." I guess I didn't hide my pained reaction well when I picked up my drink and took a big swig.

"I'm sorry if that seemed insensitive of me, Alan. I wasn't trying to be hurtful. But I think you need to know how your mother felt," Frances explained. "She wanted to be a singer in a Big Band very badly. She would have done anything... anything... to make it... even sleep with a Big Band leader like Louis Prima." Frances described Dorothy as a "party girl", someone who could show a fellow a good time. But said she always had her eyes focused on that bandstand. She wanted to be up there and gravitated to the men who might help her career. Clearly, being pregnant and out of action for nine months was something that would put a damper on the career of a 21-year-old woman. And so I was the baggage... the burden she was very willing and, in fact, very eager to leave behind in Far Rockaway.

As we were winding down our conversation, Frances felt we had bonded enough to give us her home address and phone number. She also had a sister, Edie Foyke and gave us Edie's address and phone number plus the name and phone number of George Berkowitz, her divorce attorney from so many years in the past. She theorized that, since Dorothy was a witness in her divorce, perhaps George Berkowitz had records that could show where Dorothy was born and where she grew up.

"I can't thank you enough for being so open and honest with me, Frances," I said sincerely, "you have shown so much compassion and I will be forever grateful." "It certainly is a trip down memory lane, Alan, and I am so pleased that my mother and I could have helped back in 1944 and then again today," Frances responded as all four of us stood up and prepared to leave. "I learned a lot too," Irv chimed in. "I never knew my charming wife had such an interesting past." We all chuckled at Doctor Yasney's reaction and I told Frances I would call her in a few days once Lou and I were back in New Jersey. She said that I was free to call at any time. We had our hugs and goodbyes and parted company in the hotel lobby.

"Hey paisan," Lou said in his best Italian accent as we walked to the car. "Did you ever think you'd find out for sure that you had a famous father like Louis Prima?" "I'm just numb by all this, Lou," I responded as my mind still swirled. "I can't believe we got so lucky that we found Frances.

It's really... it's really something else." Lou and I were certain Frances was telling the truth. We talked about how she had nothing to gain by lying... plus she had all the other facts to go with the story. When we combined what Frances said... with Rabbi Schwartz's letter... and Rocco Ferrucci's remembrance... I was certain that we had struck pay dirt. We went back to the motel where I called Ronni and blew her away with the story Frances had just told us. Ronni couldn't wait for me to get back home so I could share every detail with her.

Lou was firm in his belief that we had to go to California... and he proved he knew what he was talking about. But we certainly weren't feeling optimistic the day before. We had gone from the depths of despair to pay dirt within 24 hours! Feeling very satisfied with ourselves, we picked up Yanco and he drove us to the airport for the "red eye" flight back to New Jersey.

On that flight, I made thorough notes about all the different topics that Frances talked about...including the time I spent in Los Angeles years before. Then I compared what Frances told us with the information I had gotten from my well-meaning relatives. My Aunt Miriam provided the name "Margaret Weltsch" but not much else and no one knew it was spelled so strangely. Margaret Weltsch, contrary to what my relatives had said, was alive, not dead... though she was in a coma. Margaret baked at home and never professionally or full-time. But she would bake some pastries for Frances and her second husband to sell at a Hot Dog stand called "The Kosher Pup," which was next to CBS Television City. Frances told me that I had been there "maybe once or twice" but was never a regular customer. There was also one other piece of information provided by my relatives that Frances thought was highly improbable: Frances doubted that Dorothy would EVER marry and certainly she would never have three children.

I was grateful to my relatives for their help though their faulty memories sometimes inadvertently led me astray. Their most positive contribution, though, was that they led me to Frances Yasney and she had the first-hand knowledge that resolved the questions surrounding Dorothy McDonald. I had that vital information now but I wanted the absolute certainty that I believed only my birth mother could now provide. But was Dorothy McDonald still alive? And if so, would SHE confirm that Louis Prima was my birth father?

CHAPTER NINETEEN

Depression and Desperation

Connie Henley met Dorothy at the Greyhound bus terminal in Atlantic City when the bus from Philadelphia arrived late that night. Connie helped her with her bags and walked with her back to her apartment on Illinois Avenue several blocks away. It was closing in on midnight but Connie was still alert and talkative. "Child... your daddy must've really woke up on the wrong side of the bed to be so nasty to you," she said almost matter-of-factly. "I've been with him and seen him do some crazy stuff... but nothin' like this. You musta got to him on a real bad day." They walked for another half block in silence before Dorothy finally blurted out, "He hates me... He always hated me, Connie. Ever since I was a kid I was never good enough for him... I was never the hot-shot he thought Tommy was. Tommy got all of his attention... and I was just this good little Catholic girl that wasn't gonna amount to nothing." Connie looked at Dorothy, and with the wisdom of a sage said, "Well, we just gotta prove him wrong… now don't we, child?" At that moment a warm feeling swept over Dorothy and she knew she had made the right move by hooking up with Connie Henley.

Dorothy slept on Connie's couch that night as she did for the next several weeks. Connie got her fixed up with a waitress job where she worked at the Haddon Hall Hotel and shepherded her through the process of joining the Hotel Worker's Union. She even helped Dorothy apply for a Social Security number. Dorothy never needed one before. The club owners back in New York had always paid her in cash and so did her gentlemen "friends" so she never even filed an income tax return. But here in Atlantic City, she was turning legit and she had to play by the rules. And since she was still legally married, Connie encouraged Dorothy to use her legal, married name, Dorothy J. Cafferty on all her paperwork.

Just as soon as Dorothy could save up a few dollars for a place of her own she moved out of Connie's apartment… but she didn't go far. The place she rented was on the second floor of a building on S. North Carolina Avenue, five short blocks from Connie and just a few blocks from the boardwalk. It was close enough that the two of them could meet in the morning and walk to their job and walk home again in the late afternoon.

But Dorothy's apartment was far enough away that she could indulge her appetite for alcohol without having Connie snooping around. Her job as a waitress was the first truly legitimate job Dorothy ever had and she tried her best to stay away from the bottle, but the demon always beckoned to her and she began to succumb to its spell… slowly at first, and then with more regularity. She couldn't afford her Jack Daniels anymore so she turned to the far-cheaper "bottom shelf" brand, Old Smuggler Scotch, and she downed it by the glassful whenever she could. Connie was always around during the daytime hours to keep her on the straight and narrow but at night Dorothy couldn't hold it together without some "fortification."

Dorothy was lonely. She wasn't the ravishing young beauty anymore. She was nearing 50 and was looking every bit her age... a middle age woman harboring an intense bitterness. She also smoked too much... a pack a day... maybe more. Connie had her hands full trying to boost Dorothy's self-image while also trying to keep her occupied. Dorothy seemed to love cats so Connie got her a kitten from the local animal shelter. For a while, "Sandy" seemed to do the trick. Dorothy fawned on that beige and white-colored kitten and spent many evenings playing with it, holding it, and caressing it. Sandy would purr like a motorboat and Dorothy responded warmly to the sound of affection.

In April of 1972, Dorothy struggled with a chest cold that just wouldn't quit. She went to a doctor whose name she picked out of the phone book. He immediately sent her to the hospital where she was diagnosed with pleurisy and possible pneumonia. The doctors treated her pain with Demerol. They gave her Codeine for her cough. And to be sure she slept well they gave her Seconal at night. Dorothy had never slept as soundly and restfully in her life.

Despite her doctor's pleas, Dorothy kept on smoking... and she kept on drinking. She got a second cat, a tabby she called "Rosie." Rosie was the added diversion that seemed to keep her fairly straight for a while, but even the companionship of two cats couldn't keep Dorothy preoccupied enough to keep her away from the bottle. "Honey... you still be drinking too much," Connie would say when she'd meet up with Dorothy on the way to work. "I can tell... I can see it in your eyes... I know what's going on...but I don't know WHY it's going on... do you, child... do you know what's going on?" Dorothy would always slough it off by saying she was okay... and that she just had a drink or two at night... but no more than that.

Then there were the pills. The years of partying until sunrise made it difficult for Dorothy to sleep through the night and wake up at sunrise. She longed for the deep, restful sleep that she experienced while she was in the hospital so she went to her doctor to ask for medication to help. He wouldn't prescribe Seconal, though, because of its reputation as being addictive. Instead, he wrote out a prescription for Dalmane, a drug that was thought to be not as ripe for abuse. He wasn't aware of Dorothy's fondness for the bottle because she never made him aware of her drinking problem. If she had, he would have nixed Dalmane too. Alcohol raises the risk of addiction to Dalmane and the combination can be lethal.

The Dalmane worked well. And Dorothy took it almost every night. It relaxed her and helped her drift into a peaceful slumber. She awoke feeling refreshed and ready to tackle the onslaught of customers that would keep her running all day long at the restaurant. "You're looking a lot better," Connie told her as they walked home from the job one night. "It seems like you got some energy back in your step, child… so you must be doing something right." "It's these sleeping pills the doctor gave me," Dorothy responded proudly. "I never realized how much better I could feel after a good night's sleep." Connie was very savvy and she didn't like the thought of Dorothy taking sleeping pills. "Oh child…. now you be careful with them pills. They is nothing to fool with.. uh-uh… I seen lots of people get screwed up on them things… and I don't wanna see anything bad happen to you." Dorothy put her mind at ease by promising that she was being responsible and that, after all, she WAS under her doctor's care.

But the pills could only do so much. Even after a good night's rest, Dorothy woke to the daily routine of life as a waitress in a sleepy seaside town. Atlantic City bore no resemblance to the glory days in New York and Dorothy was growing weary of the routine. To counter the boredom, Dorothy would dress up some nights and go out with "the girls," her fellow waitresses at the restaurant. They'd go bar-hopping… from one seedy bar… to another. But every time they went out on the town they'd run into the same scene: The bars would be populated by the men they called "low-lifes" who would try to pick them up… "low-lifes" with smelly breath, and body odor to match; guys who hadn't shaved in days and who didn't equate manliness with cleanliness. Some of the other girls would dance with these men to the sounds of the juke box but Dorothy just couldn't bring herself to even get close to them. These were not the high-rollers from "Leon and Eddies" or "The Three Deuces" or "Club 52" in the heyday of 52nd Street. They were way down near the bottom of the social food chain.

Dorothy was living day to day, coping as best as she could. But then there were days when she would fall apart and fall into the pits of depression. Those were the days when the booze beckoned. The Old Smuggler Scotch gave her a cheap buzz and she'd knock back a glass… and then one or two more. One night, she found that she could escape the feeling of despair by taking a Dalmane and "chasing it" with a glass of Old Smuggler. The combination would numb the pain as it knocked her out. She'd wake up feeling groggy and she'd stumble over the furniture until she made herself a pot of coffee but she was blissfully unaware of the depression that had gripped her the night before.

As her dark thoughts deepened, though, Dorothy took even more Dalmane and mixed it with even more Scotch, sending her into a downward spiral that became harder and harder to control. She'd go back to her doctor again and again to complain about her sleeping problems and he'd prescribe more and more Dalmane. Dorothy, after all, was a "performer," someone who knew how to play a sympathetic role and play it well. So her doctor remained unaware of the addictive cocktail she was downing every night. Another waitress, Sally, had tried Dalmane herself and didn't like the way it made her feel so Dorothy bought her unused prescription as "backup."

The addictive cocktail of booze and pills gripped Dorothy with demonic speed and she found herself watching the clock at work and praying for five o'clock to come around so she could head to her apartment and relieve her growing mental anguish. "Lordy, child… you be walking mighty fast to get home these days," Connie would say as they took off their aprons and put on their overcoats as they left work behind late on that Thursday afternoon. "But I wish you'd get out more... instead of locking yourself up with your cats every night. The girls say you never join them when they go out on the town anymore... and I don't see you coming up to my place neither." Dorothy would put on the "act of innocence" she had honed to perfection and would scoff at Connie's comments. "Well, maybe I just like to stay in at night and watch TV and enjoy Sandy and Rosie's company... There's nothing wrong with that, is there?" she'd reply defensively. "Besides, I ain't no spring chicken anymore... and I just like to put my feet up and relax after a day's work." It always worked. Connie would back off... and Dorothy wouldn't have to listen to another lecture on the things she should and shouldn't do.

"You have a good night, Connie," Dorothy shouted after her as she opened the door to her building and went inside. But just as soon as Connie was out of sight, Dorothy stepped back outside and walked back down North Carolina Street to the liquor store where she bought three bottles of Scotch and a couple of packs of Chesterfields.

Back at her apartment, she poured herself a glass of Old Smuggler, fixed something to eat, and then sat down in front of the television with her cats on the sofa next to her or in her lap. She tried her best to get involved in whatever was on TV but the shows didn't engage her enough to distract her from the anger and frustration that brewed inside. She got up from the couch and walked over to the closet door to stare at herself in the full-length mirror hanging on the inside. In her alcohol-induced haze she touched her face and ran the back of her hand down her cheek as she wondered what had happened to the beautiful young woman who could attract any man she wanted. As she gazed at her image and turned her head to one side and moved her body seductively, a matronly woman with a thick mid-section and sagging jowls looked back at her. The stark reality of what she had become fired-up her despair and sent her straight for the bottle again.

She sat on her couch, a glass of Scotch in one hand and a Chesterfield in the other. She tried to focus on the TV screen but it all became a blur. And the pain grew to become too much to bear. Dorothy reached for her bottle of Dalmane and popped a pill. Her cats were playful and jumped up onto the couch and rubbed their faces against her leg, craving attention and affection. She stroked them aimlessly as she became woozier and the room began to spin. She began to lean to one side... and passed out... as her head came down and rested on the padded armrest of the couch.

The hours passed and Dorothy didn't budge from that spot. But the sound of several wailing sirens woke her as fire trucks passed under her window. She was in a stupor and looked vacantly at the test pattern on the television set in front of her. She was barely in tune with reality at that moment and she had a splitting headache. She reached for a cigarette, fumbled with the pack until she plucked one, and then lit it. Everything around her looked and felt so dreary and dull and even through her haze, the feelings of self-loathing crept into her consciousness. She reached for the closest liquid at hand: her bottle of Scotch... and she guzzled several mouthfuls. "Aw... what the hell," she mumbled to herself. "Who gives a rat's ass?" And with that, she reached for her Dalmane and popped the three pills remaining in the bottle into her mouth. Then she grabbed the bottle of Scotch again and washed down the stubborn pills with several mouthfuls. It only took several minutes until the mixture kicked in. Dorothy slumped over on the couch... and then her body slid off and onto the floor.

Just as she did every working day, Connie Henley arrived at Dorothy's apartment building at 8:30. But on this Friday, the 8th of December, Dorothy wasn't standing there, bundled in an overcoat, smoking a cigarette. Connie went into the lobby and buzzed Dorothy's apartment but got no reply. Dorothy had been moody in recent weeks and Connie was fearful that something had happened so she walked up the stairs to Dorothy's apartment and knocked. No answer. She knocked again… and thought she heard some faint moaning from inside so she reached into her purse and took out the spare key Dorothy had given her. She unlocked the door and went inside. "Dorothy, honey…. You here?" she called out. "Honey… you okay?" Then, she spotted Dorothy's limp body on the floor in front of the couch. She rushed over and tried to rouse her. Dorothy moaned softly but remained still. Connie rushed to the phone on a nearby table and dialed "O." When the operator responded, Connie said breathlessly, "We need an ambulance over here to 33 South North Carolina Avenue… up on the second floor!" "What's wrong?" the operator asked. "I don't know," Connie replied, "my friend here… is… well she's lying here on the floor… all passed out… you gotta send somebody fast."

Connie went back to Dorothy and tried to rouse her again. She shook Dorothy's limp body and tried moving her head from side to side. Her breaths were very shallow but Dorothy eventually moved an arm… and then a leg… while remaining nearly comatose. Connie saw the near-empty bottle of Old Smuggler on the coffee table and the empty bottle of Dalmane next to it. It wasn't hard to figure out what happened and what Dorothy had tried to do. The ambulance arrived in a matter of minutes. The rescue workers loaded Dorothy onto a stretcher, made note of the Scotch and the empty bottle of Dalmane, and knew they had to get Dorothy to the hospital fast.

The hospital workers noted on her chart that Dorothy was "admitted for drug overdose and acute alcohol intoxication." They began to treat her in the Emergency Room, and when she began to respond they moved her into a hospital room for her continued recovery. The doctor's notes the next day indicate Dorothy "was on Dalmane for sleep… was drinking heavily – one pint of Scotch and 4 Dalmane – was depressed."

The treatment Dorothy received at the hospital helped her recover quickly. Connie came to visit her and told her that she lied to the restaurant manager and said that Dorothy had a stomach virus and would be to work on Monday. Connie didn't want to see Dorothy lose her job. She knew that would be the final blow for this woman who was clearly on the verge of imploding.

On Sunday, Dorothy was well enough to be discharged. A cryptic note was entered as the last entry on her hospital chart: "Patient states she hates a lot of things."

Dorothy had the hospital call Connie Henley to tell her that she was going home. She was still a little weak but she wanted to stay in Connie's good graces especially since Connie had covered for her at work. Dorothy took a cab to her apartment where Connie was already camped out waiting for her. "I didn't want anybody to know 'bout this, honey," Connie reassured her. "I didn't call Madeline or your daddy... cause I didn't want to worry them none. But you sure got ME worried, honey... yes indeed... you sure got me worried."

Dorothy settled onto the couch, looking like someone who had flirted with death. "Aw, Connie... it was an accident... that's what it was," she lied. "I just made a mistake and drank too much." But Connie was quick to point out, "And you also took them damn pills along with it...that's what you did... I warned you 'bout them damn pills... They is something you don't wanna mess with." Dorothy nodded her head in agreement. "Could you get me a glass of water?" she asked. "From now on... that's what I'm gonna be drinking... yeah... just water." Connie went to the kitchen sink and filled a glass of water but she didn't fall for Dorothy's line. She was savvy enough to know that Dorothy had a long history with the bottle and she wasn't going to break the habit that easily.

The two of them sat in Dorothy's living room for the next hour and talked about the restaurant and casino gambling... and why it could or couldn't have been an "accident" that Dorothy mixed booze and pills. As the time passed, Dorothy grew weary and began to yawn. "Why don't you just go to bed and rest now, honey," Connie recommended. "Maybe you'll feel strong enough to go to work tomorrow... but if you can't... don't worry... I'll cover for you." Dorothy thanked Connie and said she would try her best to be downstairs at 8:30 the next morning. She stumbled over to her bed and sank into it. Connie let herself out.

The next morning, Dorothy was waiting for Connie promptly at 8:30 with a Chesterfield dangling from her lips. "I made it, Connie... just like I said I would," she called out with a smile on her face as Connie approached. "Honey child, you be looking good this morning," Connie said as she tried to assess Dorothy's true condition. But Dorothy was indeed looking and feeling good as she bragged, "Hell, I slept all the way through the day and the night and I'm feeling like it did me a world of good." "You musta needed it, child," Connie said warmly. "After what you been through it don't surprise me none that you slept so long... heh-heh... Oh, honey... you put a real scare into me.... Don't do that no more... promise?" Dorothy vowed to stay sober and straight and the two waitresses picked up the pace and headed for work.

Dorothy gained a steady customer at the restaurant, a guy named Stan, who was a dapper dresser and had a wild sense of humor. He'd regale Dorothy with jokes on a daily basis and she got a kick out of his humor and his upbeat nature. Stan finally asked her out on a date and Dorothy readily agreed. He was the first man she had socialized with in years that seemed to be the real thing. The two became an item and that gave Dorothy a diversion from the demons that had been haunting her. Stan kept her busy at night with long walks on the boardwalk along with dinners and dancing at the nicer night spots.

But even with Stan's steady involvement over the next year, Dorothy couldn't keep away from the bottle. Gradually at first, and then with more and more regularity, she went back to her old ways. Dinners on the town always included a drink or two, which whetted her appetite for more and proved to be too great for someone who had struggled with an alcohol problem for years. Stan told her repeatedly of his concern but Dorothy wasn't able to alter the habit that had grown into a curse. The final straw came on Christmas Day of 1973, when Dorothy got so drunk that Stan finally had enough. He looked around at the Christmas tree decorated with odds and ends... at the mistletoe hanging from a doorway... and Dorothy passed out cold on the couch. Sadly, he shook his head. Stan took a few steps to the couch, leaned over, and said, "I'm sorry, honey," as he planted a kiss on her cheek. She never budged. She never saw him walk out the door for the last time.

Dorothy's life began to spiral out of control again. Connie watched as it happened but was powerless. Connie was a patient woman and she was a strong woman but nothing she did or said could change Dorothy's ways. Connie even called Madeline to express her fears but she found that Madeline was in no mood to listen. "You know, Connie... that girl got no sense... and she got no feelings for right and wrong," Madeline said into the phone, her fury building. "Hell, I paid for everything while she was here with us... I bought her booze... and lemme tell you I bought her food... and that's why Angus was so.... so mad.... And now, me too... Hell, I loaned that girl 200-dollars of my own money to get herself a new start... and d'ya think I ever seen that money again? Hell no. She done spent it on booze... and she keeps lying to me about it... and it proves after all I done... she don't give a crap for me... or Angus... or nobody.... And now I'm sorry I got you involved too.... I figured you could help her... but I wouldn't be surprised if she took your money too...."

"No... she been good about that with me, Madeline," Connie responded. "But she is a real tough cookie... and she got a real big problem... drinking... and taking pills... She about done herself in one time… and I expect… I expect that it could happen again." Madeline wasn't moved. Connie ended by saying she was sorry she couldn't do more to help Dorothy… and the two said their goodbyes.

Dorothy, meanwhile, found another doctor, one who didn't know about her near-fatal overdose. She told him she was new to town and needed thyroid medication and medication for her blood pressure. The doctor gave her a complete physical examination and wrote out prescriptions for the diuretic and thyroid medicine she needed. "One other problem I am having, Doctor," Dorothy said plaintively, "I just cannot sleep at night and I have had this problem for a long time. Years ago, a doctor gave me Dalmane and it worked like a charm." The doctor saw no harm in her request so he wrote out a prescription for Dalmane. "I'll give you enough for two months if you need to take it every night," he said innocently. "That way, you won't have to come back too soon for another prescription." Dorothy could hardly conceal her delight.

Dorothy dealt with her growing depression using her trusted combination of Dalmane with a Scotch "chaser." She became fixated on her younger days on 52nd Street and on the succession of good times and naughty nights. It was no longer an option to look at herself in the full-length mirror that hung on her closet door, and one morning in a raging fit, she ripped it off the door and tossed it in the dumpster behind her building. But she even found it too painful to look at herself in the bathroom mirror as she applied her coat of make-up. The face that looked back was puffy and haggard. And the more she drank, the more Dorothy fell into the dark abyss of self-pity and helplessness. But somehow, she was able to hide her darkest side from Connie. Connie was still her one true friend.

On Wednesday night, May 1st, 1974, Dorothy was feeling the deep, searing pain of a deepening depression. To counter the growing melancholy, she took two Dalmane and downed them with a tumbler full of Scotch. In a matter of minutes she was fast asleep. When she woke up in the morning, though, she couldn't get out of bed... and she really didn't want to.

Then came the knock on the door. She looked at the clock and saw that it was 8:30. "Dorothy, honey... it's me, Connie... you in there, honey?" Connie bellowed from outside the door. "Let yourself in, Connie," Dorothy called out, and Connie did. "I'm just not feeling good today, Connie," Dorothy complained, "not feeling good at all... I'm not gonna make it to work... will you tell them for me... tell them that I'm sick." Connie came over to the bed and looked into Dorothy's eyes as she asked, "Well... what's ailing you, honey... what should I tell them at work is wrong with you?" "I got terrible cramps in my stomach... You know how I had this a while back," she said as she winced convincingly. "Can I get you anything?" Connie asked. "No, I just gotta wait it out in bed... that's all," Dorothy responded. Connie started moving to the door. "Okay then," she said, "but I'll check in with you on my way back home... okay?" "Sure enough, Connie... I really appreciate it." Connie closed the door as she left and locked it behind her.

The morning sunlight was streaming into the room as Dorothy remained under the covers. She reached into her nightstand to fetch the bottle of Scotch she had stashed inside. She also pulled out a bottle of Dalmane and placed both bottles on top of the nightstand next to her. Though she remained groggy from her flirtation with her dangerous drug cocktail, her lungs ached for another drug: nicotine. Her hand fumbled across the nightstand until she felt her pack of Chesterfields and knocked one out. Dorothy turned on her side to face the nightstand and grabbed a lighter to fire up her smoke. Her eyes stared blankly at the liquor and the pills as the minutes ticked by while she inhaled lungfuls of smoke again and again before dropping the butt listlessly into the ashtray. Then she poured a handful of Dalmane pills into her hand and shoved them into her mouth.

She reached for the Old Smuggler and chugged back the burning liquid, swallowing the pills, two or three at a time, until her mouth was empty. Her throat was feeling inflamed from the Scotch but she kept drinking it. She forced herself to swallow again and again as her eyes watered from the pain. She drained the bottle and let it fall to the floor.

Connie Henley, meanwhile, had begun her shift at 8:45 as she did every day. Even as she was taking orders for omelets and pancakes and coffee, Connie's thoughts remained with Dorothy. There was something about the way Dorothy talked that morning that just didn't feel right. Try as she might, Connie couldn't shake the feeling that something was VERY wrong with Dorothy. So, when the morning "rush" ended as it did every day around 10:30, Connie asked to take off for a bit and promised she'd be back in time for the lunch crowd. She headed directly to Dorothy's apartment.

Connie didn't bother to knock. She used her key to let herself in... and when she opened the door she saw the bottle of Scotch on the floor and the open pill bottle on the nightstand. "Dorothy!" she screamed as she realized what Dorothy had done. "Dorothy, honey.... Oh Dorothy!" she continued, as she shook her by the shoulders. There was no movement... nothing to indicate a living being. This time, Connie knew that Dorothy had done it. She feared it was too late but she called for an ambulance anyway and she rode in the ambulance to the hospital. Dorothy was still barely alive but Connie could tell there was little hope.

Connie was at Dorothy's side when the doctor in the Emergency Room first examined her friend. The doctor noted on Dorothy's chart: "52 year old.. admitted unconscious - a friend stated had overdosed on sleeping pills – Dalmane – known alcoholic and had done this before." A priest was called and Dorothy was given the last rites. But Dorothy's body wouldn't give up without a struggle no matter what Dorothy wanted. Hospital records state: "Patient had stormy hospital course – never recovered from coma – died 5th hospital day." Other hospital notes show: 5/7/74 – "Patient is moribund! Comatose – no pupilary response....5/8 – 2AM - completely unresponsive... 8:15AM – "no obtainable blood pressure or pulse – no apparent respirations"... 8:30AM – "CTB (Cease To Breathe) Relative in Philadelphia and friend notified."... 8:45AM – "Body to morgue."

The Death Certificate shows: Dorothy J. McDonald Cafferty died on May 8, 1974. The Cause of Death is listed as: "Aspiration bronchopneumonia, coma of undetermined etiology."

CHAPTER TWENTY

Cry Me A River

I first heard of Louis Prima when I was entering high school. He and Keely Smith had a hit recording of "Old Black Magic" which was played on the radio endlessly. But as the years passed and I learned more about the consummate singer, songwriter, trumpet player and entertainer... the more I understood his impact on American music. He wrote the classic song that Benny Goodman made famous in 1936, "Sing, Sing, Sing." He wrote the Swing classic "Jump, Jive and Wail"... and was the first to connect the songs "Just A Gigolo" and "I Ain't Got Nobody"... and that was back in the 1940's! Louis Prima's genius bridged the New Orleans sounds in the 1930's... and the Big Band sounds of the 1940's. With Keely Smith as his foil, he created the definitive Lounge Act that helped bring Las Vegas into prominence in the 1950's... and he carried that tradition into the 1960's and early 70's with his new singing partner, Gia Maione. Louis Prima was the role model for Frank Sinatra, Dean Martin, and the rest of the "Rat Pack"... and his pairing and bantering with Keely Smith was said to be the inspiration for Sonny and Cher. And to top off a career that spanned more than four decades, Walt Disney patterned the character of King Louie in "The Jungle Book" after Louis Prima. Louis Prima also performed the role of King Louie in the animated classic. If Louis Prima was indeed my birth father as Frances Yasney had told me with certainty and Rabbi Schwartz and Rocco Ferrucci had hinted, then I was part of an entertainment legacy that would make anyone proud and humbled by the genius of such a great showman.

So it became critical to my Search that I find my birth mother. I knew that Louis Prima had died. But even if he had been alive, I doubted that he would have confirmed anything about his involvement in my birth. No... that confirmation would have to come from my birth mother IF I could locate her. The team of Jeannette MacDonald and Nelson Eddy had a hit song in the 1930's called "Indian Love Call." As I was reaching out, trying to find my birthmother I often wondered if Dorothy Jeannette McDonald had been named after the famous singer and film star. Perhaps Dorothy craved the fame of her namesake and that desire drove her to want to be a "singer in a band." Since Louis Prima was now only performing for the Holy Hosts I would have to find Dorothy if I wanted proof that she was my birth mother and Louis Prima was my birth father.

Lou reached out to Bob Pentatore to ask again if a Dorothy McDonald or a Dolly McDonald had ever sung with Louis Prima's band. Bob remained emphatic that she never did, at least not on any recordings or in any large concert venues. He couldn't be certain though that, at some time in some small town, someone named McDonald didn't sing with Louis. He was absolutely positive, though, that a Dorothy or Dolly was never "The singer" in Louis Prima's band.

So the next move was to track down the Avon Apartments in the "West 40's or 50's" that Francis had told us about. It seemed an easy enough task. Lou and I went to the New York Public Library again and checked the telephone books and City Directories. The Avon Apartments were listed at 301 West 46th Street... the same address that I found in the New York City phone book for "Dorothy McDonald" in 1944, and the same seedy apartment building on the corner of 9th Avenue in New York City that my first private investigator, Bob Fitzpatrick, and I had already checked out.

That address had now been confirmed through several different sources: The Manhattan phone book for 1944... Frances' recollection that she and Dorothy lived in the Avon Apartments... and Rocco's comment that he took some money to Dorothy at a "hotel in the West 40's." Despite the dead end that we reached there, I felt confident that this was surely the address that could lead me to Dorothy. I reviewed my notes and saw that "Dorothy McDonald" was listed at 301 West 46th Street through the 1965/66 phone book... and then disappeared.

After confirming the address at the library, Lou and I took a cab over to 301 West 46th Street. Lou instinctively knew how to fit in with the people who still called that hell-hole of a building "home." His years as a cop had taught him how to put on a gruff persona and assert himself by talking to people as if he still was a cop and had the law on his side. Maybe it wasn't true. But no one had to know.

We stopped at Paco's apartment again, and just as he did when I was there several years earlier with Bob Fitzpatrick, Paco only opened the door a crack... with a security chain in place. "My name is Lou LoScialpo and I'm a private DETECTIVE," Lou said flashing his P.I. badge. "We're looking for Dorothy McDonald who lived here years ago. She also went by the name Dolly and I know you told this young man's investigator a couple of years ago that you thought she moved back to Philadelphia." Paco's eyes darted in my direction. He looked me up and down through the crack in the door before answering. "Yeah, that's what I said then cause that's the way I remember it," Paco said in broken English. "Why Philadelphia?" pressed Lou. "Cause she always said that's where she came from. I don't know nothing else about it," Paco responded.

Lou tried to get more details but either Paco didn't know or wouldn't say. After several more questions we realized we weren't going to get any more out of Paco. Lou, though, was never one to give up. He left a business card and asked Paco to call him if he remembered anything else. We started to walk down the hall and then looked back to spot Paco checking us out again just before he closed the door. "Dorothy is in Philadelphia," Lou said with conviction. "I don't care what your other private investigator was thinking. But Dorothy left here and went back to Philadelphia." Lou was convinced, he said, by Paco's demeanor. "He was tight-lipped but he had nothing to lose by saying Philadelphia. Call it a gut feeling. But I believe what Paco said."

Lou and I went downstairs and back outside where there were several stores on the ground level. We checked out Jimmy Ray's Bar, hoping to talk to some old-timers who might remember Dorothy or "Dolly" but no one did or was willing to admit it. It was the same story at Van Dyk's Restaurant a few storefronts away. These were people who lived on the edge of the law. No question they had all run into a streak or two of tough luck in their lives and that made them wary of strangers. If a snoop was looking for someone they would never let on. They had their own code of ethics and they protected each other from people like Lou and me who asked too many questions.

Since we were striking out in the neighborhood, Lou wanted to check out the Board of Elections to see if Dorothy registered to vote. If she had, it's possible that we could track her address through those records. We checked every registered voter living at 301 West 46th Street for the years 1944, 1948, 1956 and 1960. Dorothy McDonald had never registered to vote.

The next day, Lou called George Berkowitz, the lawyer who handled Frances Yasney's divorce many years earlier when she was a teenager. Dorothy witnessed Frances' husband's infidelity and she had testified at her divorce trial. Maybe George Berkowitz kept records that would indicate something more. Or perhaps Dorothy turned to him when SHE needed legal help. It was worth a try. Unfortunately, Mr. Berkowitz was in no mood to be helpful. Lou described him as "uncooperative."

A call to Frances helped. First of all she said that Philadelphia "rang a bell," and that Dorothy may have indeed come from Philadelphia. She also told Lou to call George Berkowitz again and mention Dave Marr's name. Apparently, Dave Marr had sent many clients to Berkowitz (including Frances). George Berkowitz softened when Lou mentioned Dave Marr's name. He agreed to sign an authorization allowing us to get Frances' divorce papers from the City Clerk's office. He said it would take a few days to research the document numbers and put the paperwork together.

We were on a roll and didn't want to lose momentum so we immediately planned a trip to Philadelphia. Lou's buddy, Bob, joined us. Lou figured the more eyes we had, the better. The two and a half hour trip to the heart of Philly was uneventful, but the traffic and parking in Philly were a driver's worst nightmare. We checked out the local library and found a Dorothy McDonald who was listed in the phone book in 1966, but was not listed in 1965 or 1964. As it turned out she wasn't listed in 1967 either.

I had to double-park outside City Hall because parking there was at a premium. While I sat there, motor running, I got the "eye" from every curious passing cop. Lou and Bob, meanwhile, checked out death records and birth records but found that random pages of the record books were missing, so they couldn't cross-check every Dorothy McDonald. When they returned to the car they had pages of notes but nothing tangible to go on, so we stopped at a diner for a bite and also so Lou could use a convenient pay phone to call the several "Dorothy McDonalds" he found in the current phone book. None of them admitted to knowing anything. Then, Lou called Information for Dorothy McDonald listings and found there were several others with that name, but to our dismay, they all had unlisted phone numbers.

Several days later, George Berkowitz came through. He not only had the authorization for Frances Yasney's divorce papers, he had gotten a copy himself from the City Clerk's office. The Xerox copies, though, were not very legible because the originals pages were old and yellowed so they did not copy well. But the papers included a deposition by Dorothy that she had found Frances' husband, Alfred Thomas Duze, in bed with another woman in Frances' apartment. The wording of the deposition made it clear that Dorothy and Frances were close friends who shared many personal experiences. It showed that Dorothy was 21 but it did not give her hometown, her profession, or any other identifying information about her. And there appeared to be some pages missing.

Frances' mother was alive, as Lou and I learned when we met Frances in California. But Margaret Weltsch had been experiencing memory loss and was living in a nursing home and Frances could not get her to remember any of the events of the summer of 1944. Over the next several months, she was taken to the hospital several times with life-threatening conditions. Frances called me when she eventually died. Dorothy had spent several months living with Margaret before I was born so Margaret probably knew my birth mother as well as anyone. But too many years had passed and I had found her too late in her life for her to be any help in my Search.

Lou was becoming more and more convinced that Dorothy McDonald came from Philadelphia even though we found no proof of her existence there. Call it another hunch. Lou was positive we would eventually be able to track her to the City of Brotherly Love. He had a friend who worked for New Jersey Bell and offered his friend $100 for the addresses of the unlisted "Dorothy McDonalds" in Philadelphia. We got the locations and took another trip to Philly and physically checked out the addresses. In each case, Lou knocked on the door and talked with the person who answered. In each case, no one admitted any connection to "Dorothy Jeannette McDonald" or "Dolly McDonald," who wanted to be a singer in a band in New York.

Lou had such great success with bribing his New Jersey Bell friend for the unlisted phone numbers that he came up with another idea. He knew a gal who worked for the Social Security Administration. He would ask her to locate Dorothy's social security number and then ask her to track down where she currently worked. After all, Dorothy' current employer would be deducting her Social Security payments. Lou's plan re-energized me because it didn't depend upon hearsay. It relied only on hard facts. But even that hope was dashed a few days later, when Lou told me that his friend could only track down Dorothy if she had Dorothy's social security number. If she tried to input Dorothy's name into the database it would generate an "alert" and she would have to explain her actions to her supervisor. She wasn't willing to lose her job by supplying us with inside information. And so far, it had been impossible for us to find any evidence (other than my birth records and the New York City phone directories) that Dorothy truly existed.

My frustration mounted even more and I became even more tormented when Francis Yasney sent me several pictures of herself at age 16. They were professionally-shot black and white photos. Francis, it turns out, was a real knockout! She looked a lot like Betty Grable with her blonde hair swept up into a 1940's "twist." She looked like a lot of fun... like she was plugged into the swinging- lifestyle of the era. But the pictures proved to be more of a tease. They brought me so close to seeing, feeling, and understanding what the times were like when I was born. But they fell short of answering my burning questions.

Then came the phone call from Edie Foyke. Edie was Fran Yasney's sister. They hadn't really talked in years and it soon became clear to see why. Edie sounded odd... just a little "off base." Nevertheless, in her desire to help me, Fran had called Edie to ask her what she remembered, and to tell her how to contact me if she could be helpful. Edie, though, rambled a lot and seemed to be shooting from the hip, unlike Fran, who was more grounded, more down to earth. But Edie did confirm her sister Fran's account.

I had many conversations with Edie Foyke over several months. She would usually call me to tell me of some great revelation she had. During one call she told me that my birth father was Jimmy Vincent, the drummer in Louis Prima's band, because she remembered rumors that Jimmy Vincent had proposed to Dorothy. But unfortunately, Edie always sounded either medicated or inebriated so I determined she was not a credible source that would lead me anywhere.

But I also asked myself, who else was not a reputable source? Which relatives got the facts confused and which ones mangled the truth unwittingly because they just didn't remember precisely what happened? Here I was... nine long years into my Search... trying to determine WHICH "truth" was THE truth. The facts had been so elusive that I became wracked with anxiety. My stomach churned continuously and I didn't sleep well. I reviewed every possible scenario in my mind again and again and I considered alternatives to the conclusions raised by every bit of information. I went back over research and reconsidered what people had told me. How much longer can I go on like this, I would ask myself as I considered giving up? But I had spent so much time, work, and emotional energy on my Search that I knew I had to see it through. And I knew that Lou felt the same way. We were both committed to getting answers.

In a symbolic act of spiritual desperation, I bought a 14-karat gold St. Anthony's medal. The "faithful" prayed to St. Anthony for the recovery of lost things. I had "lost" my birth mother and my birth father. I figured... it couldn't hurt.

Lou and I sat down in his office and went back to the beginning. We reconsidered every bit of information I managed to get since I first called

"Information" for the number for St. Joseph's Hospital. One of the theories that had gone by the wayside centered around the Bronx. The Borough of the Bronx was where most of my relatives lived during the time I was born. In fact, many of them still lived there through my teenage years so I was very familiar with the location of their apartments as I had visited them many dozens of times over the years. Lou was certain that Dorothy had come from Philadelphia but we weren't able to confirm that. So we questioned whether Dorothy could have been somehow connected to my relatives in the Bronx? Maybe Dorothy grew up there and had met my family members there... the same family members who "summered" in Far Rockaway? It seemed like a logical connection... a connection that Lou and I had no choice but to investigate.

The search for a "Bronx connection" meant going to the New York Public Library yet one more time. We searched through the old phone books again... this time for The Bronx. We found a listing for a Dorothy McDonald at 595 E. 170th Street in 1966 but not in 1965. That could explain her disappearance from the Manhattan phone book after 1965. It seemed very logical.

We also found another possible connection years earlier. There was a listing for a "Bernard McDonald" at 2310 Morris Avenue in 1944, the year I was born. I also found a listing for my adoptive mother's sister and brother-in-law.. at 2395 Morris Avenue... a few apartment buildings away. So it was possible, Lou and I agreed, that Dorothy could have lived just down the street from my aunt and uncle... and that would have conveniently placed them in Far Rockaway at the same time.

Lou and I drove to 595 E. 170th street first... to check out the listing we had found for Dorothy in 1966. The building, though, looked too dangerous to enter without first donning flak vests and arming ourselves with AK-47's. So instead of putting ourselves at risk, Lou jotted down the number of the manager which was posted on a sign outside. (He later called that number and got nowhere.) We also drove down Morris Avenue to check the proximity of the two addresses we had for Bernard McDonald. I remembered the area well from my teenage years but could not fathom what had happened to this once-thriving neighborhood. Just as Ronni and I felt when we drove down Vernon Avenue in Brooklyn looking for Rocco Ferrucci, Lou and I sensed a lurking danger... a feeling that we should not get out of the car. Although Lou was armed, he certainly didn't have enough fire power to take on the gangs of drug dealers and thugs hanging out on the apartment stoops.

Later that night, I called my cousin Muriel in California again. Muriel had grown up on Morris Avenue. Did she, I asked, know Dorothy from the old neighborhood in the Bronx? Muriel did not. In fact, she only had a vague recollection of her from Far Rockaway. But certainly, she said, she was not a friend or classmate from her days on Morris Avenue.

In the days that followed, I tried to get birth certificates for Dorothy J. McDonald, date of birth: December 31, 1922... from the states of Connecticut, Massachusetts, and Pennsylvania. Lou and I checked the Geneological Society. We checked birth records. We checked death records. We checked marriage records. Then we checked more than 50 phone books for the New York area... all looking for the name Dorothy Jeanette McDonald. We also checked the phone books on microfilm for the years 1966 through 1970... for The Rockaways, Staten Island, Suffolk County, Nassau County, and even Westchester County. All turned up negative for Dorothy J. McDonald. That proved to us that Dorothy moved sometime in the years 1965 or 1966 but she did not move anywhere in the five boroughs of New York or even anywhere nearby. State records from Connecticut, Massachusetts and Pennsylvania were no help either. The agencies either claimed there was no record of a Dorothy McDonald born in their state on December 31, 1922, or said that only close family members could get access to that information.

Lou called me the next night. "Alan," he said in a voice charged with excitement, "I think I'm really on to something. I know a guy who works for Equifax. That's the largest retail credit agency in the country… and he's gonna start looking for Dorothy by starting with 301 West 46th Street." Lou continued before I could get a word in, "Ya see, Equifax records come from all kinds of insurance policies so if your mother ever had any kind of insurance policy, Equifax would have a file on her. Bingo!"

It took more agonizing weeks of stalling… weeks of waiting… more weeks of frustration. In the end, Lou's friend at Equifax turned out to be a big talker, a blowhard, who was absolutely no help at all.

Lou and I had cemented a strong relationship over the many months we had worked together. So he asked me if I'd like to work for him "on the side." I still had my job anchoring and reporting for "Cablevisionews" at the local cable company but we only recorded our local news segments on Mondays, Wednesdays, and Fridays. My duties initially didn't require a fulltime commitment on Tuesdays, Thursdays, and on weekends. My evenings were also free and that's when Lou needed me most to help him with surveillance and research for other clients. So I gladly agreed and underwent the background check needed to become a state-licensed Private Investigator working for Lou's company, Eagle International.

It also helped that my twin boys had made it through the first miserable years of their little lives. They had survived being born prematurely and their parents had survived the torment of colicky crying and sleepless nights. Ronni and I had been put through the ringer. If babies were "little bundles of joy" we wondered why we weren't feeling any of that joy. It was an unfortunate fact that we had been sleep-deprived and miserable for many months while worrying if our babies would grow to be normal, active adults. But by the time our twins reached what's usually considered "the Terrible Twos," their behavior improved remarkably and life got a lot less stressful for Ronni and me. Ian and Evan turned to each other and became playmates so a sense of normalcy returned to our household. The boys' remarkable turnaround gave me the freedom to focus on my career in television news while assisting Lou in his endeavors.

But Lou and I had run out of options. So many different sources pointed back to 301 West 46th Street, though, that Lou suggested we try again to get someone there to talk. Lou's forte clearly was getting people to open up and tell him what they know. We had struck out everywhere else so why not go back to the apartment building where we knew Dorothy had lived for so many years?

We walked through the barren lobby once again and made our way through the littered, dank, dark hallways of the rundown building, searching for signs of life. Many apartment doors were open with no one living inside. In fact, it was hard to imagine anyone still living in this building among the roaches and rats and garbage. But people still did… the people who couldn't afford to move anywhere else… the people who had come to a dead end in their lives. One lady eventually responded to Lou's persistent knocking. Her name was Jean. She was a waitress and by the look of her deep-set eyes and the ruts and crannies in her face, she had lived a rough life. But Jean was still sharp. She suggested that we try the restaurant workers union, which she told us, was right across the street. She explained that a lot of people who had lived in the building over the years had worked as waitresses, and in most cases, they would have had to join the union.

Lou and I thanked her and made tracks for the stairs and the front door. The building gave us both of us the creeps and both of us were a lot more comfortable on the outside looking in. We walked out the entrance on 46th Street and over to the corner of 9th Avenue, where were startled by a large sign over the building across the street! It read: "H.E.R.E".. which, it turns out, is an acronym for "Hotel and Restaurant Employees Union." But we didn't make that connection at first. We were a couple of guys who were so desperate that we would grasp at any glimmer of hope... even the musings of a gypsy fortune teller. So we wondered if seeing that sign WAS a sign. At this point, we would believe just about anything. "Could it be that we have been here so many times and never seen the sign across the street that points HERE... HERE is the answer to your search?" Lou asked like a man who had nowhere else to turn.

We walked across 9th Avenue and into the Union lobby. "I'm a Private Investigator," Lou said in his most charming manner, "and we're trying to find out if a lady named Dorothy McDonald was ever a union member. Do you think you could find out for us?" "I don't see why not," the receptionist answered as she wrote down Dorothy's name along with Lou's name and phone number. "But it'll take a day or two before someone can check it out and get back to you." "Thanks," Lou said with a smile, "you're very nice to do that for us. We appreciate it."

Someone from the union called Lou the following day to say that there were no records that Dorothy McDonald had ever been a waitress in New York. The person said that they had even "checked the basement" for records back to the 40's but no one by that name had ever registered with the union.

Then we decided to also check cabaret licenses. We figured... if Dorothy McDonald had indeed been "a singer in a band" then she would likely have needed a cabaret license. We struck out there too. Lou and I were dismayed to learn that all the old cabaret licenses had been destroyed. My birth mother, I surmised, must have had a very shady past. There was no Social Security number for her. She never voted. There were no birth, death, or marriage records. She never registered with a union. And no one recollects her singing with a band. So how would she have supported herself? The only profession that seemed to fit the pattern was "the world's oldest profession"... a lady of the night who had an "accident" during one of her trysts.

Lou, meanwhile, was becoming more frustrated than me. He had found HIS birth parents but he didn't run into nearly as many brick walls as he had searching for mine. His reputation was on the line. He had been certain he could wrap up my Search for me and he was clearly annoyed at his apparent shortcomings. Every one of his sources also crapped out. And now it was becoming a case of pride. He knew he was the best. I knew he was the best. Yet we were both in the emotional "dumps" considering that neither one of us could find my elusive birth mother and solve the riddle of how I came to be.

Out of desperation, Lou decided to try his friend at the Social Security Administration again. He begged, he pleaded, he cajoled. He hit her with every argument in his arsenal. He was desperate, he said. His reputation as a Private Investigator was on the line. Couldn't she do something? After much hesitation, she finally admitted she could. She could run a computer check on every Dorothy McDonald in the Social Security database and try to pinpoint one that was born on December 31, 1922. But she cautioned it might take her a few days because she'd have to wait for her Supervisor to be away from his desk to be certain there were no prying eyes watching her.

Several days did pass as we waited... and then Lou called me with some definitive news but this time it was not about my birth mother. "I finally got it, Alan," he said rather smugly, feeling a sense of relief that something had finally turned up. "The hospital finally released Joe Grantonio's blood type. It sure took 'em long enough. Anyway, it's 'B Positive'. Since your blood type is 'A Positive', that means that Joe Grant was likely not your father and you are not related in any way to Rocco Ferrucci." Though Lou was self-satisfied that he had turned up some solid information based on fact, the news about Joe Grantonio came as a big letdown to me because it merely ruled out who WASN'T my father. It didn't help to confirm who WAS.

Then, about a week later, another devastating blow... Lou's friend from Social Security called him back. There was no listing in the Social Security database for ANY Dorothy McDonald, born December 31, 1922. It was a maddening revelation that I could not fathom. I was reeling! How could that be? I had uncovered hospital records with Dorothy's name and birth date. Fran Yasney's divorce papers and court documents also listed Dorothy's birth date. Was the woman who I believed to be my birth mother just some con artist? And did that mean that nearly a decade of my life was wasted in the Search for a birth mother whose name was usurped from a 1930's movie star? At this point, I didn't know what to think. So where do we go from here? It seemed that Lou and I had exhausted every possible avenue and checked out every detail of every lead. We were demoralized but Lou would not admit defeat. He did admit, though, that he didn't have a clue where we should turn next.

I tried to call Frances Yasney several times, but got no response until she returned my call about a week later and told me she "had been away in the desert". The "desert" was how she described Palm Springs, California where she met up with her ex-husband, Bob Silverman. Frances told me she went to Florida to work as a dancer in the winter of 1944 and that's where she met Bob. He had gotten out of the Army and proposed after just a few dates. Frances cautioned him, though, that she couldn't marry until after her divorce to her first husband was finalized. They returned to New York City together and she must have kept her old apartment in The Avon at 301 West 46th Street since Bob said he met Dorothy there. He called her a "looker" and also remembered, as Frances had, that Dorothy gave them their first "joint" (marijuana cigarette). Bob also said he heard Dorothy sing on several occasions, particularly at "The Three Deuces" on 52nd Street. Bob then rattled off the names of other people they knew, who also knew Dorothy: Roy Hart, Bingy Garfield, and Robby Royal. Bob also theorized that Dorothy was "Southern and sharp"… that she was street-wise and must have come from a big town and not out in the Styx. Bob and Frances lived at the Avon through the Spring and Summer of 1945 and so did Dorothy.

In any case, the conversation Frances had with Bob apparently also stirred up other memories. Frances now recalls that she and Bob DID operate a "restaurant" in Los Angeles. It was really a hot dog stand, "The SNEAKY Pup," near CBS Television City (not "The KOSHER Pup")... and that her mother, Margaret DID, in fact, bake linzer tortes. So some of what my relatives had told me several years earlier was indeed correct. Mrs. Weltsch WAS a Hungarian baker at a restaurant in Los Angeles. It was a bit of a stretch to call a hot dog stand a "restaurant" but at least there was some truth behind the story.

Frances' conversation with husband #2 made Lou and me I rethink husband #1. His name was Alfred Thomas Duze'. We had some of Frances' divorce papers that lawyer George Berkowitz had given us. There were pages missing and we theorized that one of those pages might contain some identifying information about Dorothy since she had been Frances' witness. So Lou and I naively thought we would talk to the City Clerk, David Dinkins, to try to retrieve those missing pages. When we got to the City Clerk's office, though, we were put in our place. David Dinkins was not just some "clerk"... he was THE clerk. And you just did not walk in and expect to talk directly to David Dinkins. (He later became mayor of New York City.)

Lou and I were a little taken aback and embarrassed that we confused the title of "clerk" with that of a low-level city employee. So with our tails between our legs, we left Mr. Dinkins' office and went to the records section to talk with a REAL clerk to request the divorce records of Frances Duze in 1943 or 1944, the approximate years of the divorce. The clerk disappeared for a bit and came back with a thick folder. We were told to use one of the booths along one wall that were designated for reading documents. Those booths shielded us from prying eyes, and as we read through them, we realized there was no real system for checking these documents in and out. So, I took the pages with my birth mother's signature on them... along with transcripts of the court proceedings, folded them neatly, and tucked them neatly under my shirt as Lou shuffled the other papers as a distraction. We then returned the somewhat thinner folder to the desk where it was added to dozens of other folders that had to be re-filed. No questions asked. We walked out with the documents clinging to my stomach, covered by my shirt and jacket.

Unfortunately, when we later checked them thoroughly we were disappointed again that there was no real identifying information other than the confirmation that Dorothy lived at 301 W. 46th Street. She also listed her Place of Birth as "Philadelphia." The pages also contained her signature in several places. At least I had something tangible to focus on. I could look at her signature and realize there was a person who signed her name in a flourishing cursive style and that person was my birth mother.

So, after nearly ten years of obsessive searching, what had I learned? I had fairly positive proof of the identity of my birth mother and her birth date and believed that she was from Philadelphia. I had copies of her signature but I knew precious little else that could connect me to my birth father. Rabbi Schwartz and Rocco Ferrucci both told stories that alluded to Louis Prima but it was all just hearsay. I did, though, put a great deal of weight on Fran Yasney's account, since she was personally so close to Dorothy and because Lou and I had quizzed her so thoroughly. But I still wanted to learn for certain if my birth mother was alive and I wanted more definitive proof that Louis Prima was indeed my birth father. I clung to the hope that one day I would locate my birth mother and she would confirm the identity of my birth father.

When I inquired about Louis Prima, I learned from various friends and musicians that Louis Prima was married five times and that he had a mesmerizing effect on women... many women. That might explain why Keely Smith and Gia Maione never responded to my letters. I guessed there was a lot of legal maneuvering after Louis Prima's death... and no one wanted to deal with an interloper who might come in and demand money as a legal heir to the Prima estate. As a prospective heir, I would certainly be "persona non grata" among any close family members and other illegitimate children who might be already squabbling over the estate. I knew enough about Louis Prima at this point to know that he was very successful in the music business. I speculated that a lot of money could be involved… money that legitimate heirs might be fearful of having to split with a child born outside of marriage. I knew I wasn't interested in the money at all, but just try to convince feuding family members who might be locked in battle over his estate.

Lou and I had seemingly tried every avenue, and every avenue brought us back to 301 West 46th Street. We had confirmation that Dorothy McDonald, my birth mother, was the one actually listed at that address and we knew from my earlier research that the phone number, Columbus 5-4144… remained listed through the 1965/66 phone book and then disappeared. So who was that number assigned to now? Lou wanted to know so he dialed the number, which was answered by The Broadcast Center on West 57th Street and 10th Avenue, where a number of network television shows were taped. It was 1985… at the same time that I was working in the television news business!!

Lou became even more curious. Was someone else listed at Columbus 5-4144 AFTER the listing disappeared for Dorothy McDonald and BEFORE it popped up as the number for The Broadcast Center? Lou made a trip to the New York Public Library once again and pulled out the microfilm copy of the New York City phone directory for the years 1966/67… the year after Dorothy's last listing. He first verified there was no listing for Dorothy McDonald as I had told him. But the library was closing soon and Lou had no desire to return another day so he "pocketed" the microfilm and took it home with him. Then several days later when he had the time, he went to the public library in Hackensack, New Jersey near his home and spent the better part of one full day using the microfilm machine there to sift through the listings. He merely ran down the column with the phone numbers looking for Columbus 5-4144. It was easy to scan each page because the number would pop out at him. The problem, though, rested with the fact the phone book was so big. He went through the A's...and the B's... before reaching the C's... where he spotted the magic number: Columbus 5-4144. It was assigned to "Dorothy J. Cafferty." Bingo!!! This, he thought, has to be the same person. How many Dorothy J. "Any last name" would you find with the same phone number? Dorothy, Lou theorized, may have gotten married and kept the same phone number but listed it under her married name. (Lou, by the way, returned the microfilm to the New York Public Library days later.)

Now Lou had a name he could work with: "Dorothy J. McDonald Cafferty." He went back to his friend in the Social Security Office and asked her to plug in the name "Dorothy J. Cafferty" with a birth date of December 31, 1922 whenever she was able.

Several days later, Lou showed up at "Cablevisionews" unannounced... and told me that we needed to go outside so he could talk to me. Lou had never done anything like this before so I knew something had to be up. We took a walk.

"I found her," he said with a gravitas that was unnerving. "After all this time, I found your mother."

The saliva dried up in my mouth as if a dentist had suctioned it out. I had a lump in my throat that made it nearly impossible for me to speak. It was if the whole world stopped in its tracks and nothing mattered except for the words: "I found her." Even before Lou continued, I felt my life over the past decade running by me like a videotape in fast-forward. I had reached the moment I had longed for... for so long. I stared at Lou numbly as he took a piece of paper out of his pocket. "I'm sorry to have to tell you, though, that she's dead. Dorothy is dead," he said sadly, "but at least we now know where she is."

Lou showed me the paper he was holding. It was a printout from the Social Security Administration with holes down each side of the paper as it came off the printer. It was headed: "Investigate possible SSN's"... and listed: "Possible numident records." Under that heading was a Social Security number 141161845... assigned to Dorothy J. Cafferty, dob 12/31/1922, Sex F. It went on to list DOD (date of death) 05/08/74, Atlantic City, New Jersey.

My mind was in panic mode as it tried to process the information. "She died? In Atlantic City?" I questioned suspiciously to no one in particular even though Lou was standing in front of me. "This.... Is... uh... is her?" I asked again before answering my own question. "Yes... it has to be... the right birth date... Dorothy J.... and the Cafferty name from the phone book." As I considered the name and dates on the paper I felt some small sense of consolation that Dorothy died in 1974, two years before I even began my Search. But then a rush of angst filled me with the remorse that I would never be able to ask her to identify my birth father.

After the initial shock wore off I gave Lou a hug. "You did it, Lou," I told him very appreciatively, "you found my birth mother. You did the impossible. You found her." But Lou wasn't fond of taking accolades before he finished what he set out to do. "Yeah, but we still have to confirm the identity of your birth father," he said with resolve. "And you know where we have to go next... right?" I answered affirmatively, "There's no question about it... Atlantic City."

CHAPTER TWENTY-ONE

What If You Held a Funeral and Nobody Came?

Connie Henley's reputation as a caring, nurturing woman had been tested repeatedly since Dorothy became a part of her life, but Dorothy McDonald Cafferty wasn't through... even in death. She put Connie to the test one last time. Connie had promised Madeline that she would look after Dorothy and she fulfilled that obligation until the very end. After the hospital notified her that Dorothy had died, Connie went to the office of the waitress' union where she applied for and received Dorothy's 500-dollar death benefit. Connie used that money to pay for the cost of a casket and for the burial. She also made arrangements to get a burial plot in the Egg Harbor Cemetery in the section of the cemetery reserved for those who couldn't afford a proper gravesite.

Five days after Dorothy's death... on May 13th, 1974, Connie Henley took a cab to the cemetery on the outskirts of Atlantic City. It was a dreary, drizzly day... perhaps a fitting metaphor for Dorothy's life. Connie met the hearse at Block Y – Row 15 – Grave 12... and said a silent prayer as Dorothy's body was lowered into the ground. The funeral director placed a cross made of wires and covered with carnations where a traditional headstone would have been erected.

Connie Henley stood there alone in silence alongside Dorothy's grave. Once the hearse drove off, Connie watched the workers laboriously fill in the six-foot trench as a chilly wind blew over the expanse of unmarked gravesites. She was by herself... the only person who attended Dorothy's funeral. Dorothy's father, Angus, and stepmother, Madeline, remained committed to their grudges and refused to make the trip from Philadelphia. Tommy had dropped out of sight because of one of his schemes had soured and he couldn't be located. Blackie was still in prison. And the other waitresses at the restaurant where Dorothy worked didn't feel close enough to their co-worker to lose money by taking time off from work.

Dorothy Jeanette McDonald Cafferty died unceremoniously after living an unfulfilled, lonely, bitter life. She died by her own hand. But Connie Henley did not let her go to her final resting place alone.

CHAPTER TWENTY-TWO

Post Mortem

By now, road trips had become old-hat for Lou and me. Another day spent on the roads: another day talking to strangers who might be able to help us. We were comfortable in our roles at this point... and VERY eager to seek a resolution to the remaining questions surrounding my birth.

Lou felt strongly that since Dorothy had died in Atlantic City, she probably died in the hospital there or at least had been brought to the hospital by ambulance. In any case, the logical place to start: the Atlantic City Hospital. We had the name Dorothy J. Cafferty. We had her date of birth and her date of death. This was the Fall of 1985 and long before the HIPPA laws were enacted to protect a patient's privacy. I wasn't certain we could get information from the hospital, but then again, Lou was a master.

After the two-plus hour drive from North Jersey to Atlantic City, Lou and I meandered around what had finally become the gambling mecca of Atlantic City until we located the hospital. We went straight to Medical Records where Lou prepared to turn on the sympathy and the charm. We watched and waited as several people were served before us and Lou picked out the clerical assistant who seemed the most empathetic to the people in line in front of us. We heard other clerks refer to her as "Sally" so when it was our turn, he asked for "Sally" by name. Before starting his spiel, though, Lou first beckoned her down to the end of the counter away from prying eyes and ears. "My friend here is named Alan. My name is Lou. I'm a private detective. And we need your help." He proceeded to lay it all out to Sally about how I had been searching for my birth parents for ten years and how we had finally located my birth mother but that she had died, he believed, in this hospital back in 1974. "There is no way he can meet her and talk to her and tell her how much he loves her," said Lou in his most sincere voice. "It's too late for that. But maybe he can find some of her family members and share his love with them. And that's where we need your help." Lou then asked if she could find any records that would help lead us to family members. His story had reduced Sally nearly to tears and she took the information we had for Dorothy and disappeared into the cavernous stack of records in the room behind her.

Lou and I waited. But we didn't have to wait long. Sally soon returned with a large file folder containing Dorothy's records. She began rummaging through them to find a form that stated: Registration of Death… and made a copy of it for us. "Here. This should help for now," she said, "It should give you a starting place to try to locate family members and it shows where she was buried." I, of course, used my "Method Acting" training to look stunned, saddened, and nearly in tears. Both of us told Sally how grateful we were but before we could finish she told Lou, "If you give me your business card, I will make copies of all of these records and mail them to you. It's the least I can do for you and your friend." We offered to pay her for her time and for the copying costs but she would not hear of it. "We care about our patients and their families here and I am proud to be able to help you," she told us, brushing off our attempt at payment. Lou and I thanked her again and left satisfied that we had made all the right moves.

Once outside, we studied the paper Sally had given us thoroughly. It was headed: DOROTHY J. MCDONALD CAFFERTY, date 5/8/74, Atlantic City Medical Center. Again, Lou was correct in his assumption: when someone dies, check with the nearest hospital. The document had Dorothy's date of birth as December 30, 1922, instead of the 31st, but it had the correct Social Security number and indicated that she was born in Pennsylvania. It also spelled out the principal cause of death as "aspiration bronchopneumonia... coma of undetermined etiology." It listed a doctor's name... M. Ackerfelt, 1652 Pacific Avenue... but more importantly, it listed as "Informant": Connie Henley, 212 N. Illinois Avenue. That would have been the person who brought Dorothy to the hospital or the person to be notified in case of her death. It also showed that Dorothy was buried at the Egg Harbor Cemetery, Egg Harbor, New Jersey. But there was more. Dorothy's father's name was Angus McDonald. Her mother's maiden name was Rita Shelfein. Lou and I had hit pay dirt again.

First off, Lou wanted to check with the doctor listed on the death certificate. We stopped at a gas station and asked how to get to Dr. Ackerfelt's office on Pacific Avenue and learned it wasn't far. Once we got there, Lou suggested I stay in the car while he would make inquiries. So, I sat and I waited. It took about a half hour but Lou finally emerged and settled into the passenger seat. "The doctor remembers her," he said, "but not too much. After all, it was eleven years ago. But he did tell me that she had committed suicide with pills and booze." He looked at me for a reaction but I wasn't really surprised by what he said. Dorothy, I had learned over the years, led an unconventional lifestyle. I felt also that suicide didn't seem out of character for someone who would get pregnant and skip out on one couple to sell her baby to a family who made a higher cash offer. So I really had no reason to linger over her cause of death... at least not now. "So where do we go from here?" I asked Lou. "Let's find Connie Henley," he responded in a heartbeat.

We searched for a pay phone with a phone directory and found one several blocks away. There was no longer a listing for Connie Henley on Illinois Avenue, but there was a listing for a Connie Henley on Main Street in Pleasantville, New Jersey, on the outskirts of Atlantic City. Lou put a quarter in the slot and dialed her number.

I stared intently at Lou as he held the phone to his ear, waiting for someone to pick up at the other end. It seemed to take an eternity, but finally I could see a twinkle in his eye and heard him say, "Hi, my name is Lou Loscialpo and I'm looking for Connie Henley." After he listened to the response he said, "Oh, hi Connie, I'm a private investigator and I'm looking for a Connie Henley who was friends with Dorothy McDonald..." But before he could continue, he was apparently interrupted by the person at the other end. "Oh, I'm so glad I reached you. I'd like to talk to you about Dorothy and about what you know about her life. I know she died but I have some questions. May I come over?" The response, from what I could tell, was a positive one and Lou quickly got directions.

We had to drive several miles to reach the apartment building where Connie Henley lived and my mood swung from wild enthusiasm to cautious pessimism. I had been burned too many times before and would not allow myself to fall prey to the excitement generated by this new lead. We didn't really know who this Connie Henley was or exactly what her relationship was to Dorothy McDonald Cafferty. And we had no idea how she would respond to questions from Dorothy's son.

We arrived at the address Connie had given Lou and found an attractive apartment building that was well-maintained though it looked like it had been a fixture in the neighborhood for decades. The lobby had a list of tenants with a buzzer next to each name. Lou pushed the button next to Connie Henley's name and she soon buzzed us in. We took the elevator to the sixth floor, walked down the hall to number 602 and knocked.

Connie Henley opened the door wide. Connie was a sweet, black woman of retirement age who welcomed the two strangers in front of her into her comfortable, cozy apartment. We sat and Lou wasted no time in introducing me as Dorothy McDonald's son and explained how we had located her. "That's so strange," Connie said shaking her head from side to side, "Dorothy never talked about having a son... but then, she never really did talk about much in her past. It was like it was something she was trying to forget." Lou and I took turns telling my story and explaining to Connie how intense my Search had been and how grateful we were that she was talking to us. Connie was charming and talkative and my fears that she would become defensive and uncooperative evaporated. Though Connie knew nothing about me, she knew a lot about Dorothy.

Dorothy, she told us, went back to Philadelphia after she soured on the scene in New York City. Dorothy's mother, Rita Shelfein, had died several years before and her father Angus McDonald then married a black woman named Madeline Jackson. So Madeline became Dorothy's stepmother. And there was another connection: Madeline and Connie had known each other for decades and Madeline was the one who encouraged Dorothy to go to Atlantic City where Connie would help her find work. Connie also sketched in some of the family's background. Angus McDonald, she said, was a Ward Boss in Philadelphia, someone who could put the pressure on anyone who dared challenge the corrupt politicians that held the city's purse-strings. Angus was rough-and-tumble, Connie told us. In fact, he had been shot twice and lived out his life with two bullets lodged in his torso. The McDonald clan, it seems, was not your typical law-abiding American family with strong middle-class values.

Dorothy also had a brother who went by the nickname "Tommy." Tommy followed in his father's footsteps and was sent to prison a number of times. During his last ten-year stretch he became friends with "Blackie" Cafferty and introduced "Blackie" to his sister when they both got out of the slammer. That meeting led to the marriage that was never dissolved. When Dorothy left New York, she left Blackie in a prison cell and never bothered with the formalities of a Separation or a Divorce. That's why she had been listed in the hospital records as "Dorothy J. McDonald Cafferty." Lou and I shook our heads and looked at each other knowingly. It all now made perfect sense.

Connie had been listed in Dorothy's death certificate as "Informant" because she was the one who called the ambulance when she found Dorothy unconscious in her bed. She and Dorothy were waitresses at a restaurant in a hotel just off the Boardwalk. They worked the same shift and they would walk to work together and back home again. Dorothy, she said, had tried suicide before but Connie felt that she was coming around and could be trusted not to harm herself. Connie, though, was wrong. When Connie stopped by Dorothy's apartment one day to walk off to work together, Dorothy told her she wasn't feeling well and would stay in bed that day. Connie went on to work by herself but had second thoughts and checked back in with Dorothy a few hours later. That's when she found Dorothy passed out with an empty pill bottle and bottle of booze on her night table. Though she called the ambulance, Connie told us, she knew it was too late for Dorothy. She knew it was unlikely Dorothy could ever be revived. She knew the end was at hand.

Dorothy was buried in a pauper's grave and Connie was the only person who was there for the burial. Dorothy's father and stepmother didn't attend. Neither did anyone else. As we listened to her tales, Lou and I realized that Connie Henley was the needle that wove a thread through the fabric of Dorothy McDonald's middle-age years. She seemed to know everything about Dorothy including where to find Dorothy's stepmother. She told us that Madeline Jackson was in a nursing home in Philadelphia. Connie was able to find the address and phone number of the home and also said she would call Madeline and tell her to expect a call from us. Madeline, she said, would likely have more information that could be helpful to us.

Lou and I wound up spending the better part of an hour with Connie. When we were about to leave, Connie told us that she would look for pictures of Dorothy and of some items that Dorothy had given her. She promised to stay in touch and tell us anything else she could remember

Connie was true to her word, and in the weeks and months that followed, she sent me pictures of Dorothy that she had taken from Dorothy's apartment after she died. Dorothy was definitely a "cat" person as witnessed by the cats in almost every photo. Connie also sent me a charm bracelet with a "cat" charm on it, as well as a porcelain cat, and salt and pepper shakers in the shape of cats. I have tried but have never have had a great deal of emotional attachments to these personal items that said so much about my birth mother. I am grateful, though, that Dorothy didn't attempt to raise me herself. I am also thankful that she didn't sell me to the Ferruccis.

When we left Connie's apartment, Lou and I didn't plan to leave Atlantic City. We now knew where Dorothy was buried and I wanted to visit her gravesite. So we got directions to the Egg Harbor Cemetery and headed there before heading home.

When we reached the cemetery on the outskirts of Atlantic City, Lou and I knew we would have to go to the cemetery office to locate Dorothy's burial site. We followed signs to the office, a small one-room building in a back corner. The cemetery itself was like so many others. It was neat and well-kept, with rows of tombstones, and a smattering of above-ground family vaults. It was lush, with flowers and trees adding shade and softness to the final resting place of so many souls.

"We're looking for the grave of a Dorothy McDonald," Lou said to the worker who greeted us at the office door. The man told us that he didn't have the records there but he would call the main office to determine where the grave was located. But he said he would also need to know the date she was buried. We told him the date was May 13, 1974. The man got on the phone and fed the information we had provided to someone at the other end, and then he paused. "What name did you say you were looking for?" he questioned us. "Dorothy McDonald," Lou and I said almost in unison. The man repeated the name into the phone and then looked at us suspiciously. "Are you sure?" he asked us curiously. "Yes," I answered. "I don't know," the man said awkwardly, "I don't know if I can help you." I suddenly had a flash. "Dorothy McDonald Cafferty," I blurted out! The man smiled. "That's what I wanted to hear," he said. "I wanted to be sure we were talking about the same person."

The man stepped outside the office with Lou and me and pointed to an area to one side of the cemetery that was devoid of trees, flowers, shrubs, and even tombstones. "She's buried over there, in Row 15... Grave 12" he said. "Just look for the marker at the end of each row and then count down the graves until you reach 12." We thanked him for his help and got back into the car for the short drive to this barren section of the cemetery. "This is what they mean by a pauper's grave," Lou said as we approached. "This is where people with no money are buried and then forgotten."

Lou and I got out of the car and looked across at the desolate plot of land about the size of a football field. Here, far away from the well-kept headstones and crypts that were packed next to each other and surrounded by well-manicured vegetation, was the spot where my birth mother was laid to rest. We began scouting the grounds, looking for the small markers the man in the office had told us about. It was a gray, overcast day, and the barren area that spread out in front of us was bleak and depressing. There were no signs that loved ones cared about the people buried here, in fact, no signs that anyone cared. These souls all just had a patch of earth so they could rest in peace for all eternity. It was not at all the kind of place where I wanted to think my birth mother, or anyone else for that matter, would be buried.

Lou and I found a plastic marker with a "15" on it and then counted down the row of graves to the twelfth gravesite. There, sprouting from the barren soil was a wire frame of a cross about a foot and a half tall. It was just a bundle of spindly interwoven wires that were shoved into the ground. But the reality set in. This was the spot. This was where Dorothy McDonald, my birth mother, was buried. Tears welled up in my eyes. I crouched down and touched the cross as I looked across this melancholy piece of land, knowing that after all these years I had reached the end of the Search for my birth mother. I screamed a silent scream as I faced the reality: My recurring teenage dreams would never play out in real life. I would not be knocking on my birth mother's door and berating her for giving me away. I would never, ever gain any morbid satisfaction from that confrontation. It was over. It was over. I felt relief… but had no satisfaction.

"That wire cross was probably filled with flowers and put there when she was buried," I heard Lou say as his voice snapped me out of my funk. "And look at it… It's still standing there after eleven years… still standing." The flowers had withered, died, and had been blown away over the years, but since this was an unkempt pauper's grave, no one cared for, or groomed the gravesite. No one even pretended. I can't say I was angry or relieved or surprised. I just never thought the Search for my birth mother would end eleven years after her suicide… in a desolate pauper's grave near Atlantic City, New Jersey.

CHAPTER TWENTY-THREE

Another Solid Source

Lou and I felt a great satisfaction in knowing we had cracked the case. But it was only part of the mystery. What about my birth father? I had several sources who named Louis Prima. And now that I had put the questions surrounding my birth mother's demise to rest, both Lou and I knew that we would turn our attention to confirming the identity of my birth father. The next step would be a chat with Madeline Jackson, Dorothy's stepmother, who might have the key to unlock even more doors leading to my past.

We were on a roll and wanted to keep the momentum going so Lou called Madeline Jackson the very next day. As she had said she would, Connie Henley had already made a call to Madeline so Madeline was not surprised to hear from him. She was eager to help, so Lou and I got in my car just one day later and drove to the nursing home in Philadelphia where Madeline was staying. I vowed to be prepared. This time, I took along a small tape recorder. It slipped neatly into my shirt pocket with its microphone on top. As we arrived at the nursing home and walked down the hall to Madeline's room, I pushed the "Record" button and let it capture our conversation.

Madeline was waiting for us, sitting in her wheelchair. She was a frail, elderly black woman, whose body may have failed but whose mind was as clear as ever. She welcomed us and we sat in chairs near her. I pulled my chair up close to her so that the tape recorder would pick up our conversation... and what a conversation it was! When we asked about the family's background we found that Madeline was eager to share. The entire McDonald clan, she told us, was involved in questionable, even unlawful activities. She confirmed that her deceased husband, Angus, was a Ward Boss, a tough character who mixed it up with the "wrong people." And Angus's brother apparently wasn't any better. He had been a Numbers Runner in Ocean City, New Jersey, the guy who picked up the illegal bets from the gamblers in town and paid them off when they won.

"And sweetie, I think I knew that Dorothy better 'n any of 'em," she said proudly. "She was one helluva lady an' her and her daddy... well, they din't see eye to eye... if ya know what I means. I can't say I blame her daddy none, though.... cause'n she was a no-good chile... Oh, she tried and all that... but she was a mean drunk... if ya knows what I means." Madeline went on to tell us that there was drinking and screaming every night. She admitted she was a willing drinking partner with Dorothy and they spent many days and night together sharing their booze and retelling stories from the past. She also told us they spent many sober hours together as she tried to wean Dorothy off the bottle. Madeline drank too but said she could stop at any time. Dorothy, though, had a real problem.

Lou began pressing her about Dorothy and her illegitimate child and Madeline proved to be an encyclopedia of knowledge. "I tried.... And I tried to get that chile to talk about her troubles... Oh, sweetie, I tried," she said with a chuckle in her voice, "but she would have none of it.... til one night... and that one night changed everythin'. An' from then on... she talked about it mo' and mo'... jest to get it out... ya' know what I means?" Then Madeline looked at me squarely and took her time before she went on to say, "You know who your daddy is...? Well... lemme tell ya.... He was that jumpin' trumpet-playin' guy.... that Louis Prima... that's who he was... and you can make book on that, sweetie."

I was having trouble responding to Madeline's pronouncement because it seemed so eerily similar to our meeting with Fran. So Lou chimed in, "Madeline... let me ask you... how can you be sure Alan's father... was Louis Prima? How do you know for certain?" Madeline said that Dorothy had told her many times of her affair with Louis Prima. Dorothy was a singer, she said, and wanted desperately to join Louis' band. She would do anything... yes anything... to further that goal. Dorothy was a "party girl" and tried everything to get closer to the famous bandleader. She was invited along as a guest when the band toured the West Coast in the Fall of 1943 and that's when she made her move on Louis. "I hears that Louis Prima liked his women... and I suspect that he did... cause Dorothy was a real good-looker, if ya knows what I means," Madeline said almost conspiratorially. "A real hot potato... and she knew how to make the mens want what she had to give... but she was tellin' me that HE was no saint. He was known aroun' town for bein' a real ladies' man... so I guess they be a perfect match," Madeline said with a hearty chuckle.

It doesn't take a math genius to take my birthday, August 11, 1944, and subtract nine months to figure that I was conceived in November of 1943 during the time Louis Prima was married to Wife #2, actress Alma Ross. The events at the time of my birth, as Madeline related them, now bore that out. It was clear that she was relishing her role as the lady with all the answers. "And ooh-ooh-ooh... that Dorothy really had a thing for that Louis Prima," Madeline said with a twinkle in her eye. "She really thought he was the cat's meow... and she wanted him mo' and mo'... and she really thought he wasn't jivin' her when he was sayin' that he was gonna let her sing wit' the band... tha's what she really be wantin'. But after they got together one night and she got pregnant he was just like all them other mens... He just didn't want to have no part of her af'er that."

Once Madeline had finished regaling us with her stories about Dorothy and Louis Prima and Lou and I ran out of questions for her, we shook her hand and thanked her for her time. We left her knowing that we had solidified the identities of both my birth parents. Madeline Jackson was now the fourth source that traced my conception back to Louis Prima.

- First, was Rabbi Schwartz saying my father was "the leader of the band."

- Then came Rocco and Rose Ferrucci, who said my father was a "fellow in Louis Prima's band"... who later told Mr. Andre that "Alan's father was dead."

- Then there was Fran Yasney, who was Dorothy's neighbor, close friend and confidante, who told me with absolute certainty that "Louis Prima was your father."

- Now, Madeline Jackson also made that definite connection.

During the drive home from Philadelphia, my mind was spinning so fast it felt like I was going to have a stroke. The pavement of the New Jersey Turnpike was racing by in a blur as I became consumed by my newly-confirmed "identity." Here I was... an adopted Jewish boy from the little town of Westwood, New Jersey, but I had a Catholic heritage. And much more than that... I had answers to those burning questions about who I really was: I was the biological son of one of the greatest Italian-American musicians and entertainers of the 20th Century!!!

CHAPTER TWENTY-FOUR

The Not-So-Saint Louis Blues

Now that I had determined through four separate sources that Louis Prima was my birth father I was overcome by a nearly-rabid desire to absolutely confirm our connection as father and son. Louis Prima was a huge star, an incredible showman, and a musical genius whose legacy has endured through the generations. But it wasn't his name and star-power that motivated me. I wasn't looking to hitch my wagon to the financial estate of this musical icon. I just needed to know for certain if my musical talent and my outgoing nature as a performer had evolved genetically. Everything pointed to Louis Prima and believing that I carried his genes helped me understand how and why a "nice Jewish boy" from New Jersey played Dixieland music in high school. It answered the questions that had haunted me since childhood. It validated who I was. But I still needed confirmation. And so, it became even more important to reach out to Louis Prima's family, hoping that someone might know something. But how?

My question was answered when the phone rang and it was Louis' biggest fan, Bob Pentatore. Bob had cable television service provided by Cablevision, the same company I worked for as a newscaster, and he watched me frequently. And whenever he had a complaint about his cable service he would call me to vent and to ask me to help resolve his problem. This call was no different. His reception was getting "snowy," he said, could I talk to someone in our station's Service Department. Of course, I said I would.

Then I told Bob about what I had learned from Madeline Jackson about Dorothy and her connection with Louis. Bob didn't flinch. He didn't seem unduly surprised. "Alan," he said matter-of-factly, "your father was a notorious lady's man. Make no mistake about it. He screwed every woman he could and there were many. He was a great musician but the ladies in the audience really loved him and showered him with attention." I wanted to know more but didn't want to be too direct so I chimed in, "Well, everyone knows about Louis musical talents, Bob, but I never heard about his way with the ladies." "I wouldn't be surprised, Alan, if you have a number of other half-brothers and sisters," he blurted out, "that's in addition to the children he had from his marriages. You know, he was married five times, don't you? And I'm real close with Louis' fifth and last wife, Gia Maione Prima."

Bob also told me that a TV station in New Orleans, WYES, had produced a one-hour documentary on Louis Prima which included Louis' entire history. "You're in the news business. Why don't you try to get your hands on a copy of the videotape," he said, as if I could just make a phone call and snap my fingers. "That way, you can find out a lot more about the man and his music through the years."

I was a neophyte in the television news business but I did know about something called "professional courtesy" and I relied on that to get a copy of the documentary from that New Orleans station. Since I was working for "Cablevisionnews," I sent a request on company letterhead to WYES, the New Orleans station, saying that I was going to be interviewing Keely Smith in the near future and I had heard about a documentary the station produced. I said that I would like to view a copy of the Prima documentary, promising not to "air" any of it, only using it for background information. (At least THAT part was true.) I also promised to return the tape within days.

The videotape arrived in the mail later that week with a letter wishing me the best in my interview with Keely. I immediately made two copies of the videotape and mailed the original copy back to WYES with a note expressing my gratitude for sharing the "remarkable documentary." I then sat and watched the tape over and over again. Sure, it featured Keely, who was Louis' wife #4 and on-stage partner during the peak of his career. But it also had a scene with Joyce Prima, who was my half-sister from Louis' first marriage. Joyce only made a brief appearance in the film but I was watching MY SISTER and I was thrilled to know I had a blood connection with at least one other person on this planet.

I called Bob Pentatore to tell him about my latest exploit. He was excited to hear it because he had been trying to get a copy of that videotape for his collection. Bob's collection included every recording Louis Prima ever made, plus newspapers articles, journals, posters, and films. Bob even had some "masters" of Louis' songs that were never released. He got them through a friend who worked in the archive section of a record company. They kept these "masters" in a vault and kept them in pristine condition on the chance that Louis or someone involved with his estate might want to release them. Well, Bob had them and he cherished them. I suspected that I would cement my relationship with Bob by offering one of my two copies of the documentary... and I was right.

Because of that one gift, Bob made copies of Louis' recordings for me, copies of songs I might not ever have. For example, Bob put together four different versions of "Just A Gigolo/I Ain't Got Nobody." The first was recorded by Louis and the Big Band back in the 1940's. The second was the classic "Gigolo" recorded during the Las Vegas years. Then, there was a disco version recorded by the Village People, and also the David Lee Roth classic that is word for word, note for note, identical to Louis' version in the 1950's. Bob and I became close and spoke often and he eventually embraced the belief that I WAS Louis' son.

To help me confirm my genetic relationship with his idol, Bob also agreed to make some further inquiries of Gia Prima, Louis' fifth wife. Bob told me that at that point in time, seven years after Louis died, the estate had still not been settled. He feared they might see me as an opportunist who would come in and demand an inheritance as a child of Louis Prima and that might complicate matters and tie up the estate for many more years. It would be a tough task to bring Gia and me together, he said, but he said he would try.

Bob Pentatore also suggested that I contact Jimmy Vincent, Louis' drummer and long-time friend, who might know something more about the connection between Louis and Dorothy. But Jimmy Vincent's wife had called me several years earlier in response to the ad I place in the musician's union newsletter and that conversation went nowhere. So I had Lou make the call now. As a dispassionate third-party with years of experience in friendly interrogation, I knew Lou would stand a better chance of ferreting-out information.

Lou actually reached Jimmy Vincent Junior, who did the talking, claiming his father wouldn't be home for several days. Lou said he was very cordial but claimed he knew nothing and said his father would not have known anything either. It seemed like a cover-up, Lou told me. It seemed that no one wanted to talk about Louis Prima's illegitimate child.

Then several weeks later the phone rang and I answered it eagerly. "Is this Alan?" the voice on the other end asked. I paused. I don't know if it was the tone of the guy's voice or the way he asked the question but I became apprehensive. "Yes, this is Alan," I responded cautiously, "who is this?" "I'm Dorothy's brother, Tommy, and I got your name from Madeline Jackson." Okay, I thought, this is bizarre. I am talking to my Uncle and yet I'm not really feeling comfortable with this. But if this was indeed my mother's brother I had to press on. "Oh, that's right. Now that I think of it, someone had mentioned you as I was looking for my birth mother," I said, trying to put a subtle "feeler" out there. I thought that this Tommy might know something about me and my birth. But it soon became clear that Dorothy had never told him a thing. Tommy's only real connection to his sister was that he was the one who introduced her to "Blackie Cafferty," one of his cellmates in prison. Tommy then told me that he had spent ten years behind bars. (Lou would tell me later that anyone who spent ten years behind bars had to be a real bad-ass, someone who had committed a felony not just some petty crime. No one spends ten years behind bars, Lou said, unless they were really dangerous people.)

Then Tommy dropped the bomb. "When I went into the slammer," he said almost nonchalantly, "I left my gun with somebody in the family and now nobody seems to remember anything about it. I thought that you might know who has my gun, that maybe somebody spilled the beans to you over the years." This wasn't really happening, I thought, as I stammered and tried to figure out what to say next. "Naw, not me," I said as my mind raced through several scenarios. "I don't really know anyone in the family except I met Madeline once. But it was all about my adoption... and nobody ever said anything about a gun." Tommy went on, "Well, it's important that I find it. Now that I'm out of prison again, I'm planning to make a lot of trips back and forth between here and Florida and it would be a good thing if I was packing heat... because of all the traveling I'll be doing. That's why I want to get my hands on it again."

By this time I was sweating bullets. This guy Tommy, my uncle, had spend ten years in prison and as a convicted felon and wanted to get his hands on his gun, another illegal act, so that he could have it to travel back and forth between New Jersey and Florida.... running drugs I surmised. This is great, I told myself sarcastically. I had opened a Pandora's Box but at this very moment, I wanted to shut the lid on it tightly while not pissing off my felonious uncle. I had learned from Connie Henley that my birth mother's family was not the upstanding, squeaky-clean All-American family. But I never imagined that I would be talking to my uncle who had done a 10-year stretch in prison. This was the guy who Connie said was also in prison 20 years ago where he met Blackie Cafferty. And now here he was again... ready and eager to break the law in his future endeavors. "If I hear of anyone who has your gun, I'll get in touch with you," I told Tommy. "But I can't help you right now because I don't know anything." I would have said just about anything to end the conversation. We hung up and I immediately began to worry about my involvement with my birth mother's family. (It is now more than twenty-five years later and thankfully, I never heard from Tommy again.)

My next step was to pick Bob Pentatore's brain again. I called him, but this time he sounded down in the dumps. "Gia's mad at me," he told me. "She told me not to get involved and not to help you in any way, and that your friend, that private detective guy, called Jimmy Vincent's son and now Gia isn't talking to me." I told Bob how sorry I was that I had driven a wedge between him and Gia. I vowed to try to make it right and asked him for Gia's address. He hesitated, but I told him he had nothing to lose and that I wanted to write to Gia on his behalf. So Bob gave me her address. It was October 5, 1986, and I wrote:

Dear Mrs. Prima,

I am the person who has been making inquiries about your late husband, Louis Prima. As this letter is quite difficult for me to write, I hope you'll bear with me.

I was born on August 11, 1944, and was adopted ten days later – and have spent the past ten years searching for my biological mother, Dorothy

(Dolly) McDonald. I found her last December but she has died. In the course of my investigation I found out that your late husband was my father.

I am writing this letter in my own handwriting to assure you that I want nothing from you, or from the estate of Louis Prima. I am sure that your late husband knew nothing about me, and I feel that I have no rights whatsoever.

I also have no desire to malign the memory of your late husband by publicly acknowledging the information I know to be true. If it will put your mind at ease, I am willing to sign any legal document you care to draw up that will state what I have already made clear – I wish nothing.

I really have only one request, which has nothing to do with me. It concerns Bob Pentatore. Bob, as you know, worships Louis Prima. He lives about 20 minutes from me and I have been privileged to see his collection of Prima records and memorabilia. When I first spoke with him he would not give me any information without first checking with you.

He has always been loyal to you – and to the memory of Louis. However, he seems to be truly heartbroken that you seem to have broken off your relationship with him. As the timing is coincidental with my inquiries, I feel that I may somehow be responsible for creating a problem between you.

Bob is not a well man but the spirit of Louis Prima still burns inside him. If you could somehow find it in your heart to call him, it would mean the world to him. I ask for nothing else.

I hope you find contentment in your life and I apologize for any emotional distress I may have caused you. If, on the remote chance, you wish to contact me, I would always be happy to speak with you.

Most Sincerely, Alan Gerstel

I never heard back from Gia Prima but Bob Pentatore did. It was months later and she had softened. She told Bob, though, that for them to remain friends he could not give me any more information about members of the band or about her. Bob left me no reason to believe that her position would ever change.

So, here it was... December of 1986... a full decade into my Search... and I had run into a brick wall and was emotionally drained. The probing, the revelations, and the rejection I had confronted over the past ten years had sapped me of the strength to reach an absolute conclusion about the identity of my birth father. But at least I could take satisfaction in knowing without doubt the identity of my birth mother and the story of her life and her relationship with Louis Prima. I now also had four separate sources who told me Louis Prima was my birth father but I had no expectation that I would ever learn anything that would confirm it further.

I can't say that I was completely satisfied with the outcome of my Search but my life at the time was changing radically. My sons were almost four years old and I was starting a new job at News-12 Long Island (which would require the "commute from hell" every day... 45 miles each way from North Jersey to Long Island on the most traffic-clogged roads on the planet.) I was gaining success in the News business and had a fulfilling professional life ahead of me. It was time to accept the fact that I was the illegitimate son of Louis Prima but also realize that no family member would acknowledge that fact. And, at this point, I really didn't care. My Search was never about money or any kind of recognition. It was only to gain knowledge about my roots so I could understand why I was who I was. So I packed up all my notes, my diaries, and my audiotapes, and closed the door to my past.

CHAPTER TWENTY-FIVE

"*The Wildest*"

Nearly 15 years passed. I spent the first 5 of them at News 12 Long Island, developing my craft as a News Reporter and Anchor. Then in 1990, I got a job at WPEC, the CBS Affiliate in West Palm Beach, Florida… and the Gerstel family moved south. Our twin boys did well in their new school and my wife, Ronni, became a puppeteer while I anchored the weekend newscasts for WPEC and became the country's first "Drug War Correspondent" during the week. I was able to put the obsession with my Search in the past. Lou LoScialpo and I remained friends and would call each other occasionally and I could count on Lou to call me EVERY August 11th to "bust" me about being older than he was. His birthday is August 27th. So for 16 days each year I was technically older than him. And he would jokingly remind me of our "age difference" on each passing birthday.

I remained friendly also with Fran Yasney and with Connie Henley. We would share phone calls and holiday gifts, but I no longer had the burning desire to get more information from them. I had made peace with who I had been and who I had become.

There were moments that rekindled the fiery frustrations of my Search but the joy I derived from my loving family and my growth as a credible television journalist reduced those feelings to a simmer and they would quickly fade away. One such incident involved a call from one of Ronni's friends in 1996 who asked if we had seen the movie "The Big Night." We hadn't, and didn't even know what it was about. She told us that it was about an Italian restaurant that was in financial trouble. Its owners had invited Louis Prima to dine there to help establish a clientele. In the movie Louis Prima never shows up, and in the end, the restaurant goes belly-up. But the movie soundtrack contained several Prima songs. So of course, Ronni and I HAD to see the movie... which we thoroughly enjoyed. But I was still able to keep the Louis Prima connection in perspective and let it be.

Then in 2000, some friends in New Jersey sent me a movie review from the "New York Times." It was for a documentary called: "Louis Prima – The Wildest." The reviewer was very upbeat about the movie and reported that it was only going to play in New York and Los Angeles and would not have wide distribution. I was disappointed that it wouldn't be playing in Florida but I already had a copy of the documentary made by WYES in New Orleans so I figured that I wasn't missing much. Life went on.

Less than a year later, though, I got a catalog in the mail from an electronics store in New York. I wasn't in the market to buy anything but I leafed through the catalog anyway to see if some gadget or another would strike my fancy. Nothing did. One page, though, featured ads for movies that were available on VHS. One such film was "Louis Prima – The Wildest," and it was on sale for only $14.95! I couldn't resist... so I ordered it.

The tape arrived several weeks later and my family gathered around the t-v to watch it together. We were all interested in what the film had to say about the man I believed to be my birth father and whether or not I could piece together any definitive information from it. This was no real obsession, just an idle curiosity at this point.

Near the beginning, Gia Maione Prima appeared in an on-camera interview. I remembered seeing her years before on the Ed Sullivan show when she was first married to Louis. Of course, she had now aged but I still recognized her and was interested in what she had to say about Louis. Then Gia's daughter, Lena, was interviewed on camera. It occurred to me that she was my half-sister and that knowledge made me want to watch more. It was a wonderful moment but it couldn't prepare me for what was coming up next.

It was a shocker… an on-camera interview with Louis Prima, Junior. Wham!! My wife said "Wow… he's cute. He looks like a younger version of …oh my God! He looks like YOU 20 years ago!" My boys were also stunned. They had to stop the tape and rewind it to take another look at Louis Junior. He looked just like me or vice versa. There were so many similarities. We played the tape over and over again. I was stunned. I had a brother! And he looked like me!

In the days that followed, the passion… the obsession… returned… and it returned with a vengeance! My God, I had at least one brother and two sisters, maybe more! I had blood relatives. And that was enough to get the juices flowing again. But now I had the Internet, so the first thing I did was to check out "Louis Prima Junior" at "People Search" on the web. He was listed!!! And so, I now had an address and phone number for him in Las Vegas. I wanted to reach out to him but that same crippling fear of rejection that had plagued me throughout my life took over once again. I opted for the safe route. I called Lou LoScialpo with the information and asked HIM to make the call.

Lou called me back the next day and said that he had called Louis Junior and got his wife instead. She told Lou that she would have Louis Junior call him back. (But she called her mother-in-law, Gia Prima, instead.) I waited for several days expecting another call from Lou telling me that he had spoken directly to Louis Junior. But when the call came from Lou, it wasn't about Louis Junior. It was about Gia. She had called Lou back and berated him for calling her son and daughter-in-law. She was incensed that someone was meddling in her family's business and was angry at Lou for not calling her directly instead of going through her son. She claimed she was listed in the phone book. Lou reached into his bag of tricks and, dripping with sincerity, explained as well as he could that no one knew where she lived and that she did not appear on "People Search" on the web, leaving her son as the only way to contact her.

Lou told me that he was finally able to calm Gia down and convince her that neither he nor I was a threat. Lou wove his spell and eventually brought Gia around, making her understand that his inquiries were not about money. They were only about gaining knowledge about my birth parents. But when Lou called me to tell me that he had spoken to Gia he also told me that Gia wanted me to speak with her lawyer, Tony Sylvester!! "Oh boy," I thought. "I'm in hot water now. This is not a good sign!!" I was worried, really worried that I was going to be hit with some legal action to bar me from contacting the family or maybe something worse: a lawsuit claiming mental anguish and stalking. My mind was racing, pondering, and worrying over all the possibilities. I really thought I had gone too far this time. I thought that I was going to rue the day I ever started my Search. I thought I was in big legal trouble.

But it was too late to turn the clock back now. So I summoned up the nerve and called Tony Sylvester the next day. His secretary put me through to him and I introduced myself. "Tony, my name is Alan Gerstel. My private investigator spoke with Gia Prima and she told him that I should speak with you," I offered with as much confidence as I could muster. "Oh yes," Tony replied, "Gia told me about you. Tell me, Alan, what is it that you want?" I wasted no time in telling him what I DIDN'T want. "Tony, first of all, I don't want any money. I believe that I am Louis Prima's son but I don't believe I deserve any money. I'm not looking for any money. I don't want any money." "That's good," he said in a reassuring, almost humorous way. "That's a very good way to begin. I'm glad to hear you say that."

Tony and I talked for about twenty minutes. I told him about my Search and how I was just looking for confirmation about my birth parents. I told him that my birth mother was dead. He told me that my birth father was dead, which I already knew from Bob Pentatore years before. I also told him of the strange coincidences in my life that I couldn't understand... about the musical talent and about my early aspirations in show business. I also reassured him again and again about not wanting or needing any money. I explained that I was a News Anchor at WPEC and even gave him the station's web address. That way, I said, he could check up on me, see my picture, read my bio, and determine that I was legitimate. There was no talk of lawsuits or legal action, and by the way the tone of his voice changed, I figured I must have said the right things. He said he would get back to me.

As he said he would, Tony Sylvester called me two days later. "Gia wants to talk to you," he told me in a non-committal manner. "She was a little annoyed that you called her son first instead of her. But when she saw your picture and bio on your Station's website she told me to give you her phone number." I was stunned and more than a little fearful at the thought. As Tony recited the number and as I began to write it down, my hand started shaking. After all this time, Gia was willing to talk to me! The news sent jolts of nervous excitement surging through my body. But that growing anticipation cranked up a nausea-inducing knot in the pit of my stomach. Gia had snubbed my overtures in the past and there were no guarantees that Gia had softened. So I braced myself for another round of rejection.

When I hung up with Tony I hungered to dial Gia's number in a nanosecond but… I couldn't… bring myself… to make that call. I sat at my desk looking at the phone and found myself paralyzed. I looked at the number I had written down and then back at the phone again. I took a deep breathe and exhaled slowly. This was it, I thought, this was the moment of truth. But what if Gia rejected me flat-out? What if she berated me for pestering her? What if, despite Tony's calm demeanor, she made it clear that she would pursue legal action against me if I tried to contact her again? I was a bundle of nerves but finally summoned the nerve to dial Gia's number.

"Hello," a woman's husky voice said as she answered the phone. "Hello, Gia," I responded somewhat sheepishly. "This is Alan Gerstel. Tony Sylvester gave me your phone number and said I could call." There was a brief silence followed by, "Oh, Alan… yes… you wanted to speak to me… tell me, Alan. What is it that you want?" Again, I felt it was necessary to spell out what I DIDN'T want so I said in an increasing rapid tempo, "First of all, Gia, I don't want your money. I don't believe I am entitled to anything…. But, I have been searching for my birth parents for many years. I was adopted when I was just a baby… and after a lot of work I found my birth mother… and… I believe that Louis Prima is my birth father… and I have so many questions… there are so many coincidences in my life… that I need to know who I really am."

In rapid fashion I then went on to explain that I had played in a Dixieland Band in high school and that I was the Emcee of the talent shows… and that I was an "entertainer" deep down inside. I just wanted validation, I told Gia, and I just want to understand my background… and to learn who I came from and what my genetic background was. With each comment I made I could sense that Gia was taking it in and softening. Perhaps she was beginning to feel that I was not the threat she had feared. "How did you learn that Louis Prima was your father?" Gia asked. I quickly responded with a touch of humor, "How much time do you have?"

It turns out that Gia had plenty of time and also a growing interest in what I was telling her. We talked for nearly an hour as I told her step-by-step how I went about my Search and how that Search led me to Louis Prima. Gia asked specific questions along the way to clarify my comments and to try to understand what I had gone through. As the minutes ticked by and I revealed the intimate details of my Search I grew more and more confident, and Gia became more accepting. Then she made a startling pronouncement: "I knew you could be Louis' son the minute I saw the picture of you on your television station's website." I was speechless! She went on, "and I sent that picture to my daughter, Lena, who lives in Las Vegas so she could also see what you look like."

That knot in the pit of my stomach began to unravel with every word out of Gia's mouth. The years of paralyzing uncertainty and mind-numbing frustration were finally over! There could be no question now about my origins for here was Gia… accepting me as the offspring of her late husband. I could feel an explosion of emotions rumbling deep down inside me. I took a deep breath as I let the protective layers of my inner defense mechanism melt away and I began to bask in Gia's acceptance! It had only taken me 24 years!!!

By the time we ended our first phone conversation Gia had become a warm, caring voice on the other end of the line. My words must have struck a harmonious chord because we were chatting like old friends. We talked about our ages and how she is only 3 years older than me and then laughed at the prospect that she was my "stepmother." I told her that I would like to stay in touch and she agreed, saying that I could call at any time. When I hung up the phone I felt exhilarated, while at the same time, drained of all emotion. My Search was finally over… and my genetic identity was being validated by the fifth wife and widow of my birth father!

I became crazed in the days that followed as I relived my conversation with Gia, moment-to-moment and detail-to-detail, while my thoughts darted back to the twists and turns and half-truths that permeated my Search and how they had finally unfolded and led me to this moment of certainty. I had done it! I now could say with confidence that I was the illegitimate son of Louis Prima and Dorothy Jeannette McDonald. I understood how I came to be, and how the turn of events surrounding my birth took me from "Baby Boy Ferrucci"... to "Baby Boy McDonald"... and then "Frank McDonald"... and finally "Alan David Gerstel." (Though, to this day, I do not know why I was named "Frank.")

Several days later Gia did something that proved to me that I was not hallucinating or that I had misunderstood our conversation and her acceptance of me: She sent me flowers! The door bell rang and a deliveryman handed me a bouquet of beautiful white flowers with a note that read: "I'm so glad that we talked. Welcome to the family. Gia."

If I was crazed in the hours after our phone call I can only describe my feelings as "out of control." I screamed... I wept... I shuddered... as I went on a dizzying emotional bender. Gia Prima, the woman who would not respond to my letters in years past and wanted me excluded from her life, had now spoken with me, validated me, and had sent me flowers!!! And she had welcomed me to the family!!!

I responded to Gia's loving gesture by sending her a hand-written note thanking her for her kindness and expressing my desire to forge a long-term relationship. I tried not to come on too strong because I had been burned so badly by the Ferruccis that I feared that might happen again. Gia had been kind to me on the phone but I really didn't know her well so I felt that I had to walk on eggshells and measure my words so that she would not misunderstand and be put off by anything I said.

Those fears of rejection, though, were short-lived. Gia called several weeks later and cemented our relationship. She told me, "Your sister, Lena, is coming to South Florida. She performs a tribute show to her dad and will be playing at a group of retirement communities near you... and she wants to meet you." I probably sounded like a blustering fool when I responded, "Oh, Gia.... I'm... I don't know what to say.... Lena wants to meet me... I can't believe it... Oh, WOW... I can't believe it." "She saw your picture, Alan," Gia said, "and she felt just like I felt when I saw it. And she wants to meet you in person." Gia gave me Lena's phone number and said, "Give my daughter a call and set something up."

For the first time in my life I was going to meet someone who was born to the same father who had fathered me!

CHAPTER TWENTY-SIX

The Bond

My sister Lena has a rich, throaty voice that's unmistakable. It seduced me during our first phone call. "Lena, this is your brother Alan," I said when she answered the phone. "Your mom gave me your number and told me to call." "Oh my God," Lena practically screamed into the phone. "I can't believe it... I can't believe it's... it's... I have another brother." She seemed as excited as I was that we were hooking up. Then she went on, "My mom sent me your picture from your TV station and I have kept it on my kitchen counter for the past week... and I walk by it again and again... and every time I look at it, I see my brother! From the minute I first looked at your picture, I knew. I knew. And I've been wondering when... and if... you were going to call."

Lena had lots of questions about how I had tracked down my birth parents so I obliged with the Cliff Notes version of my Search and told her I would go into more detail when we met. She rattled off the dates and places she would be performing in South Florida and the first gig was on February 16, 2002, at Century Village in West Palm Beach not far from my house. We set a time and made plans to meet before Lena's performance. She also invited Ronni and me to watch her act from backstage.

Ronni and I met up with the van carrying Lena and her backup singers at the gated entrance to Century Village at the appointed time and followed the van through the security checkpoint and through the winding roads lined with 3 and 4 story condos, to the Stage Entrance at the Century Village Clubhouse where Lena would be performing. The van pulled up to the door while Ronni and I parked in one of the assigned space nearby. The excitement grew as I turned off the key and looked at Ronni in anticipation. "Well, this is it, honey!!! This is what it was all about… after all these years…" I said to Ronni as I took a deep breath. "So stop talking and let's go already," Ronni fired back lovingly.

We walked across the parking lot to the van which now had the side door open revealing several people inside. I leaned forward into the somewhat dark interior, looking immediately to my left at the back seat where two attractive women were sitting. One had a video camera pointed at me and the other smiled warmly and gestured to the woman sitting in the center seat just in front of me. There she was! Lena was an arm's length away with a huge smile on her face. I looked at her. She looked at me. And we both screamed simultaneously!!!! Then the women in the back seat started screaming too!!! Lena and I stared at each other… our eyes locked on each other's face. "Oh my God!!" we both screamed in unison. "Oh my God… Oh my God… Oh my God….!!!" We reached out to each other and hugged each other and looked at each other even more closely as if to validate our secret bond.

The women in the back seat began to applaud! "It's amazing," one of them said. "You two look just like each other… It's an amazing resemblance!" Lena introduced the two women as her back-up singers who happened to be her oldest and dearest friends. "This is Kari, Alan… She's the one who's taking the videos…. And this is Kelly. We even went to high school together." "And this is my wife, Ronni," I said as I took Ronni's arm and nudged her closer. "Hi everybody," Ronni beamed. "You have no idea how much this means to Alan and to me too… It's been such a long time coming." Lena and her friends rushed to respond and we all wound up talking simultaneously while gesturing excitedly. I found myself wrapped in the warm blanket of genuine affection that radiated not only from Lena, but also from the friends who meant so much to her.

Lena's piano player and arranger came out of the Stage Door and ushered us all into the backstage area. He helped the ladies with their costumes and their boxes and they got settled into their dressing room. "You and Ronni can hang around here if you'd like," Lena told us. "We'll be out in a little bit and figure out the best place for you to watch the show." She reached forward and gave me a hug. "I needed to do that," she said warmly. "I can never get enough," I said reassuringly. And with that, Lena disappeared into the dressing room leaving Ronni and me basking in the toasty glow of acceptance.

We watched as the musicians set up their instruments and even took a peek at the auditorium. It probably seated 600 people and tonight's show was Sold Out, a tribute to Lena and our mutual father, the wildly popular entertainer who had such an impact on generations of music lovers. The title of the show: "Louis Prima, That's My Dad!" was a sure bet to bring the adoring senior citizens out to the show but I hadn't even heard Lena sing yet. I was betting, though, that she was going to be a knock-out!

As Ronni and I walked around in a state of disbelief that this was really happening, I was aware of people checking me out. Even when we sat down to wait for Lena to get ready I could see eyes darting in my direction, and everyone who passed nearby also took another look. Lena, I later learned, had told everyone on her tour about me… and about our relationship. Lena's piano player and musical director finally broke the ice. "There's really no doubt," he blurted out, "there's no doubt that you're

Lena's brother. It's really pretty cool. I've even met Lena's other brother, Louis Junior, and you even look a little like HIM... I gotta admit I was a little leery about you when Lena first told me but not any more. Welcome."

He smiled a huge smile of acceptance and then walked away to take care of the setup on stage. I turned to Ronni and said excitedly under my breath, "This is getting better all the time. I can't believe that Lena told all these people... and that these people are really good with it. They're believers too!" Ronni squeezed my hand and then threw her arms around me and hugged me tight. "You deserve it, honey," she told me. "You worked so hard for so many years... and it's so nice to see how you are finally being accepted. You earned it." I squeezed her tightly as I held her in my arms and basked in her love AND in the love of my newfound sister and her bevy of friends.

The audience was filling up the auditorium when Lena and her two back-up singers emerged from their dressing room. They were all dolled-up and ready to do a show. "Here, Alan... why don't you and Ronni move your chairs over here so you can see the show?" Lena said while gesturing to an area that looked onto the stage from between the side curtains. "You ought to be able to see just about all the action from here." Ronni and I took her advice and moved our chairs and got ready for the show. "I'll see you at intermission," Lena added, "and then we can talk about where to go out to eat after the show. I hope that's all right. But that's when we get hungriest." I assured her it was no problem as I wanted to spend as much time with my sister as I could.

The curtain went up on Lena's show and she had the audience eating out of her hand from the moment she opened her mouth. Wow, what a voice! Lena is the real deal, loaded with talent and the looks and personality to match. Ronni and I were thrilled to hear her sing, and every so often Lena's friend and backup singer, Kari, would look over in our direction and give us a big smile. I couldn't believe how this adventure was turning out.

Here I was, listening to my sister wow the audience with the songs that made our father famous... and what was more amazing to me... many were songs that I had actually played myself in my teenage years as a member of the Dixie Cups! The evening was a little slice of heaven.

The show ended around 9 o'clock (remember, this was for a "senior" audience who go to bed early) and we all headed to a Tommy Bahamas restaurant in downtown West Palm Beach. There, Lena and I sat side-by-side and talked up a storm all evening. The other members of Lena's entourage were as interested in my Search as Lena was so I shared my saga with everyone, and everyone seemed amazed that I was able to overcome all the obstacles to learn the truth. But the real focus for all of Lena's friends seemed to be how alike we were. We do, in fact, have similar features. But we also both love spicy food... we both are very organized... we both talk with our hands more than our mouths... and we both even gesture in the same way.

The evening turned out to be an incredible "high" for me and was far more personally gratifying than I ever dreamed it would be! Lena and I made plans for Ronni and me to attend another of her concerts a little later in the week.

Ronni and I didn't actually get into that next concert because the "Condo Commandos" at the senior citizen venue didn't allow guests. But we DID meet up with Lena and her friends outside the gates of that cloistered senior community. Lena hopped into our SUV for the ride to a restaurant near the hotel where she was staying. I was driving. Lena was in the passenger seat. And Ronni graciously sat in the back so Lena and I could talk. And we DID! We talked about show business and about the music business and about the news business. And somehow, the conversation turned to make-up: the kind of stage make-up that Lena uses versus the make-up I use for television news. "MAC make-up... that's the brand that works best for television," I told Lena. "No way!"

Lena shot back. "That's the brand of make-up I use too." We both broke into laughter at the silliness of what we were saying. Ronni was in stitches too when she posed the question: "How many wives can honestly say that they've had the experience of listening to their husband and his sister compare make-up notes? This may be a first!"

The incredible feeling joyous spontaneity continued once we reached the restaurant and caught up with Lena's friend, Kari and her Manager, Ron. As we sat around the table Lena and I began to talk even more feverishly about all the things we have in common. "Do you like seafood?" she asked me. "Of course," I replied, "particularly shrimp and lobster." "Shrimp… that's my favorite too!" Lena beamed. "How about Cajun?" she asked again. "Bingo!" I responded, "the hotter, the better!"

No one watching the two of us carrying on could help but spot the way we both talked with our hands and how our gestures were nearly identical, as if we had studied each other's movements to try to copy them. I looked across the table to catch Kari practically staring at me and smiling. "You know, the two of you…. well, there's no way you could NOT be brother and sister. It's even kind of freaky how much alike you are," she gushed. "I am so happy that you found each other… because you really are family." Lena and I looked at each other again in amazement as we both connected with what Kari said.

After dinner we drove Lena back to her hotel with Kari and Ron following in their rental car. I remained overwhelmed by Lena's warmth and welcome and told her, "You know, this is pretty amazing. It took me so many years, and it was such an incredible hassle to find my birth parents… that I can't believe my good fortune… and that we are together… that we finally met!" "Me too," Lena said warmly. "It was pretty freaky at first when my mom sent me your picture. But now that I met you, it all seems so right." As the evening unfolded Ronni didn't say a great deal. She thoughtfully gave Lena and me the space we needed to discover each other as sister and brother but she was always at my side, holding my hand, and squeezing it tightly with each new revelation.

As we approached the hotel, I parked my car near the entrance. But before we all went in to the lobby bar for one last drink I had a present to give Lena. "Here," I said as I held out a small box, "I want you to have this... because I don't need it anymore." Lena opened the box to find the gold medal of St. Anthony I had carried around for years. I explained, "St. Anthony helped me find my birth parents AND my sister. He's done his job and now I want you to have him to remind you of me." Lena let out a breath as she said, "Wow! This is really neat, Alan. And it's gold. Are you sure you want to give it away?" "I want you to have it," I repeated, "I really do." We looked at each other in a way I had never experienced with another woman (a woman who was my sister) and shared a great big hug.

We all went inside and sat in the lounge in the hotel lobby and ordered another round of drinks. Lena reached into her purse and fumbled around a bit before she found was she was looking for. "Here, I want you to see this" she said as she pulled out a tiny pill box. "This is one of two boxes my dad gave me when I was a little girl." The box was a brass color, an inch-and-a-quarter square. It had a wood veneer top and an Indian Head penny set it in the wood. "Dad liked to be called The Chief," Lena told me, "and that's why the penny with the Indian Chief on it. I use the box to save the pennies that I find." She told me that one of Louis Prima's big hits was 'Pennies from Heaven' and that gave the pill box a truly special meaning. "I have the other one in my house in Las Vegas," she said. "I want you to have it... so I'm going to mail it to you when I get back." I was overwhelmed by Lena's gesture and as my eyes welled-up with tears, I had difficulty saying anything other than a feeble, "Wow!"

The promise of that gift from Lena was something I could never have anticipated but it said so much about our time together: Lena felt comfortable with me. She felt our blood connection. And she was willing to part with one of two identical gifts from her dad. Louis Prima could never have dreamed when he gave them to her that one day she would be sharing that gift with a newfound brother, a child that he could never acknowledge as his own. I keep it with me always.

Lena and I said goodbye that night knowing she was returning to Las Vegas the next day. And since her shows were so well-received, she expected to return to South Florida the next winter. We hugged a lot… and Ronni joined in too. We had a real feeling of family.

I didn't have an opportunity to meet Gia in person until the next Fall, nearly a year after our first conversation, when Ronni and I headed to Italy for a much-needed vacation. We had to fly from West Palm Beach to Newark, New Jersey, to catch our overseas flight. We arranged to arrive a day early so we could rent a car and drive to Gia's home on the Jersey Shore. By this time we were old friends. Lena had shared our experiences together with her mom and Gia and I had talked extensively. We all seemed to be at ease with who I was and how I fit into the family.

When we arrived at her home, Gia greeted me at the door with a huge hug followed by another one reserved for Ronni. Gia and I looked at each other fondly as if we were looking at the face and into the soul of an old friend. We had spoken so often on the phone that we had already developed a comfortable relationship. But here we were, finally able to touch each other and to share in each other's love more than fifteen years after I had first reached out to her. For me, it was a dream fulfilled! Neither of us experienced so much as a nanosecond of discomfort as we talked about the past and the circuitous route that had brought us together. I felt so "at home" and finally at peace with myself knowing that I was basking in the aura of this wonderful, accepting woman who had been so much a part of my birth father's life. They say "timing is everything", and the timing of the start of my Search negated any chance of every meeting my birth father. But in Gia, I had something very real and very warm and very caring:

someone who had welcomed me into the family that was so much a part of my birth father.

Gia indulged me in memories of Louis and showed Ronni and me a number of videos of old television performances that featured him. One particular song stood out. It was from her first solo appearance on The Ed Sullivan Show in October of 1962. Gia sang "How High the Moon," during a broadcast that, coincidentally, I remembered watching live. As the evening progressed Gia had lots of questions about my Search and I gave her a blow by blow description of the massive effort that eventually brought us together.

Gia graciously put Ronni and me up in her guest bedroom and made breakfast the next morning. When we finished our omelets and were nursing our second cup of coffee, Gia offered an apology. "I have to tell you, Alan," she said rather woefully, "that I now really regret that I treated you so badly when you first tried to contact me so many years ago. We could have had all these years together as friends. But I was afraid... afraid of anyone else who might hold up the finalizing of Louis' estate. He died in 1978 and Keely served papers on me as soon as I arrived home from the hospital... on the day Louis passed away. He had been in a coma for three years and then she served me with papers! The estate was tied up for years because of her... and I had a really tough time making ends meet as I raised my kids without their father."

Gia told me the legal wrangling went on for more than fifteen years and when I first contacted her, the last thing she needed was another "heir" who would file a lawsuit for a share of the estate and tie the money up even longer. "But I really wish I hadn't done that, Alan," she told me ruefully again, "I really wish I hadn't." I wish she hadn't, either, because it might have save me years of anguish and doubt. But I had forgiven Gia years before and I explained that I understood her tribulations and the predicament I posed when I first contacted her.

It was then that Gia hit me with a bombshell that acted as the glue to cement the various accounts of my birth and adoption!! It also explained why she seemed so certain that I was Louis Prima's son. She took a breath and began, "After you first contacted me, Alan, and told me the story of your birth in Far Rockaway, I called Jimmy Vincent. He was Louis' best friend and ONLY friend for so many years. I knew Jimmy was playing drums with Louis back in the 40's so I asked him what he knew about you. It turns out he knew a lot. He told me that your mother was an usher who wanted to be a singer with the band but she never got the chance. He also said that Louis had a "one-nighter" with your mother and that she got pregnant. Louis couldn't do anything about it because he was married to Alma Ross, his second wife. And he couldn't even go to see your mother in the hospital because he knew we would be recognized and the story of your birth would wind up in the gossip columns. So Louis gave Jimmy some money to buy her a cross and chain."

As I was listening to this tale unfold I could feel my muscles twist nervously as I grasped the magnitude of what Gia was telling me. This was the undisputed account that confirmed all the other stories. But Gia was not finished, "And Alan... Louis... asked Jimmy to marry your mother! Being Louis' best friend Jimmy said he would. And he told me he took the cross to St. Joseph's Hospital in Far Rockaway where he proposed to your mother. But she wanted nothing to do with his proposal. She didn't want to be a mother. She had this dream... this fantasy... to replace Lily Ann Carol as Louis' band singer. She turned Jimmy down flat. So Jimmy left the cross and chain with her and told Louis that he did what Louis asked him to do... And that was that."

My mind was in overload! I didn't know what to say. But there it was... the confirmation of the Far Rockaway connection! It all made sense now. All the different stories and all the different facts now added up. I could now say with certainty that I was the illegitimate son of Louis Prima.

Amid my whirlwind of discoveries, Gia told me that the cold winters of New Jersey were becoming too harsh for her so she was making the move to a home she owned in Destin... in Florida's panhandle.

Several months later, Gia called to tell me that Lena was getting married! Tim Fahey was a bass player and Lena's "Mister Right." They were going to be wed on the beach in Destin... and when I called Lena to congratulate her, she told me that Ronni and I were invited to her wedding!

The invitation came in the mail a few weeks later... a parchment-like scroll rolled up in a plastic bottle like the kind that would wash up on shore with a note from a sailor shipwrecked on a desert island. Lena would become Mrs. Tim Fahey on Tuesday, November 1st. I opened my appointment book to make a note of the date and I immediately realized that I could not take off work because it was on the eve of the November News Ratings Book, a month-long period that sets a television station's advertising rates for the months ahead. Television station policy mandated that no one could take off during that time period for any reason, but that policy was unacceptable to me under these circumstances. After searching for my birth parents for nearly 30 years and developing a terrific relationship with Gia and a super bond with Lena, there was no way I was going to miss that wedding even if it meant getting fired from my job. Lena's wedding was THAT important to me. Ronni and I responded that we would be there!

I had plotted and schemed for decades to learn my true identity. Compared to that Herculean task, figuring how to beat the "system" at a mere television station, turned out to be a piece of cake. It was to be an afternoon wedding so Ronni and I figured that I could call in "sick" for just that one day and then return to work... right on schedule... at 2:30 the following afternoon.

Here's how my plan played out:

On Monday, I worked my normal shift at the station and was off the air at 11:00 that night. I rushed home and went to sleep so Ronni and I could wake up at 5AM for an early flight. But before actually boarding the plane, I called the station at 6:30 to say I didn't feel well and would not be in to work that day. We then flew to Atlanta and caught a connecting flight to Fort Walton Beach, the nearest airport to Destin. We rented a car and drove to the beachfront hotel where we were staying and where the afternoon wedding would be held. After attending the gala event... we went to bed by 10:00 and got up at 4:30 for an early flight home the next day. We arrived back in West Palm Beach shortly after noon and I rushed home to shower and change my clothes and then strolled into work at 2:30 for my evening shift, saying that I had recovered from my illness and felt a lot better. Talk about a whirlwind trip. It was the most insanely wild chain of event that Ronni and I had ever shared. But we were there for Lena's special day!

There was a glitch in Lena's wedding plan, though, but it had more to do with Lena's vision for her ceremony than my absence from work. Lena had planned an afternoon wedding on the beach but it was a rainy day in Destin. In fact, from the time Ronni and I approached Destin hours earlier, the sky was dark and ugly. As our plane prepared to land, we descended into what looked like grayish pea soup. We feared that Lena's dream wedding would be a nightmare and would have to be moved indoors.

Our hotel room overlooked the beach and had a balcony that allowed Ronni and me to look down at the arch made of flowers and the folding chairs set up in rows for the wedding. All the while, the rain never stopped. It wasn't a drenching downpour but it certainly was enough moisture to dampen everyone's spirits. Ronni and I unpacked our suitcase and paced around, watching the clock and wondering if the sky would clear. Then, the phone rang on the table next to the bed and I answered it. "Hey, Alan," the voice at the other end called out, "this is Tim. How's my future brother-in-law doing?" I was nearly overcome by the surge of emotions. "My future brother-in-law?" My eyes began to tear up at the unexpected sound of those words. I never imagined that I could ever have a brother-in-law. Yet, here was a guy who had never met me... a guy who was about to marry my half-sister... calling me his future brother-in-law!!! It was a staggering, once-in-an-eternity moment.

Tim went on to tell me that they had gotten reports that the rain was ending in Pensacola to our west... that the skies should clear in about an hour... and that they were putting the ceremony off for another hour and a half so they could still get married on the beach. Ronni and I waited in our room, and fortunately, the weather prediction was right on the money. After about an hour, the rain stopped, the clouds slowly blew away to the East, and the sun began to shine. Ronni and I got dressed and took the elevator downstairs to the ground floor where we met up with Lena's bridesmaids, Kari, Kelley and Brandy. Of course, we knew Kari and Kelley as the back-up singers from Lena's past performances in West Palm Beach. We also met Gia's lawyer, Tony Sylvester, my first real contact with the Prima family, the man who had put me in touch with Gia several years before. And then Gia walked over to our group of wedding participants gathered near the rear of the expansive lobby area. Gia and I hugged, almost in disbelief that we were there in Destin, about to be a part of Lena's wedding. Gia then hugged Ronni and proudly reminded us that she was wearing the beaded shawl that Ronni and I had sent her as a gift the previous Christmas. Everything seemed so right!

It was time for the ceremony so we all took our shoes (and socks) off and strolled past the hotel swimming pool and down to the beach. The several dozen guests were dressed in suits or gowns but we were all shoeless in the sand as we sat in the folding chairs that had been set up facing the ocean. When everyone was in place the music began and Lena and Tim made their entrance down the wooden stairs from the hotel to the beach and across the sandy aisle created by the folding chairs. The ceremony was magical! The heavens had cleared and a vivid rainbow cut across the sky in a crescent-shaped path directly over the floral arch where Lena and Tim were reciting their vows. The sun was low in the sky and pierced through the remaining wispy clouds with warm, pink beams of light that stood in counterpoint to the emerald green sea that washed up onto the shore and receded again and again. I glanced over at Gia who was beaming proudly at the sight of her daughter consecrating her love with the man who had won her heart. I held Ronni's hand affectionately and we glanced at each other lovingly. I had shared the best times of my life with this wonderful woman standing at my side. And I was now looking on as my sister and my new brother-in-law were gazing lovingly into each other's eyes as Lena's mother looked on.

I took a deep breath of the rich salt air. It transported my soul back in time to the sandy shores of Far Rockaway… and I nearly burst with the revelation:

I am not an "only child" anymore!

Reflections

Gia has since put me in touch with my half-sister, Tracy, who lives in Washington State. Tracy and her daughter, Laira, came to South Florida for a visit and stayed with us for a few days. One of the things I showed her was a scrapbook I put together showing the various stages of my life from childhood through my teen years. But when I first opened that scrapbook to a picture of me when I was probably three or four years old, Tracy didn't "ooh" and "ah" as I anticipated she would. She began to sob. It was certainly an odd reaction so I put my hand on her shoulder and asked, "What's wrong, Tracy? What brought this on?" Tracy touched the photo of me tenderly and pointed to my eyes. "I took a picture of 'Brother' (Louis Junior) when he was this age," she said through her tears, "I was like the unofficial family photographer... and Alan... he... 'Brother'... looked... exactly like you... the eyes... the hair... everything. There's no doubt. The resemblance is amazing."

Then, some six months after Katrina made landfall, Gia called to tell me that Brother would be playing a one-night-only concert in The Big Easy to try to help that city get back on its feet... and she told me that Brother wanted to meet me! At that moment there was no question that I'd be going to New Orleans, my birth father's home town! On the downside, though, Ronni could not go with me. I would make this trip with Gia.

I was enraptured by the food and the spirit of New Orleans "French Quarter" but I was also awed by the realization that THIS was my birth father's home town! This is where he grew up... and this is the city that influenced his music and his life.

For Brother's show I was seated at a table with some of Gia's longtime friends and some of the movers and shakers of the New Orleans scene. I wasn't quite sure how I was supposed to fit in with these people and what I was supposed to tell them about why I was there but Gia made it simple. She introduced me to everyone as "Louis Prima's son." That, of course, prompted a litany of questions about how I learned the truth about who I was. I was happy to oblige.

As I sat there fielding questions and basking in the warm reception from everyone at the table, I realized that Gia had just done for me what decades of searching could not: She had legitimized me as Louis Prima's son! She told the people who mattered to her that I was the real deal. No one, ever again, would question my credibility. Gia had made Louis Prima's illegitimate son... legitimate in the eyes of the world.

I was also thrilled and privileged to meet my older sister, Joyce. Joyce is about ten years older than me, the daughter of Louis and his first wife, Louise. Joyce was warm and loving and very accepting of me. We sat next to each other at the table with about a dozen other guests and she held my hand during Brother's entire knock-out show. What a treat!

I have vowed to return to New Orleans some day but only with Ronni by my side.

As I reflect on my life and the twists and turns that put me on the path to becoming the man I am today I realize how fortunate I am. First of all, I would have ceased to exist even before I was born if my birth mother had chosen to have an abortion. Abortions were illegal at the time, but given what I know about Dorothy McDonald's lifestyle and her family, it would not have been a problem for her to locate a doctor who would perform the procedure. I can only guess that her Catholic upbringing played a big role in that decision. But that's only a guess.

Dorothy could also have chosen to raise me herself. That, I fully recognize, would have been a disaster. I am grateful that she was more focused on being a singer in a band than a mother for I cannot fathom what life would have been like for a little boy growing up in the lifestyle and the environs she chose for herself.

I am also grateful that my parents, Herman and Selma Gerstel, succeeded in adopting me and raising me. I could have been named Frank Ferrucci and grown up in Brooklyn, the son of a truck driver and his wife. Rocco and Rose Ferrucci may have been good people but more than a quarter century after the fact, I still cannot fathom how they could have built my hopes up and then could cut me off without an explanation knowing that they were causing me so much grief. I doubt that I would have thrived as a child having parents with so little feeling for the heartbreak of others despite the unimaginable pain that Dorothy caused them. But I will never know.

What I DO know is there are reasons I had to seek out the truth and validate who I am. I have also learned there are extraordinary coincidences I cannot explain:

There was my musical ability and the desire to be a performer... yes, even a singer. Something in my genes drew me to music and to the stage and now I understand why. Even as a News Anchor, I was a performer... someone who uses his ability as an actor to convey the depth of feeling needed to fully articulate a news story. And I also like to have fun with stories that call for a little comedy. I somehow intuitively understood the value of having fun on stage as a musician or a performer. It was a key ingredient in my birth father's performances, an ingredient I inherited though I don't quite understand how.

I cannot explain why my first choice of a musical instrument was the trumpet. What possessed me as a young boy to choose THAT particular instrument?

I also find it remarkable that I was playing Dixieland Jazz in a high school band that featured the same songs that were a solid part of my birth father's repertoire. What drew me to Dixieland music?

I actually watched Gia's second performance on the Ed Sullivan show "live" in October of 1962... when she sang "How High The Moon." I didn't watch the Sullivan show often, so why was I watching THAT night?

My friends in Las Vegas took me to see Louis Prima perform in the Lounge of The Sahara hotel in the early 1970's although there were several dozen other shows on The Strip that they could have taken me to see. Why did they pick Louis Prima?

Why was I apparently destined to work with Keely Smith in 1963 shortly after she divorced my birth father? I worked in Summer Stock with other stars during that summer but why was Keely one of them? It was my only summer working at that particular summer theatre, and I later learned, it was the only time Keely also worked at that same theatre.

And then, there was my friend, Martha Raye. I always felt a "connection" between us, especially after she reached out to me in Viet Nam. I suspected that we had some ethereal magnetism that drew us together but as a young man who hadn't even thought about beginning a Search, I dismissed my feelings as the mind games of someone who was merely stage struck. Years later, though, I learned a very revealing piece of gossip: Martha Raye had a torrid love affair with Louis Prima back in the 1930's!! And that has always left me wondering if there was some genetic attraction between the two of us... something that Maggie saw in me that somehow reminded her of Louis. Maggie has passed on, so sadly, I will never know.

Ever since we connected and cemented our relationship, Gia Maione Prima has given me gifts of Louis' jewelry and clothing that help me connect with the birth father I never knew. But she has done so much more. She has extended her heart to me and embraced me as a member of the Prima family. At times, she's told me, "Your father would be very proud of you." And at others, she has reminded me that, "Louis would never win the Father of the Year award." As is the case with many celebrities, Louis Prima was a complex man and he was devoted to his craft. He would urge his band to "play pretty for the people." And he lived his passion for entertaining in front of the countless audiences who packed into sold-out clubs and showrooms because they cherished his music and his magnetic presence.

I am saddened that I never met him but I have my mementos. I have recordings of his music. And I have videotapes of his performances... all courtesy of Gia. And to top it off, I have a loving extended family that I never knew existed. I am indebted to them for their acceptance and their love.

When I began my search, my expectations were tempered with fears of even more rejection. My birth parents, whoever they might turn out to be, had given me up once and I had no way of knowing how they would respond to a "return engagement" decades later. Yet despite all my fears and all my fantasies I never came close to even speculating that I was the by-product of an affair between a great entertainer and one of his many mistresses. But now I know. And my odyssey has come to an end. I never had the opportunity to meet my birth parents (for better or for worse) but the tortuous journey to the truth led me to dozens of warm, caring people who helped me navigate the murky waters and put me on the path to discovery. They helped me answer the burning questions and made me understand who I am... and how I came to be who I am. There is no way I can adequately thank them.